T0278177

The Lost Princess

The Lost Princess

Women Writers and the

History of Classic Fairy Tales

&

Anne E. Duggan

REAKTION BOOKS

For Donald Haase,
whose long-time support, collaboration,
friendship and witty sense of humour
I have always cherished.

Published by
REAKTION BOOKS LTD
Unit 32, Waterside
44–48 Wharf Road
London N1 7UX, UK

www.reaktionbooks.co.uk

First published 2023
Copyright © Anne E. Duggan 2023

Printed and bound in Great Britain
by TJ Books Ltd, Padstow, Cornwall

A catalogue record for this book is available from the British Library

ISBN 978 1 78914 769 8

CONTENTS

Episode from *Hypolite, comte de Duglas* (1690) in which the hero is
about to recount the first published tale of the 1690s fairy-tale vogue
The Island of Felicity (Brussels, 1704).

Introduction

Through this book I would like to take the reader on a voyage into a fairy-tale land, a once upon a time, when the tales that we now consider classic were born. In this universe, no one has yet heard of Jacob and Wilhelm Grimm, Hans Christian Andersen or Walt Disney. Although it is a universe that includes Charles Perrault, whose tales were the main sources for Disney's *Cinderella* (1950) and *Sleeping Beauty* (1959), his tales do not dominate the cultural landscape to the degree to which they do today. It is a time when other Cinderella tales with strong heroines, such as 'Finette-Cinders', are just as popular as the one with which twenty-first-century readers and filmgoers are familiar. It is a world in which the virtuous heroine from 'Finette; or, The Clever Princess' kills her persecutor; an era when Amazonian women had princely sons, as in an early version of 'Beauty and the Beast'; a period when a female White Cat was at least as well known as Perrault's male Puss-in-Boots. This universe is not that of Rapunzel but of Persinette, a tale used to criticize arranged marriages. And it is a time of popular maiden warrior tales, with such cross-dressing, swashbuckling heroines as Constantin(e) from 'The Wild Man'. These tales were all written by a unique group of women: Marie-Catherine d'Aulnoy, Marie-Jeanne L'Héritier, Gabrielle-Suzanne de Villeneuve, Charlotte-Rose de La Force and Henriette-Julie de Murat.

For most twenty-first-century readers, these women authors are probably unfamiliar. However, they used to be household names at different times and in different places, with d'Aulnoy enjoying a renown in Europe, from the seventeenth until the end of the nineteenth century, as great as and sometimes greater than that of Perrault, the Grimms and Andersen. *The Lost Princess: Women Writers and the History of Classic Fairy Tales* traces the story of these French women writers of the seventeenth and eighteenth centuries who were essential to the emergence of the fairy tales that are considered classic today, including 'Cinderella', 'Beauty and the Beast', 'Rapunzel' and 'Puss-in-Boots'. Through our voyage we uncover some of the breadcrumbs, the threads, the ashes, that link past and present, in ways that challenge our assumptions about who collects or writes fairy tales, what kinds of heroine we find in these narratives, and for whom and why they were written. We will see that many 'Cinderella' tales and many 'Beauty and the Beast' tales, along with cross-dressing maiden warrior tales, coexisted, often through the centuries, appealing to different audiences and including many enterprising heroines who did not need a prince to save them, and who in fact did a pretty good job at saving princes themselves.

Like the archaeological excavation of a lost city, here I attempt to unearth part of the history of these lost princesses: those women authors, and especially d'Aulnoy, to whom we are unknowingly indebted for tales that are familiar to us, and who also shaped earlier fairy-tale canons that are different from 'our' contemporary one. Their impact was enduring, even if their legacy goes largely unacknowledged in the twenty-first century. These women authors were essential to the development of the genre that today is so influenced by the hegemonic hold of Disney, a circumstance that blinds us to their prominent positions within fairy-tale history. We also too often assume that the history of women, gender and feminism is a teleological one about progress, about women who didn't have a voice before the twentieth century, about women's lot only improving. The tale I tell here seeks to dispel some of these assumptions, showing that women – and women writers of fairy tales – had a voice, challenged patriarchal norms and asserted female agency. Moreover, their tales were popular; these were not marginal writers, but bestselling authors whose works were translated into English, German and, in the case of d'Aulnoy, Czech, Italian and Spanish, among other languages. Indeed, the idea that a European fairy-tale princess in the seventeenth, eighteenth or nineteenth century would not have immediately evoked images of passivity or a damsel in distress might seem strange to a twenty-first-century reader, but it would come as no surprise to the many fans over the centuries of d'Aulnoy's fairy tales, adapted to theatre and music as well as comic books, with many a plucky and sovereign heroine.

The *Oxford English Dictionary* defines 'classic' as 'Of the first class, of the highest rank or importance; constituting an acknowledged standard or model; of enduring interest and value'. When we think of classic fairy tales, such stories as 'Cinderella', 'Sleeping Beauty', 'Beauty and the Beast', 'Snow White', 'Rapunzel', 'Little Red Riding Hood' and 'The Little Mermaid' immediately come to mind. Apart from 'Beauty and the Beast' – whose author many ignore, or have come to believe is by Disney – these tales were published by Perrault, the Brothers Grimm and Andersen. In other words, our conception of classic fairy tales revolves primarily around publications *by men*. Even twentieth- and twenty-first-century fairy-tale writers, such as Angela Carter, Margaret Atwood, Robin McKinley and Emma Donoghue, tend to take this group of tales by the Perrault-Grimms-Andersen 'trinity' as defining the genre as it has existed from time immemorial to the present. And yet, a history of classic fairy tales that foregrounds the seminal role women authors played historically reveals other conceptions of 'classic', other notions of 'standard or model', other ways of determining 'enduring interest and value' that might surprise us. Digging deeper, underneath the layers and traces of different versions of the 'classic' tales, it becomes evident that women writers, indeed feminist writers, shaped their very foundations.

I started researching fairy tales some three decades ago, and was particularly struck by the history of French women writers of fairy tales, known as the conteuses, or women tale tellers. Marie-Catherine d'Aulnoy (1652–1705), Charlotte-Rose Caumont de La Force (1654–1724), Marie-Jeanne L'Héritier (1664–1734), Henriette-Julie de Murat (1668–1716), and later Gabrielle-Suzanne de Villeneuve (1685–1755) and Jeanne-Marie Leprince de Beaumont (1711–1780), among others, wrote fairy tales that resemble those that have become part of 'our' twentieth- and twenty-first-century canon. Yet these tales, importantly, present several contrasts with the versions that are familiar to us today. First and foremost, these seventeenth- and eighteenth-century women writers produced fairy tales in which queens could rule over their own realms, Amazon warriors demonstrated military prowess, and clever heroines outwitted evil kings and evil fairies, as well as ogres and ogresses. Stylistically, their tales resemble novellas in their complex plot development – far from the succinct style of tales by Perrault or the Brothers Grimm.

Over the years I have continued to research and teach about the ways in which these women writers challenged seventeenth-century gender norms and promoted the equality of women and men through their tales. The *conteuses* based many of their plots on fairy tales by the Italian writers Giovanni Francesco Straparola (*c.* 1485–1558) and Giambattista Basile (*c.* 1575–1632), both of whom cast more empowered heroines than those we typically find in the fairy-tale canon today. The more I learned about these women fairy-tale writers, the more it became clear that their impact was not limited to France or to late seventeenth-century society. Indeed, d'Aulnoy in particular had a lasting impact throughout Europe with tales that were initially written for aristocratic adults and then re-branded for younger bourgeois readers by the end of the eighteenth century, only to be adapted for the stage in both France and England in the nineteenth century. Some of d'Aulnoy's tales even made it to such places as French Canada and Missouri, feeding into the oral traditions of French settlers in the United States.[1]

The community of the *conteuses*

Numerous studies have been written about the *conteuses* and their social context in both French and English.[2] Despite critical attention, somehow word still hasn't reached the general public or even folklore and fairy-tale scholars outside French studies that, first, countless fairy tales that historically enjoyed acclaim and fed into oral traditions and popular culture were written by women; second, these women were aristocrats who wrote tales for elite adult listeners and readers; and third, in their tales they treated mature subjects ranging from pregnancy and the problem of arranged marriage to gender equality and criticism of monarchy. So, who exactly were these women?

In France in the 1690s a fashion for publishing fairy tales emerged that was dominated by women writers of the nobility, many of whom were marginalized at court owing to their transgression of gender and social norms; that is, because of their refusal to accept their assigned place within an autocratic and patriarchal society. At the head of this movement was d'Aulnoy. Born Marie-Catherine

Le Jumel de Barneville, d'Aulnoy was from a distinguished noble family who arranged her unhappy marriage, at the age of thirteen, to François de la Motte, baron d'Aulnoy, thirty years her senior. Marie-Catherine's troubled marriage was punctuated by her husband's financial problems and his infidelity, which led her to plot against him with her mother and their two lovers. They attempted to get the baron accused of lese-majesty – speaking out against the king – which was considered treason in that period. The attempt failed, however, resulting in their lovers' execution and mother and daughter fleeing the country; it is likely that d'Aulnoy spent time in both England and Spain. Allowed to return to Paris around 1685, d'Aulnoy was subsequently arrested by order of Louis xiv (possibly at her husband's request), sequestered to a convent in the town of Blois, then transferred in 1687 to a Parisian convent, where she remained until 1695.[3] D'Aulnoy was the first of the fairy-tale writers to publish a fairy tale, 'The Island of Felicity', which she included in her novel *The Story of Hypolite, Comte de Duglas* (1690). Her two other collections were published in 1697 and 1698; d'Aulnoy thereby proved to be the most prolific – and, in the end, the most successful, given her enduring legacy – of the *conteuses*.

Also from a prominent noble family, Charlotte-Rose de La Force served as a maid of honour at Louis xiv's court and began to fall out of favour when she was accused of possessing a pornographic novel; she was also believed to have had numerous love affairs.[4] In early modern France, children were forbidden to marry without the consent of their parents, and La Force violated this law by marrying Charles de Briou in 1687, against his family's will; they had the marriage annulled. Accused of writing satirical songs in 1697, the same year her fairy tales appeared in print, La Force was then banished from court and from Paris and forced to live in an abbey in Gercy, northern France. It should be noted that in early modern France, convents often served as prisons for women who had behaved in a way that was deemed unbecoming. Husbands had the legal right to confine their wives to a convent indefinitely for an accusation of adultery (no proof needed), and of course the king could use confinement as a punishment for a woman's behaviour at court.

Henriette-Julie de Murat's biography shares features with that of her cousin La Force, and of d'Aulnoy. Murat was from a prestigious noble family, and she frequented the king's court until she was accused of sexual transgressions, including lesbianism. Murat was eventually sent into exile in 1702 to the Château de Loches, 'from which she attempted to escape in March 1706 wearing men's clothing, a hat, and a wig'.[5] Her attempt was unsuccessful, but by 1709 Murat was granted limited freedoms, which stipulated, however, that she could not return to Paris. She published her collections of fairy tales in 1698 and 1699, a few years before being forced into exile.

One might say that Marie-Jeanne L'Héritier was the 'upstanding' woman of the group – she remained unmarried and without scandal – who was also an unequivocal advocate of women's rights, following in the footsteps of her mentor, the feminist writer and philosopher Madeleine de Scudéry (1607–1701).[6] L'Héritier was related to and visited Charles Perrault and his family, and dedicated a tale to Perrault's only daughter. She also knew Murat, a fact that is evident from her dedication of 'The Clever Princess; or, The Adventures of Finette' to the countess. This also shows L'Héritier's familiarity with Murat's works: 'You write the prettiest Stories in the world in Verse.'[7] As we will see in Chapter One, d'Aulnoy was clearly familiar with L'Héritier's work, borrowing the name 'Finette' for her version of 'Cinderella', 'Finette-Cinders'.

We know that these women associated with one another to some degree, and scholars continue to speculate on the precise nature of their community. Murat and La Force were cousins, as we have seen, and in her journal, Murat discusses frequenting d'Aulnoy's salon on the rue Saint-Benoît in Paris (possibly after 1695), declaring, 'I knew Mme d'Aulnoy very well, and one never became bored in her company. Her lively and playful conversation went far beyond her books; also, she didn't make a study out of writing, she wrote as I do, out of fancy, in the midst, and among the noise, of a thousand people who came to her house.'[8] Bronwyn Reddan further notes that there is 'evidence that d'Aulnoy, [Catherine] Bernard, La Force, and Murat frequented the weekly salon of the Marquise de Lambert during the 1690s'.[9] Catherine Bernard, another *conteuse*, probably spent time at the salon that L'Héritier inherited from Scudéry after her mentor's death. As we will see in the following chapters, connections between the *conteuses* resided as well in 'their knowledge of each other's work', evident in the many intertextual references found in their tales.[10] As such, they formed an intellectual community that met in physical spaces (the salon) and also communicated with one another through their literary productions.

The French salon emerged in 1610, launched by Catherine de Vivonne, marquise de Rambouillet. It was a space in which women could engage in literary, philosophical and even scientific exploration and debate. Women and men frequented the salon, but the tone of each salon was largely determined by the women who ran it, such as Madeleine de Scudéry, whose novels were shaped by her salon gatherings; Madeleine de Souvré, marquise de Sablé, who composed moral maxims and was associated with the well-known maxim writer François de La Rochefoucauld; and Anne-Thérèse de Marguenat de Courcelles, marquise de Lambert, whose salon, launched in the 1690s, was frequented by fairy-tale writers.[11] The salon was both a physical place, where members met in person to share their work and discuss literary and philosophical trends, and a virtual one: correspondence and literary production served as extensions of the salon and of the social relations, discussions and debates associated with that particular space and group of intellectuals.

While we do not have sufficient historical evidence to understand the exact relations between the fairy-tale writers and the different salons they may have frequented, the salon was indeed a space important to them. The fairy worlds these writers created, where women were empowered and could thrive, could be viewed as so many salon-like spaces. Rather than a 'room of one's own', the salon provided a 'room of their own', where women could hone their literary skill and support one another to produce poetry and novels as well as the fairy tales that became bestsellers in France in

Marquise de Rambouillet's salon by Abraham Bosse (1604–1676).

the 1690s, and that enjoyed, as we will see in the following chapters, a cultural legacy that has yet to be fully acknowledged.

It is clear from this brief overview of the *conteuses* and their cultural context that we are far from the image of peasant women telling tales, which were then collected by men – the stereotype of the 'authentic' folk tale promoted by the Grimms. It is significant, however, that in their notes, the Grimms often acknowledge the seminal role played by French women writers in the tales they collected, even if the brothers slowly edited the women's influence out of their celebrated collection *Children's and Household Tales*, which was first published in 1812. In fact, many of the Grimms' informants were middle-class, even noble women of French Huguenot (Protestant) backgrounds who were familiar with tales by the *conteuses*, either having read them in French or in German translation (the earliest German translation of d'Aulnoy's fairy tales was published in Nuremberg in 1702), or having learned about them through their folklorization, their transformation from literary into oral tales, a phenomenon we will examine more closely in Chapter One.[12]

The impact of the French *conteuses*, and especially of d'Aulnoy, on nineteenth-century German women writers of fairy tales was significant. Inspired by salon culture and the fairy tales of the *conteuses*, German women writers also created tales with many empowered heroines. There are connections between d'Aulnoy's tale 'The Bee and the Orange Tree' and the story the Grimms collected for the 1812 edition from Jeannette Hassenpflug, 'The Okerlo', which they 'removed from later editions because of its relationship to d'Aulnoy and French tradition'.[13] The Grimms collected but did not publish a tale related by Ludowine von Haxthausen, 'Prettyflower, Finette and Tiny Ears', a folklorization of d'Aulnoy's 'Finette-Cinders' (see Chapter One). Maintaining that 'Friederike Helene Unger (1751–1809) was one of the most beloved and talented writers of her day,' Shawn Jarvis foregrounds the influence of d'Aulnoy's tale 'Babiole' on the German writer.[14] In 1818 the renowned German writer Karoline Stahl (1776–1837) published 'Princess Elmina', which blends elements drawn from d'Aulnoy's tales 'The Blue Bird' and 'Beauty with the Golden Hair'.[15]

Jarvis has also examined the impact of French salon culture on the formation of the Berlin *Kaffeterkreis*, literally the 'Coffee Circle', which ran from 1843 to 1848 and was formed by the sisters Gisela, Armgart and Maximilia von Arnim, whose parents, Achim and Bettina von Arnim, were both collectors and writers of folk and fairy tales and frequented the same circles as the Grimms. Like the French salon, the *Kaffeterkreis* fostered female community and encouraged women's writing, particularly of fairy tales. The various influences between the French *conteuses* and German women writers of the late eighteenth and the nineteenth century merits a book-length study of its own to document adequately the transnational and transhistorical community of women fairy-tale writers who, despite all their differences with respect to social class and political tendencies, came together in challenging gender norms and women's place within the public and private spheres of their respective societies.[16]

Fairy tales for adults?

Contrary to popular belief, for centuries adult women and men were writing and reading fairy tales containing mature subject matter. Straparola's sixteenth-century tale 'The Pig Prince' is an animal bridegroom tale in the spirit of 'Beauty and the Beast' in which the pig-hero sleeps with his third wife, Meldina, who, after her wedding night, awakes happy and contented in a bed 'full of dung'.[17] Basile, who provided an early seventeenth-century model of the tale that La Force reshapes, later translated into German to become 'Rapunzel' (see Chapter Three), casts a single mother who gives birth to the heroine who later chooses her own mate. From d'Aulnoy and Murat to the eighteenth-century writers known for their versions of 'Beauty and the Beast', Villeneuve and Leprince de Beaumont, fairy tales were often deployed to criticize and reflect upon the practice of arranged marriage, a pressing subject for young women. Even in the nineteenth century, when children's literature was on the rise, French vaudeville *féeries* and British pantomimes and extravaganzas appealed to both the child and the adult, with many a burlesque quip, as we will see in the staged versions of such tales by d'Aulnoy as 'The White Cat' (Chapter Three) and 'Belle-Belle; or, The Knight Fortunio' (Chapter Four).

The conventional scholarly narrative goes like this: fairy tales were written for adults in the early modern period, and these fairy tales were adapted to the children's library beginning in the late eighteenth century and especially in the nineteenth century, the golden age of book illustration and the rise of children's literature. However, as we examine tales written by women and in particular by d'Aulnoy, whose influence was enormous, we will see that translations and adaptations of tales aimed at children continued to coexist with those aimed at adults. Risqué, gender-challenging, gender-fluid adaptations of tales by women authors continued to appeal to adult readers, listeners and theatregoers. This is nowhere more evident than in the account from the *Illustrated London News* of 1 August 1874 of the fancy dress ball hosted by the Prince and Princess of Wales.[18] Costumes took inspiration from figures drawn from history, painting, various national traditions and playing cards, as well as fairy tales, including those by women authors. Miss Graham and the Duke of Connaught dressed as Beauty and the Beast (by Villeneuve or Leprince de Beaumont;

both versions circulated in England); Lady Margaret Scott and Lord Walsingham as Princess Fair Star and Prince Cheri (d'Aulnoy); Lady Florence Gower and Lord Mandeville as the White Cat and the Fairy Prince (d'Aulnoy); Lady Theresa Talbot and Lord Berkeley Paget as Fair One with the Golden Locks and Avenant (d'Aulnoy). The other fairy-tale costumes included the Goose Girl and the king (Grimms), Red Riding Hood and the Huntsman (Grimms), Undine and Hildebrand (Friedrich de la Motte Fouqué), Cinderella and the Prince (Perrault), Babes in the Wood (English tale), Bo Peep and Little Boy Blue (English nursery rhyme), Fatima and Bluebeard (Perrault), and Mary Quite Contrary and Puss-in-Boots (English nursery rhyme; Perrault).

This account of the ball illustrates, first, that there continued to be a place for fairy tales within adult and elite culture, even as tales were adapted to the children's library and the popular stage; and second, that tales by d'Aulnoy, Leprince de Beaumont and Villeneuve were as 'canonical', as 'classic', as those by Perrault and the Grimms. Indeed, d'Aulnoy upstages her peers at this event by the number of characters represented from her tales, and this anecdote reveals that Princess Fair Star, Prince Cheri, the White Cat, the Fair One with the Golden Locks and Avenant were all household names in Victorian England. As such, the tales considered 'classic' in Victorian England – as well as in early modern France and nineteenth-century Germany – included those written by women that featured powerful female characters.

Each of the following chapters takes as its point of departure a particular type of tale whose history I trace from the early modern period to the nineteenth and twentieth centuries, from literary texts and chapbooks to oral, musical and theatrical adaptations. In Chapter One we follow the different types of Cinderella tale, from Basile and d'Aulnoy (via L'Héritier) to the folklorization of d'Aulnoy's tale, which eventually makes it into the Czech national folk corpus through an adaptation by the feminist writer Božena Němcová, and finally to a popular film enjoyed in Germany, the Czech Republic and Scandinavia, *Three Hazelnuts for Cinderella* (1973). In Chapter Two I show that, while d'Aulnoy's tales 'The Ram' and 'The Green Serpent' were invaluable to the creation of the tale we know today as 'Beauty and the Beast', shaped by Villeneuve and attaining its 'classic' form with Leprince de Beaumont, these two tales also enjoyed enduring legacies of their own, evident in British adult and children's literature and French music. Chapter Three focuses on the creation of d'Aulnoy's 'The White Cat', which draws importantly from early modern cat tales and La Force's Rapunzel tale, 'Persinette', and its amazing legacy on the London and Parisian stage in the nineteenth century. As we will see, the tale was so popular in Europe and North America that it made its way to a Mexican comic in the twentieth century. In Chapter Four, I explore the history of maiden warrior tales by Murat, L'Héritier and d'Aulnoy to show that in early modern France, such tales were part of the 'classic' fairy-tale canon, a fact that puts into question any universalizing assumptions about fairy tales and passive princesses. Moreover, d'Aulnoy's tale about a cross-dressing heroine who saves a kingdom not only made it to the British stage, but became a board game in the nineteenth century, showing the extent of its popularity and appeal in Victorian England.

As we move between the different adaptations of these female-authored tales across linguistic and cultural boundaries, we will see how tales by the *conteuses* could accommodate many different audiences and ideological objectives. Tales by d'Aulnoy were regular fare in France and England, read by adults and children, by Honoré de Balzac and Gustave Flaubert, set to music by Maurice Ravel and adapted to stage by the famous Cogniard brothers in

Paris and James Robinson Planché in London. While we will explore contributions to classic tales by different women fairy-tale writers, Marie-Catherine d'Aulnoy will consistently remain front and centre, given the prominent position of her tales within the European pantheon, not only in France and Britain (where her tales were popularized as 'Queen Mab' and 'Mother Bunch' tales), but in Germany, the Czech Republic, Spain, Mexico and Italy.

Recovering the history of tales by d'Aulnoy in particular, and women writers in general, complicates our understanding of both fairy-tale history and women's history. Sometimes projecting 'our' idea of passive princesses as being the norm of fairy tales in fact obscures a much livelier, more feminist history than a twenty-first-century reader might expect. So let's move back in time, to a pre-Disney period when many Cinderella, Beauty and the Beast and cat tales circulated freely alongside tales of cross-dressing heroines; a time when women fairy-tale writers were as well known as male writers like Perrault and the Grimms. Let's enter fairylands where heroines decapitate ogresses, lead armies and contract their own marriages to the men they love – and even sometimes save.

1

A Not-So-Passive Cinderella

Imagine a Cinderella who kills her stepmother, or decapitates an ogress, or triumphantly splashes mud on her sisters on her way to trying on the famed slipper. These are not the first images that come to mind when we think of Cinderella tales in our post-Disney world. But all these variations of the Cinderella story competed with one another for generations, and one woman author, Marie-Catherine d'Aulnoy, produced a variant – 'Finette-Cendron' or 'Finette-Cinders' – that not only was frequently reproduced in France, England and Germany, but fed into oral traditions in these countries as well as in the United States and Czechoslovakia. In fact, her version of Cinderella was adapted by the writer Božena Němcová – known as the Czech George Sand – which subsequently served as the inspiration for the celebrated German-Czech film of 1973 known as *Tři oříšky pro Popelku* in Czech, *Drei Haselnüsse für Aschenbrödel* in German and *Three Wishes [Hazelnuts] for Cinderella* in English.

In today's world the most dominant version of Cinderella is that of Walt Disney Studios, produced in 1950. The fact that it was remade as a live-action film in 2015 only speaks to its ongoing popularity. Few viewers probably notice the opening credits to the earlier film, which read: 'Cinderella, from the original classic by

Charles Perrault'. Perrault's version, whose heroine is rewarded with the hand of a prince for her ability to endure abuse patiently and without anger, resentment or retaliation, has become the canonical one, to the point where, even as early as 1949, Simone de Beauvoir wrote in *The Second Sex*, 'Woman is the Sleeping Beauty, Cinderella, Snow-White, she who receives and submits.'[1] Cinderella, who is often cited in criticism about the heroine's lack of agency in classic fairy tales, 'plays as passive a role [as Sleeping Beauty] in her story . . . Cinderella can remain quietly at home; the prince's servant will come to her house and will discover her identity.'[2] Feminist and gender scholars, critics and writers continue to fight against the figure of the passive Cinderella emblematized in Perrault and Disney. However, more active, spunkier Cinderellas have enjoyed and in some places continue to enjoy popularity. Whereas Perrault's Cinderella made her way into a Disney film, d'Aulnoy's Finette-Cinders reached a more empowered place in *Three Hazelnuts for Cinderella*, directed by Václav Vorlíček, which continues to be an enormously popular film in Germany, the Czech Republic and Norway, among other countries.

This chapter traces the history of these competing Cinderella stories, with a focus on the legacy of d'Aulnoy's 'Finette-Cinders'. On the one hand, it is important to recognize that Perrault's passive Cinderella did not always enjoy the monopoly on Cinderella narratives that it does today. On the other, it becomes clear that d'Aulnoy's Finette-Cinders has a fascinating history of her own through the twenty-first century. We will first trace the birth of Finette-Cinders in the seventeenth century, examining how d'Aulnoy drew from other fairy-tale writers to produce her own unique take on a Cinderella story, then explore her legacy in literary, oral and cinematic traditions in France, the Francophone United States, Germany and the Czech Republic. While many scholars and fairy-tale enthusiasts think of d'Aulnoy's influence as being one of the past, we will see that traces of her legacy remain part of contemporary fairy-tale culture.

A murderous Cinderella

The very first Cinderella story that is the mother of the classic version we know today, giving the heroine her name, was written in the first half of the seventeenth century by the Italian author Giambattista Basile. Both Perrault and d'Aulnoy would have been familiar with 'The Cinderella Cat', published in Basile's *Tale of Tales; or, Entertainment for Little Ones* (1634–6). Importantly, this earliest European Cinderella is a far cry from Disney's post-Second World War domesticated heroine. Basile names her Zezolla, although after her demotion by her stepmother her family refers to her as 'Cat Cinderella', because she sits by the hearth, where cats would warm themselves. She is also the daughter of a prince, whose wife had passed away. At the beginning of the story, Zezolla has a wicked stepmother, about whom she complains to her sewing teacher, Carmosina, wishing that her teacher was her stepmother instead. Carmosina advises Zezolla on how to kill her stepmother, which Zezolla succeeds in doing, and shortly thereafter Zezolla's father takes Carmosina as his wife. But, as they say, be careful what you wish for: Carmosina brings her six daughters into the household, raising these commoners above Princess Zezolla, who is forced to carry out the lowliest work in the household.

In Basile's tale, female figures have the power to halt a ship. A fairy dove informs Zezolla that should she wish for something, she need only send her request through the dove of the fairies in Sardinia and her wish will be granted. When Zezolla's father prepares to leave for Sardinia on business, the stepsisters ask him to bring back luxury items, while Zezolla asks him to promise to give his regards on her behalf to the dove of the fairies and to ask her to send Zezolla something. If he forgets, he will not be able to move forward or backward. Of course, the father forgets, and his ship is stuck at port until it is brought to the prince's attention that he broke his promise to Zezolla. He thus goes to seek the fairy, who gives the prince a date tree, a hoe, a golden pail and silk cloth to bring back to his daughter. Zezolla plants the date tree; it grows, and a fairy emerges from it to grant her wish, which is to attend a feast. Zezolla rides to the feast on a white thoroughbred – the white horse will become a recurrent theme in Finette-Cinders tales – and the king falls in love with her. She attends two more feasts, and after the third, as she rushes off, she loses her shoe. As we can expect, the king issues a proclamation inviting all women to try on the shoe, and when Zezolla finally gets her chance, it fits like a glove. She is crowned, and the last line of the tale describes the sisters' anger. The moral? 'Those who oppose the stars are crazy.' The idea that fairy tales always conclude with a clear moral message is challenged in this earliest incarnation of 'Cinderella'.

Basile's Cinderella wields more authority – backed by fairy power – than her later incarnations in Perrault and Disney. Zezolla kills her first stepmother, and despite her apparent lack of female virtues – innocent maidens don't usually kill anyone – the fairies assist her in attaining the hand of a king. Although for the second and third feasts she travels by luxury coach, to the first she rides a beautiful white thoroughbred, which paints a rather adventurous picture of our heroine. The feast is not being given to find a wife for the king or his son; the king simply falls in love with the mystery woman, who continually evades his men when they try to discover her identity as she flees the festivities, until she loses her shoe. Zezolla is a Cinderella who kills to improve her lot; she can overpower her forgetful father – a prince, no less – through the assistance of (female) fairy magic, and she is able to outsmart the king's men. Cat Cinderella is oppressed by her stepmother and stepsisters; however, it is her initiative and assertiveness – supported by those other strong women, the fairies – that lead to her being crowned queen at the end of the tale.

The fact that Perrault adapted Basile to create his own version of Cinderella only foregrounds the ideological changes he made to accommodate his more conservative perspective on gender. For his 'Cinderella; or, The Little Glass Slipper', which appeared in *Stories or Tales of Past Times* (1697), Perrault makes the hero a nobleman instead of a prince, and streamlines the story, including only one stepmother and two stepsisters, and two balls. He emphasizes the fact that Cinderella submits with great patience to abuse from her family. When the sisters prepare for the prince's ball (as opposed to the king's in Basile), they call on Cinderella to dress and coif them because they value her fashion sense, and the narrator remarks: 'Any other than Cinderella would have done up their hair awry.'[3] Cinderella receives help from her fairy godmother only when she is crying, after her sisters leave for the ball, and she then arrives in great style at the ball, where she is kind to her sisters, who fail to recognize her. The fairy godmother serves a parental role in setting a curfew of midnight to Cinderella's evening excursion, whereas Basile's heroine simply wants to arrive home before her stepsisters. At the end of the tale, when it is discovered that Cinderella is the mystery lady at the ball and will now marry the prince, the stepsisters ask her forgiveness, and Cinderella not only forgives them, but has them move into the palace with her and finds them noble husbands.

Perrault's Cinderella is much more self-effacing than Basile's heroine. Zezolla does not display any particular patience; she is commanding, even in her oppression, with respect to her father; and there is no evidence that she readily submits to or forgives her stepsisters. In the case of Perrault's Cinderella, however, the moral of the story valorizes the heroine's 'good grace', which in the period could signify doing a favour or service for someone without being obliged to, without payback, so to speak. While such values could be viewed as laudable in broad, abstract terms, within the context of gender relations in the tale, this suggests that *good women* should give without expecting anything in return, and in so doing, in the long run, they will win the hand of a prince, who will come to the rescue. That is to say, if they submit to and endure abuse patiently, they will eventually be rewarded with a crown. This message is more blatantly communicated through another tale by Perrault, 'Griselidis', whose heroine is seriously mistreated by her husband, supposedly in order to make her patience and virtue shine all the more. Given such pre-marital training, we can easily imagine the submissive role Cinderella will continue to play in her marriage to the prince.

Let's now imagine that d'Aulnoy has read or heard both Basile's tale and that of Perrault.[4] She doesn't agree with Perrault's representation of Cinderella and is thinking of playful ways to respond to this problematic tale. She is familiar with another tale by Perrault, 'Little Thumbling' – a sort of 'Hansel and Gretel' story – in which the youngest and smallest of seven brothers saves his siblings from parental abandonment and from a child-eating ogre. She is also familiar with Marie-Jeanne L'Héritier's tale 'Finette; or, The Clever Princess' (1695), which became quite popular in England in the eighteenth and nineteenth centuries and from which d'Aulnoy clearly drew in the shaping of her Cinderella tale. Interestingly, L'Héritier and Perrault (who was 36 years her senior) were related through their mothers, probably cousins to some degree. Perrault's mother was Pâquette Le Clerc (d. 1652); also a Le Clerc, L'Héritier's mother, Françoise, would have been significantly younger (more likely Pâquette's niece and not her sister), having married Nicolas L'Héritier in 1660. L'Héritier and Perrault occupied the same circles, and L'Héritier dedicated a tale about a maiden warrior, 'Marmoisan', to Perrault's only daughter, Marie-Madeleine. However, L'Héritier did not share the gender ideology of her cousin, which is clear in 'The Clever Princess'. (The adjective is problematically rendered as 'Discreet' in most English translations from the seventeenth to the nineteenth century, thus toning down the agency of the heroine, who in French is *adroite*, meaning clever, skilled, accomplished or nimble.) One could imagine that d'Aulnoy names her heroine '*Finette*-Cinders' as a way of supporting L'Héritier's representations of women, perhaps foregrounding the implicit gender debate occurring between the two cousins.

L'Héritier's clever princess

Dedicating it to another fairy-tale writer, Henriette-Julie de Murat, L'Héritier frames her tale with two messages: idleness is the mother of all vices, and distrust is the mother of safety. The second message specifically has to do with sweet-talking men, who swoon over women in the salons without actually being in love with them. The tale takes place in the period of the Crusades, when a widowed king with three daughters is preparing to leave for Palestine. He worries in particular about leaving his two older daughters, the lazy and messy Nonchalant (Dronilla in some English versions) and the gossipy Chatterbox (or Pratilia). Finette, on the other hand, is less worrisome; she typically occupies herself with dancing, singing and playing music as well as watching over the administration of her father's kingdom and advising him on political treaties. In order to know if his daughters have behaved appropriately in his absence, the king obtains three enchanted distaffs that will break if the girls dishonour themselves, and locks his daughters in an apparently impenetrable tower.

In their boredom, Nonchalant and Chatterbox are duped into letting the prince known as Rich-in-Ruse into the tower, and he succeeds in seducing and impregnating them. Of course, Finette, who is able to negotiate treaties between kings, not only outsmarts the prince, but punishes him violently on several occasions. First, when he breaks into her room, she arms herself with a hammer, 'which she waved around as if it were a fashionable fan'.[5] Then she sets a trap, and the prince falls into a sewer, injuring himself. Later, when he wishes to throw her into a barrel lined with knives, razors and nails, she ends up pushing him in instead and rolls him down a mountain. The fairy who furnished the father with the enchanted distaffs punishes the two sisters by having them work picking peas and weeding, and they both end up dying, while Finette marries a handsome prince and brother of Rich-in-Ruse named Beautiful-to-See, who had sworn to his dying brother to avenge him, another sticky mess that Finette adeptly resolves.

The opposition between the morally compromised and frivolous older sisters and the youngest, virtuous one is typical of tales about kind and unkind girls in the tradition of 'Cinderella'. However, in L'Héritier, the sisters do not mistreat Finette. For her part, Finette is hardworking not because she is forced to be, and this work is not limited to the domestic; she is no simple housewife, but also engages in intellectual and political domains. Although Finette is considered virtuous, it is not the kind of passive virtue we see in Perrault. She protects herself actively from male violence and sexual predation, ready to harm any prince who threatens her well-being, and she even tries to protect her sisters who had children out of wedlock. The prince Beautiful-to-See does not swoop in to save

Finette. Instead, he nearly kills her because of an oath he swore to a perfidious brother, and Finette in fact saves them both from dishonour and death. More justified in moral terms than Basile's Zezolla, L'Héritier's Finette is an example of a virtuous heroine who can exercise violence to protect herself.

When d'Aulnoy wrote her own Cinderella tale, she fused the names 'Finette' from L'Héritier and 'Cinders' from Basile and Perrault to create her title heroine, Finette-Cinders. This allowed her to reconfigure the power dynamics found in Perrault's version of 'Cinderella' in ways that empower her heroine. Much like Finette, Finette-Cinders is clever, adept at getting out of sticky situations, and at times resorts to violence, all the while remaining virtuous, which also recalls Basile's 'Cat Cinderella'. Just as d'Aulnoy fuses 'Finette' and 'Cinderella' to create 'Finette-Cinders', she also blends into the first part of her Cinderella tale aspects of Perrault's 'Little Thumbling', in which an enterprising youngest son saves his brothers from parental abandonment and from ogres (much in the tradition of 'Hansel and Gretel'). D'Aulnoy regenders 'Little Thumbling' by having Finette-Cinders play the role of the enterprising youngest daughter who saves her sisters from parental abandonment and ogres, only to be abused as Cinderella later in the tale. By associating her heroine with L'Héritier's Finette and by making her a female Little Thumbling, d'Aulnoy invests Finette-Cinders with significant agency in ways that challenge our notion of what the heroine of a Cinderella tale can or cannot do.

D'Aulnoy's Cinderella tale

'Finette-Cinders' concerns an impoverished king and queen, chased from their kingdom, which they lost, and who have three daughters: Flower-of-Love, Night-Beauty and Finette. Because they can no longer offer luxuries for the spoiled princesses, the queen proposes to the king that they abandon them in the forest. Finette, also referred to as 'Fine-Ear', overhears the conversation and brings fresh butter, eggs, milk and flour to her fairy godmother Merluche in order to make her a cake and ask her advice. On her way, Finette tires and Merluche sends her a beautiful Spanish horse (a motif from Basile's 'Cat Cinderella'); she later gives Finette a ball of thread to help her find her way back home. When the queen abandons the princesses, Finette helps them all return home even though her sisters beat and scratch her. Finette overhears her parents again speaking about abandoning the princesses, and this time she brings chickens, a rooster and some rabbits to Merluche, who gives her ashes to spread to help her back home – anticipating her association with cinders. This time, however, the godmother warns her not to bring her nasty sisters back with her. Of course, Finette saves her sisters a second time, and when the third outing occurs, she fears going to see Merluche since she disobeyed her. After packing fine clothes and diamonds to bring with her, Finette drops peas to find her way home. But, as we might expect, birds eat up the peas and the sisters are lost in the forest.

Finette then finds an acorn and plants it – saying every day 'grow, grow, beautiful acorn' – and it grows into a tree. She climbs the tree every day as it grows, and one day she sees a beautiful castle. Thinking the castle might be the abode of princes, the sisters steal Finette's elegant clothes, make themselves up and have Finette pass as their scullery maid (as in 'Cinderella'). But it turns out that the castle belongs to an ogre couple. The three princesses are greeted by the ogress, who is 15 feet tall and 30 feet wide, and who wants to hide the girls from her husband so that she can eat them all up herself. Finette eventually tricks the ogre husband into getting into the oven and he is reduced to ash – a motif that probably shaped the oven scene in 'Hansel and Gretel' – and she cuts off the ogress's head with an axe while doing her hair. The three sisters take over the castle, and despite Finette's heroism, her sisters make her sweep and clean the house, and won't allow her to accompany them to the balls they attend in town.

But one evening, while sitting among the ashes by the hearth, Finette finds a key that opens a beautiful chest filled with luxurious clothes, diamonds and lace, and she dresses for the ball, 'more beautiful than the sun and the moon'.[6] As soon as she appears, guests either admire or envy this mystery woman who now goes by the name of 'Cinders'. Her sisters, who are not unattractive in d'Aulnoy's version, are jealous of the mystery lady who takes attention away from them. Importantly, Finette attends *many* balls, setting fashion standards at court, and she never encounters a prince; she simply has a good time and makes all the men unfaithful to their lovers (as the narrator informs us), suggesting that this Cinderella is a worldly one.

One night, Finette-Cinders leaves the ball later than usual and on her way home loses one of her mules, a type of backless shoe that could quite easily slip off. The next day, the Prince Chéri – not mentioned until this point in the story – is out hunting, finds Finette's mule and actually falls in love with the shoe! He can no longer eat, and the king and queen send for doctors from Paris and Montpellier, who conclude that he is in love, albeit without having seen the mistress of the mule. The prince informs his parents that he will marry none but the woman whose foot fits the shoe. Anticipating the scene in the version published by Jacob and Wilhelm Grimm in which women cut off their toes, here ladies starve themselves and flay their skin to try to fit their foot into the mule. In d'Aulnoy it is Finette who takes the initiative to seek out the prince and try on the shoe – no one comes to fetch her, and she waits for no one – dressing magnificently in a blue satin dress covered in diamonds. She rides to court on her beautiful Spanish horse, splashing her sisters with mud en route: 'she began to laugh and said to them: Your Highnesses, Cinderella despises you to the extent that you deserve it.'[7] The sisters suddenly realize that Cinders and Finette are one and the same. Finette tries on the mule, which of course fits, and Prince Chéri kisses her feet. The prince, king and queen all beg Finette to marry him. But she will not agree until she tells her story. Delighted to discover that Finette is a princess, the prince's parents also realize that they were the ones who took away the land of Finette's parents, and Finette will not marry the prince until her parents' kingdom is restored. The tale ends by informing the readers that Finette and her sisters all become queens. The moral of the story is a bit tongue-in-cheek:

> All your presents and services
> Are so many secret avengers . . . Flower-of-Love and
> Night-Beauty
> Are more cruelly punished
> When Finette grants them infinite favours,
> Than if the cruel ogre robbed them of their life.[8]

D'Aulnoy's 'Finette-Cinders' presents several important contrasts with Perrault's 'Cinderella'. First, d'Aulnoy establishes Finette's agency at the outset by showing the heroine's ingenuity through her ability to outwit her parents, albeit with the assistance

Finette about to splash her sisters with mud as she rides to claim her shoe,
18th-century print.

of her fairy godmother. But importantly, Finette doesn't simply receive help passively from Merluche. She brings her offerings of sorts, a fact that suggests a relation of reciprocity. Her agency is further demonstrated in her ability to outmanoeuvre the ogre and ogress, killing them both, thus recalling Basile's Zezolla and L'Héritier's Finette, both of whom resort to violence to overcome their oppressors. Such an action is not typically associated with normative forms of femininity, whether we think about early modern Europe or the contemporary United States. Interestingly, Finette decapitates the ogress while doing her hair, which could be a playful reference to the more obedient heroine of Perrault, who does up her enemies' hair without seeking revenge.

Second, and like L'Héritier's Finette, d'Aulnoy's Finette-Cinders, in Tatiana Korneeva's words, 'doesn't dream about her passive rescue by Prince Charming, even if she ultimately marries him'.[9] Indeed, Finette takes the initiative time and time again to determine her own future. When she learns that her parents wish to abandon her and her siblings in the forest, she seeks help from her fairy godmother. When the sisters are lost in the woods, Finette locates the ogres' castle, which eventually brings them wealth. Later Finette-Cinders finds the resources she needs to attend the ball and becomes a fashion icon – fashion, as Rebecca-Anne Do Rozario has argued, being a marker of social status and even 'political cunning' in the period.[10] When the time comes to try on the shoe, Finette-Cinders doesn't wait for someone to bring it to her; instead, she climbs on her Spanish horse and rides off to the castle to reclaim her mule. And, rather than be rescued by a prince, Finette-Cinders rescues Prince Chéri, and furthermore restores her family's wealth by negotiating the terms of her marriage with him, recalling the ability of L'Héritier's Finette to negotiate treaties between monarchs.

Finally, Finette-Cinders doesn't, technically, forgive her sisters, although she does help them to re-establish their social position by negotiating the return of her family's wealth. In fact, she takes little and bigger pokes at them throughout the tale, which only foregrounds her mastery of the situation. On the numerous occasions when her sisters describe the beauty of Cinders (for, again, there are many balls), Finette playfully replies under her breath, so that her sisters can barely hear her: '*Ainsi j'étais, ainsi j'étais,*' 'So was I, so was I.' Most importantly, as she gallops past her sisters on her way to the castle to try on the mule, she splashes them with mud, dirtying their beautiful clothes in a gesture that is both playful and vengeful. As a thirteen-year-old girl, d'Aulnoy herself showed such mischievous proclivities. Volker Schröder documents the inscription she made in one of her books: 'Adieu, Reader, if you have my book and I don't know you and you don't appreciate what's inside, I wish you ringworm, scabies, fever, the plague, measles, and a broken neck. May God assist you against my maledictions.'[11] For Korneeva, through this act of vengeance, 'd'Aulnoy's Finette assumes the position typically occupied by the male character in narratives, a position which is even more underlined by the comparison with [Perrault's] Cendrillon's passive forgiveness of her evil stepsisters'.[12] Interestingly, in Perrault, Cinderella shares fruit and is generous with her sisters at the ball; in d'Aulnoy, the sisters pay Cinders – 'made to command' – tribute at court, just like the other courtiers; that is, they pay homage to her as if she were already the queen.[13] While both Perrault and d'Aulnoy evoke the idea of 'grace' in the morals to their tales, in d'Aulnoy this has more of the sense of *noblesse oblige* – Finette giving 'from above' – than a position of subservience, or (for)giving 'from below'.

We must keep in mind that, at the time d'Aulnoy wrote 'Finette Cendron', there was no tradition of literary fairy tales with established conventions.[14] Her implicit quarrel with Perrault was not about a feminist combating a widely circulating antifeminist tale called 'Cinderella', for the two tales were published within months of each other, neither being predominant at the time. Moreover, both authors were adapting Basile's tale, with its wily heroine (which Perrault domesticates). In other words, d'Aulnoy's 'Finette-Cinders' was not what we would call today a feminist fairy-tale 'revision' of a classic tale in the tradition of such authors as Tanith Lee, Emma Donoghue and, more recently, Marissa Meyer, which tend to concern rewriting what are considered to be 'originally' misogynistic tales – a move that often ignores their more complex history, as the present chapter demonstrates. Rather, when d'Aulnoy was reacting to Perrault's 'Cinderella', it was about writing against a new story produced by her male contemporary; it was about producing a competing narrative about women and gender. And that competition didn't end in the 1690s. Although we know that Perrault's 'Cinderella' endured the test of time, for it formed the basis of the Disney film, we simply don't know the history of d'Aulnoy's 'Finette-Cinders', which enjoys its own legacy, feeding not only into oral tale traditions but into a popular filmic adaptation.

The diffusion of 'Finette-Cinders'

'Finette-Cinders' was published regularly in French and English anthologies of d'Aulnoy's tales throughout the eighteenth and nineteenth centuries, with more than thirty editions over the course of the eighteenth century in England, where the tale was known as 'The Story of Finetta; or, The Cinder Girl'. It was mostly reproduced with her other tales, but in 1895 in Boston, Massachusetts, the linguist Charles Hall Grandgent published a first-year French book, *French Lessons and Exercises*, with grammar and vocabulary exercises all organized around d'Aulnoy's 'Finette-Cinders'. For the most part, though, in France, England and the United States 'Finette-Cinders' didn't stand out from other tales of d'Aulnoy's that enjoyed particular renown, such as 'Beauty with the Golden Hair', 'Fortunio, and His Seven Gifted Servants' (also known as 'Belle-Belle; or, The Knight Fortuné'), 'The White Cat' and 'Graciosa and Percinet', all of which enjoyed numerous editions and stage adaptations in the nineteenth century.

Where 'Finette-Cinders' made a particular impact was in folk traditions in France, the Francophone United States, and even in Germany and Czechoslovakia. The tale became popular in Central Europe when Božena Němcová, one of the most important Czech writers of the nineteenth century, included it in her collection *Národní pohádky* (National Fairy Tales, 1845–6), which later served as inspiration for the film *Three Hazelnuts for Cinderella*. Through German and Czech translations as well as cheaply made and widely circulating chapbooks, d'Aulnoy's tales in general and 'Finette-Cinders' in particular moved between written and oral traditions and between languages as writers, printers and storytellers disseminated them through various media and traditions, providing Europeans and, through oral versions, Francophone North Americans with a more empowered version of Cinderella.

The folklorization of 'Finette-Cinders'

We tend to think of literary fairy tales as written adaptations of oral storytelling traditions. However, oral cultures also adapt literary tales according to certain conventions. This 'folklorization' of literary tales – that is, reshaping a written tale to oral narrative needs – entails 'the adaptation of the narrative structure and the suppression of elements that don't assume a functional role in the plot', which basically amounts to streamlining the plot and narrative descriptions.[15] At the same time, oral adaptations of literary tales often retain certain very specific details from literary tales, such as names or objects that are not absolutely necessary, which constitute so many traces of the written text in the oral tale. For instance, some oral versions of 'Finette-Cinders' retain or slightly reshape all or part of the name of the heroine. Published in 1937 by the folklore collector Joseph Médard Carrière, the version related by Frank Bourisaw, a Francophone from a mining community in Missouri, retains the name 'Finette', along with the double-pronged plot in which the heroine, after being abandoned by her parents, overcomes the giant people-eater and his wife in the first narrative sequence, then manages to attend the ball or 'party' in the second, Cinderella narrative sequence.

In oral versions of these tales, we often find aspects of Perrault's 'Cinderella' blended with elements from d'Aulnoy's 'Finette-Cinders'. In the version collected from the Poitou region of France by the historian Léon Pineau in 1891, the name of the eponymous heroine, 'La Cendrouse', could be playing on the French forms of 'Cendrillon' (Perrault) and 'Finette-Cendron' (d'Aulnoy).[16] Like d'Aulnoy, the Poitou heroine has two sisters and not stepsisters as in Perrault, but the first part of the narrative about parental abandonment and killing the ogres is absent, unlike in d'Aulnoy's tale. Instead of a ball, Cendrouse wishes to attend Mass in town, and obtains a magical hazelnut from her father, which gifts her rich clothes, two horses and a carriage (a streamlined version of Perrault's extravagant carriage drawn by six horses, and the six valets who accompany the heroine). When the sisters tell Cendrouse about the beautiful mystery woman they have seen at Mass, much as Finette-Cinders repeated under her breath 'So was I, so was I,' so Cendrouse responds, to her sisters' confusion, 'Oh! As beautiful as she may be, she's not as beautiful as me!'[17] As in Perrault, Cendrouse loses a 'slipper' (*pantoufle*) and not a mule after the second Mass. But, as with the king in d'Aulnoy's tale, here the king also finds the shoe without knowing its owner, and immediately wishes to marry the woman to whom it belongs.

Bourisaw, our Missouri storyteller, had family origins in the Poitou region. It is quite possible that versions of 'Cinderella' and 'Finette-Cinders' coexisted and often blended in the oral tradition of this region. While the Poitou version of 'La Cendrouse' focuses only on the second half of 'Finette-Cinders', Bourisaw's 'Belle-Finette' bears a much closer resemblance to d'Aulnoy's tale, yet also seems to integrate elements taken from Perrault. The context of the tale is completely changed: in d'Aulnoy, Finette-Cinders is the daughter of a king and queen; in the Poitou version, the parents are rich lords; but in the Missouri variant, the family is poor. Rather than a *fairy* godmother, it is simply Belle-Finette's godmother who endows her with a ball of string (*pelote de fil* in d'Aulnoy; *pelote de corde* in Bourisaw), ashes and grains of wheat, very closely following d'Aulnoy's plot. As in d'Aulnoy, the girls hide in a tub or *cuve* in the giant's house, and it is Belle-Finette who pushes the giant into the oven and decapitates his wife. In the second part of the narrative, the sisters go to a dance party (the English word 'party' is used in the first instance in Bourisaw's North American French version) without Belle-Finette, until her godmother – not described as being a fairy – appears. As in Perrault, the godmother provides the heroine with a pumpkin that, in this case, turns into a carriage when it is cut open, and she informs the heroine that she must return from the party by nine in the evening. Belle-Finette goes to the party three times in three different dresses (yellow, red and white), and on the third night doesn't leave until eleven; she loses her slipper (as opposed to mule in d'Aulnoy), and the son of the king wishes to marry the slipper's mistress. Again, we clearly see motifs from Perrault's 'Cinderella' (the pumpkin coach, the slipper and the curfew) that are blended with a plotline – including the 'Little Thumbling' narrative sequence not found in Perrault – that largely follows d'Aulnoy's 'Finette-Cinders'.

At the very least, 'Finette-Cinders' circulated orally in the Poitou region of France, if not elsewhere in the country, sometimes blending elements from Perrault's 'Cinderella', a fact that points to the creative transformations oral storytellers made to their sources. It is possible that Bourisaw's 'Belle-Finette' may have oral origins in Quebec, from where his family migrated to Missouri, although, according to Charlotte Trinquet du Lys, folklorists have not collected any versions from Quebecois informants. We do know that there were oral versions of d'Aulnoy's 'Finette-Cinders' in Acadia (eastern Canada); the linguist France Martineau makes reference to one collected in Yarmouth, Nova Scotia – initially populated by French Acadians – titled 'Cendrillouse, Finette and Belle-d'Amour' – from the ninety-year-old Elie Amirault in 1961.[18]

Germany and Czechoslovakia

Given the widespread print circulation among French-speakers of d'Aulnoy's tales in the eighteenth and nineteenth centuries, it is perhaps not surprising that her version of 'Cinderella' successfully entered French and Francophone oral culture. The extent of this tale's diffusion, however, is much broader. D'Aulnoy's tales were translated into German as early as 1702, in a collection that was brought out in two more editions, in 1739 and 1743.[19] In 1761 the historian Friedrich Immanuel Bierling began publishing the nine-volume *Cabinet der Feen* (Chamber of Fairies, 1761–5), which included tales by d'Aulnoy, Perrault, Murat and Charlotte-Rose de La Force, among others, and 'provided the German reading public with key French fairy-tale texts and sparked imitations of different kinds'.[20] In 1780 an anonymous collection of fairy tales aimed at children and consisting of unattributed tales by d'Aulnoy, entitled *Feenmärchen für Kinder* (Fairy Tales for Children), appeared in Berlin. After Charles-Joseph Mayer released his 41-volume anthology of French fairy tales, *Le Cabinet des fées* (1785–9), which included three volumes of tales by d'Aulnoy (volumes 2–4), the translation and production of tales took off in Germany. The writer, editor and bookseller Friedrich Justin Bertuch published the *Blaue Bibliothek aller Nationen* (International Blue Book Series, 1790–97), modelled on the French chapbook series the *Bibliothèque bleue*, in which d'Aulnoy's tales figure prominently among the corpus of fairy tales that regularly appeared in the series. In the same period *Feen-Mährchen der Frau Gräfin von Aulnoy* (Fairy Tales by the Countess d'Aulnoy, 1790–96) was published, which included fairy tales by d'Aulnoy drawn from volumes 3, 4, 9 and 10 of the German *International Blue Book Series*.[21]

As was the case in France, 'Finette-Cinders', among other tales, entered the oral tradition in Germany. In fact, one of the informants who provided tales to the Brothers Grimm, the aristocrat Ludowine von Haxthausen, recounted to them a version of 'Finette-Cinders' that they transcribed around 1818, giving it the title 'Prettyflower, Finette and Tiny Ears'. However, as Jeannine Blackwell has shown, it 'remained part of the Grimm brothers' unpublished collection of tales'.[22] In this variant, Tiny Ears plays the role of Finette-Cinders, while the name 'Finette' is displaced to the middle sister. Like d'Aulnoy, von Haxthausen makes the three sisters' father a king, but the queen is their stepmother, not their mother. Although the god-mother is not referred to as being a fairy, she is called an enchantress and a witch in the tale, attributing to her more magical powers than, for instance, the version related by the Missouri miner. Von Haxthausen's tale follows the overall structure of d'Aulnoy's 'Finette-Cinders', but does some streamlining; the children are abandoned only twice before they come upon the ogres' castle. In the oral tale we find a ball of yarn, peas, an acorn and a golden key, all objects that assist in the heroine's journey and that we also find in d'Aulnoy's 'Finette-Cinders'. Tiny Ears also splashes her sisters with mud when riding a Spanish horse (note the specificity), exclaiming 'Tiny Ears is laughing!', as in the case of d'Aulnoy. One important change in von Haxthausen's version is that when killing the ogre couple, the girls collaborate to defeat them: Finette, the middle sister, lures the ogre to the oven, and she and Prettyflower push him in; and it is Finette who kills the ogress while Tiny Ears combs her hair. Whereas in d'Aulnoy the prince falls in love with Finette-Cinders's shoe without having seen her, in von Haxthausen's version the prince accompanies Tiny Ears to the first ball, and lays out pitch to stop her when she flees at the end of the evening; her shoe gets stuck in the pitch but Tiny Ears leaves it and runs away, only to return later on horseback to try on the shoe and cure the prince of his lovesickness, again recalling d'Aulnoy.

This is only one of many examples of German women writers and tale tellers of the first part of the nineteenth century having been influenced by d'Aulnoy's tales, whether through literary or oral traditions. Moving in the same circles as von Haxthausen, Jeannette Hassenpflug, whose family was of French Huguenot background, had provided the Grimms with a version of d'Aulnoy's 'The Bee and the Orange Tree', titled 'Okerlo', which also features a powerful heroine. It was published in the first edition of the Grimms' *Children's and Household Tales* (1812–15), but was eliminated from later editions owing to its proximity to French literary tales.[23] Despite the Grimms' purging, however, d'Aulnoy's influence affected the Grimms' collection. For instance, given the wide circulation of d'Aulnoy's tales, it is likely that the scene in 'Hansel and Gretel' when Gretel pushes the witch into the oven was borrowed from 'Finette-Cendron'; the tale was related to the Grimms in 1809 by Dorothea Wild, the future wife of Wilhelm, and from a French Huguenot family. 'The Six Servants', related by the Huguenot von Haxthausen family, shares details that may have come from d'Aulnoy's 'Belle-Belle; or, The Knight Fortuné' and 'Beauty with the Golden Hair'.[24]

D'Aulnoy's tales continued to be published in German in the nineteenth century. Following the Grimms' lead, the German poet, publicist and tale collector Hermann Kletke describes d'Aulnoy's stories as being 'skilfully wrought and amiably told, but not as simple and natural' as those by Perrault.[25] Nevertheless, in his first volume of *Märchen aller Völker für Jung und Alt* (Fairy Tales from All Nations for Young and Old, 1845), the section on French tales is launched by 'Finette-Cinders' (or 'Finette Aschenbrödel'), and nine out of seventeen tales are from d'Aulnoy, with five from Perrault, one each from the Chevalier de Mailly and L'Héritier, and a folk-tale collection by the writer Marie Aycard from Marseilles. Kletke's three-volume collection was important enough by the end of the century that the writer and collector Andrew Lang drew select tales from it for his coloured books series in the 1890s. According to Margaret Ross Griffel, Finette also apparently made it to the German stage in 1830 with the production of *Finette Aschenbrödel, oder Rose und Schuh* (Finette Cinderella; or, Rose and Shoe), a *Singspiel* – a genre that blends spoken dialogue and songs – with a libretto by Julius Ribics.[26]

Specifically mentioning 'Finette-Cinders', the Czech literary historian Jan Máchal claimed in 1902 that French fairy tales travelled from France to Germany to Czechoslovakia.[27] Providing further evidence for this theory in 1930, the writer and critic Václav Tille published an overview of Czech versions of d'Aulnoy's 'The Bee and the Orange Tree' and 'Finette-Cinders', following the lines of transmission. He emphasizes the importance of Václav Matěj Kramerius, the eighteenth-century Czech publisher and writer who founded the publishing house Czech Dispatch in order to translate and adapt into Czech works 'capable of instructing or amusing the lower classes', and to foster a literary culture at a time when there was not yet an established Czech literary tradition; he translated and published a version of d'Aulnoy's 'The Bee and the Orange Tree' in 1794.[28] Tille suggests that there may have been a translation of 'Finette-Cinders' from German into Czech as early as 1761 in Jindřichův Hradec in southern Bohemia, which was reprinted several times in the nineteenth century. Later, Kramerius's son Václav Rodomil Kramerius produced a Czech version of 'Finette-Cinders' in which, according to Tille, the youngest of the three daughters is named Finette, who is assisted by the female magician Tamarinde. The heroine manages to kill the ogres and take over their castle, and rides a white horse given to her by Tamarinde to go to the palace, where she meets the prince, Otmar, whom she eventually marries. Tille documents several other oral variants of 'Finette-Cinders', including a Moravian variant published in the nineteenth century by Matouš Václavek, which includes only the first part of the narration; a version by Václav Popelka in *Pohádky z Poličska* (Fairy Tales from Policka, 1888), in which the ogress, instead of being 15 feet wide, has fifteen toes; and another Moravian variant told by the informant Kateřina Vidláková and collected and published by Beneš Method Kulda, in which the wife of the ogre is happy that her husband is killed in the oven, and Finette rides to Mass instead of to a ball on her white horse.

Along with dramatic works by such French playwrights as
Molière and Marivaux, 'French fairy tales, for example *Finette
Cendron* (*Pohádka o Popelce* [A Fairy Tale about Cinderella]) in the
version by Madame d'Aulnoy . . . represented another source of
inspiration for different Czech adaptations and for indigenous
literary production, especially in the 1840s.'[29] As d'Aulnoy's tales
were circulating throughout Bohemia via German and Czech translations and oral storytelling, Božena Němcová was coming into her
own as a writer. The daughter of a servant and a coachman, and un-
happily married to Josef Němec in 1837, Němcová frequented Czech
nationalist salons and in this spirit changed her first name from
Barbora to the more Czech-sounding Božena.[30] Alfred Thomas
characterizes Němcová and her works in the following terms:
'Influenced by the French novelist George Sand, Božena Němcová
was the first feminist writer in Czech literature. But she was also a
nationalist writer who believed deeply in the Czech and Slovak
right to equal political representation within the Habsburg Empire.'[31]
Her work collecting tales is thus grounded in the type of nationalist
and democratic impulse evident in the work of the Grimms, with
Němcová specifically identifying as socialist. At the urging of the
Czech folklorist Karel Jaromír Erben, she published her first collection of tales, *Národní báchorky a pověsti* (literally National Stories
and Legends, but translated into English as *Czech and Slovak Folk
Tales*, 1845–7), which includes 'The Black Princess', a racist Beauty
and the Beast tale in which the 'beast' is a princess turned Black by
an evil magician in retaliation for her rejection of him, and who can
be saved only by a man who is willing to love her despite her Black-
ness; 'The Three Sisters', a Cinderella tale bearing affinities with the
Grimms' 'Aschenputtel'; and her version of 'Finette-Cinders', titled
'O Popelce' (literally 'About Cinderella'). Němcová continued
collecting folklore in the region; in 1855 she released her most

renowned work, *Babička* (The Grandmother), and two years later she produced another collection of tales, *Slovenské pohádky a pověsti* (Slovak Fairy Tales and Legends, 1857), which included a third Cinderella tale, 'O Popelušce', also meaning 'About Cinderella'.

Like d'Aulnoy, Němcová was subjected to an arranged and unhappy marriage and eventually separated from her husband. Both writers sought to empower their female characters, albeit from different sociohistorical and class perspectives, so it is not surprising that Němcová found inspiration in d'Aulnoy's tale featuring a strong female character such as Finette. Němcová may have drawn her adaptation of 'Finette-Cinders' from oral tradition, but certain details are so specific that it is also possible that she adapted a German or Czech translation of d'Aulnoy's tale. In some ways, just as the Grimms initially included tales they recognized as being of French or other non-German origin in the 1812 edition of the *Children's and Household Tales* that was to embody a new German identity (although they excluded many of them from later editions), so Němcová was trying to build a national Czech identity through the collection of folk tales, which included some of French origin (she also published 'The Princess with the Golden Star on her Forehead', which has clear links to Perrault's 'Donkey Skin').

As in the case of some of the oral adaptations of d'Aulnoy's tale issuing from poorer communities, Němcová makes her heroine, Popelka (or 'Cinderella'), the daughter of a poor couple who wish to abandon their daughters to avoid having to beg; in this case, it is the father who advances this plan of action, not the mother or stepmother. (Although Francis Gregor claims that Němcová was closer to her father than her mother as a child, it was her father who forcibly married her to Němec.)[32] Němcová also creates a more realistic setting for the tale, limiting recourse to the marvellous by having Popelka consult her aunt, rather than a magical fairy godmother.

But, like d'Aulnoy's Merluche, Němcová's aunt warns the heroine, after giving her a ball of thread, not to bring her sisters Kasala and Adlina back home with her when their father abandons them in the woods. The second time the father talks about abandoning their daughters, the mother unsuccessfully begs him not to, and Popelka again seeks out her aunt, who gives her ashes and another warning. However, on the third occasion, the aunt has grown so angry with Popelka for helping her wicked sisters that she gives the heroine peas, knowing they will be eaten up by birds. Popelka climbs a tree and spies a castle belonging, in this case, to an ugly woman, who warns the girls about her cannibalistic husband. The episode where the ogres are killed recalls that of von Haxthausen: when the cannibal wants to learn how to make bread, Popelka prepares the fire and, with her sisters, pushes him into the oven, killing him; with respect to the wife, Popelka's role is to hand the axe to her sister Kasala. These changes to the story could have been made to lessen the violent role the main heroine plays in the tale, or perhaps to show the sisters working together in a moment of female solidarity.

In the second part of the narrative, Kasala and Adlina make Popelka carry out all the housework in their new castle-home, and plan to attend a feast given by the prince. Like Finette, Popelka finds a golden key that, in this case, unlocks a door in the cellar leading to a room of chests filled with silver, gems and exquisite clothes; here she also finds a white pony that will take her to the feast three times. For the first feast, Popelka dons a beautiful white dress and gold slippers; for the second, a red dress with silver slippers; and for the third, a blue dress with silver slippers and pearls. It is on the third occasion that the heroine, fleeing the feast to return home before her sisters, loses her shoe, which gets stuck in pine tar set out by the prince to prevent her from running off. Unlike in 'Finette-Cinders', in 'O Popelce' the heroine and prince fall in love at the first feast, and the prince promises to submit to her will at the second feast, wanting her to become his wife at the third. When she learns that he is seeking the woman whose foot fits the slipper, Popelka presents herself at the castle and they wed. Although she doesn't splash her sisters with mud on the way to try on the shoe, she does end up getting her revenge. The riches Popelka finds can only be removed from the castle cellar three times. After she and the prince have made three trips – Tille suggests that these magical riches function as Popelka's dowry – the heroine informs her sisters about the cellar. Kasala and Adlina try to remove some of the treasures and are attacked and disfigured by two black cats; the riches they have taken turn to stone. The sisters are punished for their greed, while Popelka and the prince live 'peacefully and happily, treated their subjects well, and in return the heavens blessed them'.[33]

Although Němcová's version of 'Finette-Cinders' doesn't quite read as a socialist fairy tale, 'O Popelce' does entail a redistribution of wealth, whereby Popelka and her sisters manage to appropriate the riches from the cannibalistic castle owners they kill, and Popelka is clever enough to unlock the riches accessible through the golden key, thus laying a level playing field between the daughter of a poor man and the son of a king. Importantly, Popelka isn't simply lifted out of poverty or low status by the prince, in the tradition of Perrault's or Disney's *Cinderella*; it is through her own wits that she obtains wealth and thus provides herself with a dowry worthy of a prince. While one could maintain that this is an exchange of women in the tradition of patriarchal marriage, here Popelka arguably exchanges herself, being the agent of her own marriage, as opposed to it being an exchange between her father and her future husband (which Němcová experienced in real life, leading to a miserable marriage). In this variant of 'Finette-Cinders', the three sisters spend a longer period working for the monstrous couple in the castle, and at one point they decide together that they must kill their 'masters'. This is an interesting moment in the tale given the fact that Němcová's parents were themselves servants in a noble household, that of Wilhelmine Zaháňská. Němcová apparently had a good relationship with Zaháňská, and features her as the princess in *The Grandmother*; nevertheless, her tale points to tension between bad masters who oppress their servants, leading to violent conflict. Drawing from d'Aulnoy's model of a Cinderella who takes care of herself and waits for no prince, Němcová challenges the class hierarchy that d'Aulnoy in fact sought to uphold in her tales, through the redistribution of wealth, the rejection of oppression by the cannibalistic (and, given their castle abode, noble?) couple, and intermarriage – on at least equal financial terms – between a commoner and a prince.

Němcová's *Czech and Slovak Folk Tales* were eminently popular. Tille contends that the 'collection of tales by Božena Němcová having broadly spread among the Czech-speaking population, it isn't surprising that so many people could tell her tales'.[34] He gives a specific example of a young woman from the northern Krkonoše mountains who recounts a tale that, while differing in some aspects from that of Němcová, includes a heroine named Popelka, the taboo against bringing her sisters back with her, and the two black cats, which in this instance kill the two sisters. It is notable, however, that d'Aulnoy's folklorized version also seems to have continued to circulate in Czechoslovakia. As late as 1923 the folklorist Josef Štefan Kubín collected a tale with a heroine called Fineta, who has a godmother, Merlusi, and is carried to her godmother's home on the horse Jindydad, a deformation of '*gentil dada*' or 'toy horse', the expression the French Finette uses to refer to the Spanish horse her fairy godmother sends her. Whether through oral folklorizations of d'Aulnoy's 'Finette-Cinders' or via Němcová's 'O Popelce', this other Cinderella tale remained so popular in Czechoslovakia that František Pavlíček decided to draw from it for his screenplay for *Three Hazelnuts for Cinderella* (1973).

The other Cinderella

From an American perspective, it is hard to imagine a Cinderella film that could compete with the global phenomenon of Disney's movie, and especially one with roots going back to a seventeenth-century French woman author. The director Václav Vorlíček's *Three Hazelnuts for Cinderella* is such a film. In 2012 it aired seventeen times on ten different German television stations between 20 November and 26 December, and it is the most frequently aired fairy-tale film on German television.[35] It has become a must-see Christmas film in Germany, the Czech Republic, Norway, Poland, Slovakia and Switzerland. The fortieth anniversary of the film was celebrated in 2013 with exhibitions at Moritzburg Castle near Dresden – one of the filming locations – and in the Czech Republic, and in 2015 Norway collaborated with the Czech Republic to finance the restoration of the film.[36] The film emerged as a co-production between DEFA (Deutsche Film-Aktien-gesellschaft; the East German film company founded in 1950 that produced many socialist fairy-tale films aimed at children) and the Czech studio Filmové Studio Barrandov, with a Czech director, Vorlíček, and a Czech writer, Pavlíček, who had already written a biopic about Němcová and the script for a televised adaptation of *The Grandmother*.[37]

For the screenplay of *Three Hazelnuts*, Pavlíček drew from Němcová's three Cinderella tales, as Pavel Skopal and Adéla Ficová have shown: 'O Popelce' and 'The Three Sisters', from her first collection of tales, and 'O Popelušce' from her second.[38] Critics tend to focus on Pavlíček's use of 'O Popelušce', which provides the film's framework of a stepsister and stepmother, both of whom abuse the heroine. In fact, Němcová's third Cinderella tale reads as an abbreviated version of 'The Three Sisters'. Both tales have the heroine go to Mass instead of a ball; whereas 'The Three Sisters' includes two rival sisters, one of whom is named Dorotka, in 'O Popelušce' the siblings are reduced to one stepsister, similarly named Dora; in both versions the persecuted heroine is given three magical nuts by her father, and they provide her with exquisite dresses, allowing her to attend Mass despite her cruel stepsisters, and to meet the prince. (As we have seen, some oral variants send the heroine to church and not to a ball or feast.)

While the churchgoing Cinderellas from these two tales by Němcová come off as rather passive, the heroine of 'O Popelce' proves much more spirited, and provided Pavlíček with a model of a feistier Cinderella. In his study of the film, Skopal remarks on distinctions between the Grimms' Cinderella and Němcová's Popelka: 'In contrast to the Grimms' take on the tale, Božena Němcová's Cinderella [from 'O Popelce'] is a much more active figure, and Pavlíček emphasizes the character's independence even further.'[39] However, from the other two tales Pavlíček borrows the motif of the three nuts and the heroine's affinity with animals.

Although inspired by the enterprising heroine of 'Finette-Cinders' via Němcová and possibly other Czech folklorizations of the tale, *Three Hazelnuts for Cinderella* leaves out the child-abandonment episode from 'O Popelce' that leads to the encounter with child-eating ogres, focusing instead on the 'Cinderella' episode of the tale. The film opens in a beautiful little village in winter, featuring the estate where Popelka lives with her stepmother and stepsister; we later learn that the heroine's father died three years earlier. In the first scene, we witness the stepmother mistreating servants, and later, when she is ready to whip the kitchen boy for dropping something, Popelka takes the blame for him. From the beginning of the film, the heroine is viewed as the ally of the household servants, trying to protect them from the cruelty of her stepmother and stepsister, and in return they show her great affection. In fact, the three hazelnuts that provide Popelka with rich clothes are from the coachman, who wanted to bring something back for the mistreated Popelka; all she asks for is the first thing that hits his nose, recalling the episode in 'The Three Sisters' and 'O Popelušce', in which it is the father who brings the heroine the nuts. We see that Popelka enjoys two sites of refuge at the estate: the barn, where her beautiful, faithful white horse, Jurášek, given to her by her father, is stabled; and a shed where she keeps a little chest of sentimental objects and is consoled by her owl, Rosie. Nature – snow-covered plains and forests – also figures as a space of freedom in the film. In a motif recalling the Grimms' 'Aschenputtel' and Němcová's 'O Popelušce', the stepmother has Popelka separate peas from the ashes as a pretext to keep her from meeting the prince when the royal family comes to their country castle, but the heroine is assisted by pigeons, which do the job; in a later scene she must separate corn from lentils, and is again helped by these birds.

Thanks to the pigeons, Popelka can ride off into the woods on Jurášek, and she happens to bump into the prince – himself in dereliction of his duty to greet the villagers – hunting a deer. Popelka throws a snowball at him to prevent him from killing the deer with his bow, after which the prince and his friends try to catch her, but she outsmarts them. On a second occasion, the prince again abandons his official duties to go hunting in the woods. Popelka opens her first hazelnut, in which she finds a beautiful hunting costume, and ends up competing with the prince's men to be the first to kill a bird of prey. (She notably protects the vulnerable deer but is ready to kill a predator.) Cross-dressed and with her crossbow, Popelka outdoes all the men with an impossible shot and wins a ring; she runs off and, teasing the prince, climbs a tree in a scene that recalls Finette's tree-climbing abilities. For their third encounter, Popelka opens a second hazelnut and finds a beautiful dress for the ball. She hops on to her white horse, saying: 'Daddy always laughed that I'd ride to my first ball on Jurášek, like a Hussar.'

Even when dressed in a feminine manner, Popelka never fully complies to repressive models of femininity. Of course, at the ball the prince falls immediately in love with the mystery woman, who playfully refuses to reveal her identity, and who also refuses to submit to the man she loves:

PRINCE: Tell me who you are!

POPELKA: Can't you see for yourself?

PRINCE: Take off that veil, then. At least give me a hint.

POPELKA: Why do you want to know?

PRINCE: Because I have just chosen a bride and I know not who she is.

POPELKA: Not so loud, they are listening!

PRINCE: I'll call right out into the world that I'm in love and getting married.

POPELKA: But you forgot something!

PRINCE: What?

POPELKA: To ask the bride if she wants you!

She gives him a riddle, which references her three meetings with him as a cinder-girl, a huntsman and her present appearance, then runs out of the ball, losing her shoe, and rides away on her white horse. The prince and his friends follow her to the estate with the shoe, shortly before the stepmother and stepsister arrive home. After tying up Popelka and locking her in a room to prevent her from trying on the shoe, the stepmother attempts to trick the prince into marrying a veiled Dora without seeing her and without her trying on the shoe, but he does not fall into her trap. The stepmother then grabs the shoe and she and Dora ride off on a sleigh. The prince chases them, the sleigh falls into the river and, realizing the step-mother's ruse, the prince grabs the slipper, leaving the two women thrashing around in the water. In the meantime, our clever heroine manages to free herself from the ropes and somehow escape from the locked room; she opens the last hazelnut at Rosie's urging, and a wedding dress appears. The prince returns, forlorn, to the estate with the shoe, when Popelka suddenly rides up in her wedding dress. When the prince approaches, she smiles and says: 'Have you brought my slipper?' She then repeats the riddle, to which the prince now gives the answers, and the final response is cheered by the servants, who say 'Our Popelka!' with the prince, more humbly than at the ball, declaring, 'And mine too . . . If you want me.' The two ride off towards a snowy horizon.

While the storyline of the film seems a long way from Němcová's (witting or unwitting) adaptation of d'Aulnoy, there are some clear connections between this tale and the film with respect to specific motifs, and more generally in terms of the representation of the heroine. A recurrent motif in 'Finette-Cinders' tales is the Spanish or white horse, which the heroine usually receives from her fairy godmother; in Němcová, the heroine finds the white horse with the other riches in the secret room in the cellar. In many Finette-Cinders tales, the figure of the white horse appears as a manifestation of the bond between the heroine and an important figure in her life, this being in the case of *Three Hazelnuts for Cinderella* Popelka's father, who before his death taught her to ride and hunt. Evident in other versions of the tale, but emphasized in the film, is the way in which the horse represents the free spirit and agency of the heroine, who takes herself to the ball, and who rides up to the prince to don the slipper. One might also understand the shed with the owl, the chest and the saddle to be akin to the secret room and chests in the cellar found in 'O Popelce'; Popelka even says as she greets the owl, 'Looking after my treasures?' Although in the film the chest is quite small – more like a jewellery box – it contains a rose cameo from her dead mother (at one point she holds it while reflecting on her mother's words about what Popelka would wear to her first ball). Later, she keeps the three magical hazelnuts in the little chest with her other 'treasures'. Finally – although this is not found in Němcová's version of 'Finette-Cinders', but featured in the Czech oral tale collected by Kubín in 1923 – the scene of Finette splashing her sisters with mud on the way to try on the shoe seems to take new shape in the film when the stepmother and stepsister are similarly humiliated and ridiculed by falling into the river. This scene suggests that Pavlíček was familiar with other variants of 'Finette-Cinders'.

In the scenes of encounter between Popelka and the prince, the heroine tends to have the upper hand. She playfully throws a snowball at him when they first meet, and can outmanoeuvre him and his friends when they try to catch her in the woods. For the second encounter, Popelka proves to be the superior archer. Even when dressed in a feminine manner at the ball, she expresses her wit through the riddle the prince cannot yet solve, and she makes it clear to him that he cannot assume she will marry him; he must take into account her own desire. Although Popelka's stepmother ties her up and locks her in a room to prevent her from trying on the slipper – the viewer practically expects to see the prince come and rescue her – she is no damsel in distress. Already a proven escape artist of sorts, she frees herself, dons the dress she has found in the last hazelnut, and rides to the prince to ask for her slipper. Referencing the Grimms' 'Cinderella', Vorlíček was very conscious of the difference in agency with respect to Popelka: 'Readers remember Cinderella as a passive, defenceless creature, tortured by her wicked stepmother and envious sisters, dependent on the help of doves and liberated by a prince charming. Our Cinderella is more like a modern girl, she is active, brave, sporty and she helps herself out of misfortune.'[40] Skopal cites East German reviews at the time of the film's release that similarly praise the heroine's independence, emancipated nature and ability to fight for her freedom. While some critics and theatregoers were aware of the relation between the film and this tale by Němcová, it is likely that none fathomed that this feisty, independent Cinderella has as her great-great-grandmother Finette-Cinders, imagined by a seventeenth-century French noblewoman, Marie-Catherine d'Aulnoy.

The film also challenges norms of masculinity. Although in some respects the prince manifests aspects of hegemonic masculinity in his constant desire to hunt, he also resists the norms of princedom by refusing to conform to court etiquette and princely education. Moreover, he evolves over the course of the film, moving from assuming that Popelka will marry him to asking her, at the end of the film, if she 'wants' him. What makes this association with hunting different from other representations of man-as-hunter and woman-as-prey is, first, that Popelka can hunt as well as if not better than the prince; and second, that the film also constructs the prince as prey. When speaking to the king and queen about the planned ball, and knowing that his parents wish him to select a bride from among the attending women, he declares: 'I thought this was to be a ball, but it looks more like a man-hunt!' In effect, both the prince and Popelka are trapped by their environments, populated by calculating and controlling family members, and both seek solace in nature, and in the end, with each other, as they playfully melt into the snowy forest and meadow at the conclusion of the film.

With respect to *Three Hazelnuts*, Qinna Shen remarks that this 'image of a new woman agrees with the socialist conception of gender relations', which was an egalitarian one; many DEFA fairy-tale films 'presented strong, intelligent, and confident female protagonists'.[41] While Pavlíček and Vorlíček's shaping of Cinderella indeed conforms to a broader vision of gender equality, they were also, via Němcová, inspired by the spirit of d'Aulnoy herself, who challenged gender norms for both women and men through her unconventional characters. Like Popelka and the prince, her romantic couples were often equal in beauty, wit and martial skill, and sought to free themselves from parental and social constraints. However, in her Czech incarnation, Finette-Cinders further becomes the embodiment of socialist ideals that also challenge class hierarchy.

It is as if Cinderella took two different paths. Rooted in Basile, the tale forks in two directions, one moving from Perrault and leading to Disney's gender-conservative *Cinderella*, the other stemming from d'Aulnoy and travelling to Czechoslovakia, making its way into Pavlíček and Vorlíček's socialist and egalitarian *Three Hazelnuts for Cinderella*. I do not mean to suggest that the respective evolution of these tales had to happen this way, but I do put forward the idea that 'Finette-Cinders' spoke to women tellers and writers, as well as male tellers, such as Bourisaw, and a feminist-minded male screenwriter and director. Ludowine von Haxthausen provided the Grimms with an oral version of 'Finette-Cinders', Kateřina Vidláková furnished the Moravian folklorist Beneš Method Kulda with another oral version of the tale, and through her adaptation Božena Němcová in effect canonized within Czech nationalist folklore a tale that later, with the production of *Three Hazelnuts for Cinderella*, became a cult film within Czech and German cultures. One branch of the Cinderella family provides us with a passive heroine who waits for a prince to elevate her and save her from oppression; the other offers a

Cinderella who is self-reliant, saves princes, kills monsters and takes charge of her own destiny.

Following the breadcrumbs, or rather – as in the case of 'Finette-Cinders' – the thread of motifs, there is a clear lineage from d'Aulnoy to oral and written tale traditions and finally to film, a thread that critics have not yet woven together to be able to view the full tapestry of d'Aulnoy's cultural impact on Cinderella tales and media. Although Basile's tale introduces the motif of the horse, it is d'Aulnoy who perpetuates what becomes a symbol of Finette-Cinders's agency and – evident in *Three Hazelnuts* – her freedom. D'Aulnoy provides us with the only version of 'Cinderella' that splices in the 'Little Thumbling' or 'Hansel and Gretel' motif of the children being abandoned in the forest – also found in versions from Missouri, Germany and Czechoslovakia – and she does so in order to high-light Finette's wit and ability to fend for herself and defend others. It is only in d'Aulnoy's variant that the fairy godmother (or, in some versions, the aunt) forbids Finette-Cinders from bringing her sisters back with her, and provides her with specific objects – a ball of thread, ashes and peas – that the heroine uses to try to make her way home. The golden key Finette-Cinders finds that unlocks a chest, allowing her to attend the ball in proper attire, is found in Kletke's German translation of the tale, in von Haxthausen's German oral variant, and in the Czech versions by Němcová and the oral version collected by Kubín. Such specific motifs found in written translations and oral and written variants from France, North America, Germany and Czechoslovakia all foreground the fact that d'Aulnoy's 'Finette-Cinders' fed into several different written and oral traditions across three centuries.

'Finette-Cinders' coexisted with 'Cinderella' over generations and in different places, providing readers and listeners with contrasting conceptions of female agency. Drawing from L'Héritier's

'Finette; or, The Clever Princess', d'Aulnoy presented her readers with an oppressed yet enterprising Cinderella who found her most recent incarnation in Popelka, the master archer, expert horsewoman and witty courtier who maintains her independence before all, including the man she loves. Interestingly, no critics have mentioned the genealogy of *Three Hazelnuts for Cinderella*, which can be traced from d'Aulnoy to Němcová. Somewhere, at some time, the thread got cut, the ashes blown away, the peas eaten up – perhaps by scholarly and literary traditions that have suppressed, ignored or otherwise marginalized the work of women writers and tale tellers. But d'Aulnoy's legacy lives on today, unbeknownst to many.

2
Beauties, Beasts and d'Aulnoy's Legacy

'Beauty and the Beast' is the exception to the rule that classic fairy tales broadly circulating in twentieth- and twenty-first-century Western Europe and Euro-North America were produced (collected, edited, written) by men. Modelling her story on Gabrielle-Suzanne de Villeneuve's lengthy Rococo tale 'Beauty and the Beast' (1740), Jeanne-Marie Leprince de Beaumont produced an abridged adaptation, which appeared in the *Young Misses' Magazine* (*Le Magasin des enfants*) in 1756.[1] In the twentieth century, the position of Leprince de Beaumont's animal bridegroom tale solidified itself within the fairy-tale canon, being adapted for the screen by Jean Cocteau in 1946, and by Walt Disney Studios in animated form in 1991 and as a live-action film in 2017. However, from the late seventeenth through the nineteenth and even into the early twentieth century, the main predecessors of both Villeneuve's and Leprince de Beaumont's 'Beauty and the Beast' – Marie-Catherine d'Aulnoy's 'Le Mouton' (The Ram, 1697) and 'Le Serpentin vert' (The Green Serpent, 1697) – continued to circulate widely in France and England. This chapter makes visible the traces of d'Aulnoy on 'Beauty and the Beast' as we know it today, as well as the continued legacy her own foundational animal bridegroom tales enjoyed in France and England.

In Chapter One we noted the diverging paths of Cinderella, with Perrault's heroine finding herself in the hands of Disney Studios and d'Aulnoy's Finette-Cinders in those of the East German film studio DEFA. In the case of the history of 'Beauty and the Beast', two d'Aulnoy narratives prove essential in the formation of the canonical tale that is familiar to twenty-first-century readers, which then continue to follow their own paths, taking new forms in chapbooks, children's books and musical compositions. As we will see, 'The Ram' most closely anticipates Villeneuve's 'Beauty and the Beast', for which Villeneuve also borrowed elements from 'The Green Serpent'. Tracing the threads connecting these narratives by d'Aulnoy, Villeneuve and Leprince de Beaumont, we can follow the genealogy of a well-known tale and its accommodation to different contexts. However, the stories of 'The Ram' and 'The Green Serpent', importantly, did not simply disappear with the birth and canonization of 'Beauty and the Beast'. Popular in British print culture, 'The Ram' was continually republished and adapted in many creative ways to such Victorian contexts as the children's library, while 'The Green Serpent' inspired prominent writers and composers, including Honoré de Balzac and Maurice Ravel.

In *Fairy Tale as Myth/ Myth as Fairy Tale* (1994) the scholar Jack Zipes remarks on d'Aulnoy's fascination with what folklorists refer to as animal or monster bridegroom tales, which include 'Beauty and the Beast'. D'Aulnoy was particularly struck by the story 'Cupid and Psyche', especially in the form of Jean de La Fontaine's adaptation, *The Loves of Cupid and Psyche* (1669), based on Apuleius's second-century Latin tale. In both versions, Cupid remains invisible to his bride and is at times described by Psyche's sisters as being monstrous. D'Aulnoy was also familiar with Giovanni Francesco Straparola's 'The Pig Prince' (1550), a different model for the animal or monstrous bridegroom tale, which she adapted to create 'The Boar Prince'. In several of her fairy tales, including 'The Golden Bough', 'The Ram' and 'The Green Serpent', d'Aulnoy reimagines and recontextualizes some of the themes from Apuleius (via La Fontaine) and Straparola. Zipes specifically points to the impact d'Aulnoy's 'The Ram' and 'The Green Serpent' had on the development of 'Beauty and the Beast': 'I must first emphasize that it was Madame d'Aulnoy who prepared the way for the literary version of *Beauty and the Beast*, not Perrault.'[2] While folklorists and fairy-tale scholars tend to lump together all animal or monstrous bridegroom tales, from 'Cupid and Psyche' (second century CE) to Jacob and Wilhelm Grimm's 'The Frog King' (1812), few scholars have closely examined the very specific motifs drawn from d'Aulnoy that can help us build a clearer genealogy for Villeneuve's and later Leprince de Beaumont's now canonical tale 'Beauty and the Beast'.

This chapter traces d'Aulnoy's important role in the birth of 'Beauty and the Beast' and showcases the fact that her foundational tales did not simply disappear with the emergence of this new variant of the animal or beastly bridegroom tale. After exploring the specific elements Villeneuve and Leprince de Beaumont borrowed from d'Aulnoy's 'The Ram' and 'The Green Serpent', I will turn to the individual legacies of these two tales by d'Aulnoy as they shifted from their aristocratic origins to more bourgeois contexts, from an adult readership to the domain of children's literature, and from literature to music. Moving from d'Aulnoy and Villeneuve to Leprince de Beaumont, we furthermore witness the historical evolution of the social conception of women's roles, with d'Aulnoy proposing more aristocratic, worldly and active heroines, Villeneuve tracing the 'fall' of the aristocratic, worldly woman, and Leprince de Beaumont ushering in a domestic, bourgeois model of femininity – an evolution that follows more general historical and cultural trends in Western Europe. This history of adaptations also reveals that tales by a woman writer who sought to empower her heroines

could be turned into stories of female self-sacrifice and even erotic
objectification.

The making of 'Beauty and the Beast'

In order to concoct a 'Beauty and the Beast' tale, you might say
that one takes 'The Ram' and blends it carefully with elements drawn
from 'The Green Serpent'. These monster bridegroom tales by
d'Aulnoy contribute important narrative components to 'Beauty
and the Beast'. Like the story of Psyche and later 'Beauty and the
Beast', both tales include the heroine's separation from her family
and isolation within the monster bridegroom's marvellous domain.
'The Ram' serves as a model for the Beast by providing the reasons
for his metamorphosis and the warning that the hero might die
if the heroine abandons him for too long. 'The Green Serpent'
includes a doubling of the hero, which we see in Villeneuve's version
of 'Beauty and the Beast', and which is reiterated in films by both
Cocteau and Disney through the figures of Avenant and Gaston,
respectively. As we will see, these antecedents to 'Beauty and the
Beast' are missing two important elements that Villeneuve will
emphasize in her version of the beastly bridegroom tale: the explicit
rivalry between sisters, and the prisoner-like status of Beauty in the
Beast's castle.

From ram to beast

'The Ram' begins with a King Lear-like narrative, in which the king
suspects the youngest and most loving of his three daughters,
Merveilleuse (Marvellous), of being unloving or disloyal to him.
This is owing, first, to her initial response to her father when he asks
why she donned a white dress upon his return from battle; and

second, to a dream she had, in which her father washes Merveilleuse's hands at her sister's wedding. Misinterpreting the dream as a bad omen, the king has the captain of the guards take Merveilleuse into the woods to kill her, asking the captain to bring back his daughter's heart and tongue. As we might expect, the captain takes pity on the princess, and Merveilleuse's monkey, Moorish servant and dog all sacrifice themselves to provide the captain with a substitute tongue and heart.[3] Merveilleuse then flees, until she spies a beautiful white ram with golden horns, who transports her in a pumpkin carriage – a nod to Perrault's 'Cinderella' – to his cavern domain, a luxurious cornucopia of gardens and delicacies worthy of Versailles. (Although Perrault published his 'Cinderella' the same year as d'Aulnoy published 'The Ram', it is possible that Perrault's tales were circulating in manuscript form; given the nature of d'Aulnoy's subtle references to Perrault's tales, I suggest that she is playing on his tales.) The Ram explains to Merveilleuse that he was a king with the most beautiful kingdom and subjects who loved him. All was lost, however, when the old and ugly fairy Ragotte demanded that the king marry her. When he refused, Ragotte condemned him to live as a ram for five years as 'penance' for having snubbed her. He then encounters other sheep who were similarly condemned by the resentful Ragotte for supposed offences towards her.

When Merveilleuse learns about her eldest sister's forthcoming wedding, she wishes to attend incognito (her father must believe that she is dead), and begs the Ram to allow her to go. He informs her that she is free to leave at any time, but that she must return promptly or he will die at her feet. Her beauty dazzles all at the wedding, and she successfully returns to the Ram. Later, upon learning that her second sister is to marry, she again asks the Ram for permission to attend the celebration, and takes leave of him, again promising to return. While at the second wedding, Merveilleuse wishes to return to the Ram, but all the palace doors are locked because the king (her father) desires to know who this mysterious woman is. He brings her a basin of water and washes her hands, thus fulfilling the prophetic dream. Merveilleuse reveals her identity, and her father and sisters are all overjoyed; the father then crowns her in his place. Meanwhile, the Ram cannot tolerate Merveilleuse's absence any longer and approaches the gates of her father's castle, but no one allows him to enter because they fear Merveilleuse will leave them again. The Ram expires at the gates, only for Merveilleuse to discover his body as she is riding in a chariot through the city, presenting herself to the people of her realm as their new sovereign. The tale ends: 'In her despair she thought she would die herself: it can thus be agreed that the most elevated people are subject, like everyone else, to the whims of fortune, and they often experience the greatest tragedies at the very moment when they believe themselves to be fulfilling all their dreams.'[4]

This pre-'Beauty and the Beast' tale is striking in its similarities to, as well as its differences from, what became a classic tale within the contemporary fairy-tale canon. First, 'The Ram' provides some possible precedents for the relationship between Beauty and her father in Villeneuve and Leprince de Beaumont that do not appear in other tales of this nature. While scholars have talked about the influence of 'Cupid and Psyche' on 'Beauty and the Beast', the Latin tale does not suggest that Psyche is her father's favourite daughter, although she is indeed the most beautiful of them; nor does this happen in Straparola's 'The Pig Prince', another tale that influenced d'Aulnoy, in which the daughter of a poor woman marries a pig.[5] In 'The Ram', Merveilleuse is the favoured sister who earns her father's crown at the end of the tale. In Villeneuve's 'Beauty and the Beast', Beauty consoles her father during their financial difficulties and is prepared to sacrifice herself for him, and the father is blamed by his other daughters for caring only about Beauty. Leprince de Beaumont further emphasizes Beauty's love for her father: unlike her sisters, Beauty does not wish to marry, so that she can keep her father company. D'Aulnoy's 'The Ram' thus provides the model for Beauty's close relationship with her father – even though he tried to have her killed.

Second, and perhaps more importantly, d'Aulnoy makes the life of the animal bridegroom the price to pay for the heroine not returning to him on time. In both Apuleius' and La Fontaine's versions of 'Cupid and Psyche', the invisible husband (Cupid) warns Psyche about visiting her sisters, whom Psyche should not trust, anticipating that the sisters will manipulate Psyche into violating the taboo of gazing upon him. Fearing that her husband is a monster, a fear fuelled by her jealous sisters, Psyche takes a lamp and gazes upon her beautiful husband. She learns that he is the God of Love himself, and in her excitement burns him with oil from the lamp,

Miranda comes upon the beautiful white sheep in Andrew Lang's adaptation from *The Blue Fairy Book* (London, 1930).

seriously injuring him, all of which brings about their separation and Psyche's trials. In 'The Ram', d'Aulnoy modifies the taboo: rather than it being about Psyche gazing upon her unknown, monstrous husband, it is about Merveilleuse/Beauty returning (or not) to the Ram/Beast before he dies from love for her. The relationship between Beauty's departure and the life of the Beast is predicated on this episode of 'The Ram'. Villeneuve and then Leprince de Beaumont clearly modify d'Aulnoy's ending – the Beast nearly dies, but Beauty returns just in time to save him – in order to close the tale with a happy ending. At the same time that this move eliminates the tragic fate of the beastly bridegroom, it also arguably takes away the agency of the heroine: d'Aulnoy concludes her tale with Merveilleuse's independent reign, whereas Beauty becomes the wife of the Beast, living in his domain. 'The Ram' could be read in terms of the difficulty women had in exercising their authority after marriage (it is important to recall here that d'Aulnoy's husband regularly had her interned in convents against her will), the author giving the heroine free 'reign', so to speak. Could Merveilleuse's fate represent an early modern version of the idea that women cannot have it all?

Third, d'Aulnoy presents the reader with the backstory explaining why the king was transformed into a ram, a narrative element that Villeneuve takes up in her version of 'Beauty and the Beast', and which becomes simplified in Leprince de Beaumont's adaptation. Well before Merveilleuse takes leave of the Ram to attend her eldest sister's wedding, the Ram relates his story to her: he was transformed because he rejected the fairy Ragotte's love. Villeneuve develops this episode, titling it 'Story of the Beast', in which the hero explains that his Amazonian queen mother left him in the care of an old and ugly fairy who, over time, went from caring for the prince as a mother to developing inappropriate feelings for him. When the prince comes of age, the old fairy wishes to marry him, but he refuses, and is condemned to live as a beast until a woman can love and marry him in his monstrous form; he notably cannot communicate his story until Beauty agrees to marry him and he is transformed. Villeneuve clearly drew from d'Aulnoy's backstory of an old and ugly fairy who condemns a handsome prince to beastliness, and she develops the narrative further, while for her part, Leprince de Beaumont informs her readers only that a bad fairy transformed the prince into the Beast, without providing any motive. This modification to the narrative reveals a shift in audience: d'Aulnoy and Villeneuve wrote their tales for adult readers who might appreciate the problematic representation of the fairy's inappropriate and even incestuous desire for the prince, whereas Leprince de Beaumont, writing explicitly for children, removes this backstory from her tale, making the fairy appear less motivated, less sexual and more arbitrary in her actions.

Both d'Aulnoy's 'The Ram' and Villeneuve's 'Beauty and the Beast' are anchored in an aristocratic context; indeed, many scenes in d'Aulnoy's tales recall descriptions of court society at Versailles.[6] Both Merveilleuse and Villeneuve's Beauty enter spaces that are luxuriously designed and decorated, with extravagant food and aristocratic forms of entertainment, which include concerts, banquets and hunting parties in d'Aulnoy and theatre, opera and the popular Saint-Germain fair in Villeneuve. D'Aulnoy's description of the Ram's kingdom is filled with rivers of Spanish wine, liqueurs, roasted partridges and foie gras; Villeneuve's Beauty enjoys tragedies with a cast of monkeys and parrots, and magically watches a Parisian opera through a glass window from the Beast's abode, almost as if she were watching television. Leprince de Beaumont greatly reduces these sumptuous descriptions of food and setting, simply noting, for instance, that the table in the Beast's castle was 'magnificently' prepared, and the palace was 'beautiful'. Rather than spending her time watching theatre and opera, Leprince de Beaumont's Beauty reads and plays the harpsichord, perhaps more appropriate pastimes for her young, bourgeois readers.

Two modifications made to 'The Ram' in the development of both Villeneuve's and Leprince de Beaumont's 'Beauty and the Beast' are, first, the emphasis on sisterly rivalry; and second, the change to the ending of 'The Ram'. The two principal texts from which d'Aulnoy draws for her animal bridegroom tales are La Fontaine's 'Cupid and Psyche' and Straparola's 'The Pig Prince'. Interestingly, each tale constructs the relationship between the sisters differently. In La Fontaine (and Apuleius), Psyche's sisters demonstrate envy and resentment towards their youngest sister. In Straparola, the sisters display no jealousy at all; the two older sisters are simply killed by the pig prince, and the youngest is the only one to survive. D'Aulnoy chooses not to have her sisters be explicit rivals, a decision she also makes in the other tale that is the subject of this chapter, 'The Green Serpent'. Second, and perhaps more importantly, Villeneuve and Leprince de Beaumont save the animal bridegroom, rather than letting him die tragically. Such an ending might seem shocking today, since we cannot *not* read 'The Ram' through the filter of 'Beauty and the Beast'. It is important, however, to keep in mind that for seventeenth- and eighteenth-century readers, the ending would not necessarily have been surprising precisely because 'Beauty and the Beast' did not come into existence until 1740, and it continued to coexist with both 'The Ram' and 'The Green Serpent' at least throughout the nineteenth century.

The serpent and the beast

In 1697 d'Aulnoy published her *Contes des fées* (Tales of the Fairies) in four volumes. Embedded in the Spanish novella 'Don Gabriel Ponce de Léon', 'The Ram' is the first tale that appears in volume three, while volume four closes with 'The Green Serpent', told by the titular character of the frame novella, Don Fernand de Tolède. Where 'The Ram' is closer than 'The Green Serpent' to the 'Beauty and the Beast' tale, 'The Green Serpent' is closer to 'Cupid and Psyche', in particular La Fontaine's adaptation of the Latin story. In fact, La Fontaine frequently refers to Psyche as 'la Belle' ('Beauty'), which may have influenced Villeneuve's choice of name for her heroine. Although 'The Ram' is an essential source for Villeneuve's 'Beauty and the Beast', Villeneuve also drew certain elements from 'The Green Serpent', in particular the doubling of the hero (as both the frightening Green Serpent and the pleasing invisible lover) – which Leprince de Beaumont eliminates in her truncation of Villeneuve's tale – as well as the displacement of the heroine from the familial domain to that of the beastly bridegroom.

'The Green Serpent' opens with a scene reminiscent of Perrault's 'Sleeping Beauty': the disgruntled, older and ugly fairy Magotine intrudes upon a banquet to which other fairies were invited to be-stow their gifts on the twin daughters of a queen and king. Because she was not invited, the fairy Magotine curses the eldest twin to become uglier and uglier with age. The parents end up naming the accursed princess Laideronnette ('little ugly one') and her younger twin Bellotte ('little beauty'), which also may have planted a seed for Villeneuve naming her heroine 'Belle' or 'Beauty'. Aware of her ugliness, Laideronnette first retreats from court life to the Castle of the Solitary Ones, which could be read as a figure for the convent – a space with which d'Aulnoy was all too familiar, given the forced sequestrations she endured.[7] During an outing, Laideronnette sees the Green Serpent, who later wishes to help her when her boat floats away from the shore, but she is afraid of the beastly hero; the boat capsizes and, unbeknownst to her, Laideronnette is saved by the Green Serpent, who takes her to his luxurious palace, staffed by little animated Chinese figurines, or 'pagods'.

While there, Laideronnette enjoys plays by the famous French playwrights Corneille and Molière, attends balls and reads. However, what pleases her most are her conversations with an unknown invisible lover, who is in reality the Green Serpent. As such, the hero's character is doubled: although Laideronnette fears the Green Serpent, she is comforted by her *amant inconnu* or 'unknown lover'. Her 'invisible king' recounts how the fairy Magotine condemned him to a penance of seven years, five of which have already passed, and he asks Laideronnette to marry him, but she cannot look upon him or he will have to start his penance all over again, and she would have to join him. Laideronnette agrees, but then reads the story of Psyche (the text suggesting it is La Fontaine's version), which sparks her desire to visit her family. During her visit, Laideronnette reveals – just like Psyche – the fact that she has never seen her husband, and her mother and sister urge her to gaze upon him, not out of jealousy but out of concern for her well-being, fearing he may indeed be a monster. Based on her reading of Psyche's story, Laideronnette insists to her mother and sister that her husband is probably the god of love, and upon her return, fuelled by her 'fatal curiosity', she gazes upon her husband, hoping to see Cupid. But, in an ironic twist, she cries out in horror upon seeing the Green Serpent instead. Several other adventures and trials occur, inspired by 'Cupid and Psyche' and with Magotine playing the role of Venus, until Laideronnette is transformed into the Discreet Queen and the Green Serpent is returned to his original, handsome form.

Laideronnette being served by the pagods. Image d'Epinal
Pellerin, 19th century.

In several respects 'The Green Serpent' represents a mediation
between 'Cupid and Psyche' and Villeneuve's 'Beauty and the Beast'.
First, unlike the Ram, the Green Serpent appears frightening to
the heroine, as will be the case of the Beast in Villeneuve and later
Leprince de Beaumont. As in Psyche's story, in which the heroine
marries and sleeps with an invisible husband, Laideronnette marries
the invisible king. However, it turns out that the Green Serpent
is also the beast, whose physical appearance initially frightens
Laideronnette – just as the Beast initially frightens Beauty – and
who must reassure her that he presents no danger to her well-
being. In Villeneuve, the heroine receives in a dream the 'real' image

of the beast, the handsome *inconnu*, modifying d'Aulnoy's splitting of the hero; instead of juxtaposing the Green Serpent with the invisible king (d'Aulnoy), we have the splitting of the hero into Beast and *bel inconnu* or 'handsome unknown' (Villeneuve). This doubling takes new form in Cocteau, who has Jean Marais incarnate both Avenant and the Beast, and in Disney, in which Gaston and the Beast are cast as rivals. In some ways this doubling of the character of the monstrous bridegroom serves to reassure the heroine that her husband or suitor is, in reality, an acceptable, even ideal mate, despite all appearances. The ironic twist d'Aulnoy gives to her version of 'Cupid and Psyche', in which Laideronnette hopes to find Cupid and instead finds a beastly serpent (whom she nevertheless continues to love), indeed clears the path to 'Beauty and the Beast'.

In her well-documented translation and critical edition of Villeneuve's 'Beauty and the Beast', Aurora Wolfgang remarks on other connections with 'The Green Serpent'. In d'Aulnoy's tale, Laideronnette regularly learns about all the most current events in the world through the pagods; Villeneuve's Beauty similarly gazes through a window that offers her 'a reliable means to find out about everything happening in the world'.[8] Later, the Lady Fairy recounts Beauty's backstory and mentions the fairy trial of having to survive living as a serpent, which Wolfgang connects to motifs found in d'Aulnoy's 'The Green Serpent', among other tales. Both Laideronnette and Beauty enjoy books, an activity associated with the heroine that endures even in Disney's *Beauty and the Beast*, in which the Beast's library is a privileged site within his palace. D'Aulnoy's 'The Green Serpent' thus represents another important link in the creation of 'Beauty and the Beast', influencing both plot elements – notably the doubling of the hero – and smaller details, such as Beauty's pastimes and interest in books.

In d'Aulnoy's 'The Green Serpent', both heroine and hero are monstrous, a circumstance that also occurs in her tale 'Le Rameau d'or' ('The Golden Bough'). By making both heroine and hero ugly, d'Aulnoy establishes a relation of 'sameness' or equality between them, undoing gender dichotomies whereby women must be beautiful in order to win a husband, even a monstrous one (Laideronnette marries the Green Serpent before becoming beautiful), at the same time that male beauty is an integral part of masculinity. It is important to keep in mind the fact that seventeenth- and eighteenth-century styles for men included the application of white powder and artificial beauty marks or *mouches* (literally, 'flies'; in fact, small black taffeta or velvet patches) to bring out the whiteness of one's face, as well as the wearing of wigs and high-heeled shoes (heels were supposed to accentuate the shape of a man's calves). Beauty thus formed an essential feature of early modern masculinity, even if writers continued to consider it a feminine quality. As opposed to 'The Green Serpent', 'Beauty and the Beast' tales reiterate more patriarchal notions of gender by returning to a dichotomy that insists that beauty is a specifically feminine quality. This is a dichotomy that d'Aulnoy's tales undermine by making it an essential quality for forms of ideal femininity and masculinity, for both hero and heroine must undergo similar trials in order to regain their beauty.

It is also notable that upon her separation from the Green Serpent, Laideronnette must oversee the pagods, who go to battle against Magotine and her marionette troops. Although Magotine wins, it is nevertheless important to keep in mind that this is a battle between two queens. Interestingly, in the Beast's backstory provided by Villeneuve, the Beast's mother leaves her son in the care of the fairy in order to lead her kingdom's troops herself, and she does so successfully for many years. However, in Villeneuve the

Amazonian queen appears to be a relic of the past, with Beauty – a more docile woman – pointing the way towards a more domestic model of femininity that will take fuller form in Leprince de Beaumont, who drops altogether any references to warrior queens. Villeneuve's iteration of 'Beauty and the Beast' could even be said to suggest that it is precisely because the mother does not take care of the child herself that disaster strikes, and her son is turned into the Beast. Moving from d'Aulnoy, who wrote several tales in which women rule over their own kingdoms ('The Island of Felicity', 'The Good Little Mouse', 'The Ram' and 'The White Cat'), to Villeneuve, in which the future is decidedly not an Amazonian one, we can follow changing trends in French society in which (elite) women were increasingly associated with the domestic, rather than the more public spaces of court or salons.

One important element shared by 'The Ram' and 'The Green Serpent' that is inspired by 'Cupid and Psyche' and feeds into 'Beauty and the Beast' is the displacement of the heroine from the somewhat realistic space of her family domain to the marvellous space of the beastly bridegroom's domain. In other animal bridegroom tales, notably Straparola's 'The Pig Prince' and later the Grimms' 'The Frog King', the beastly heroes are not associated with a particular magical space that can fulfil all the heroine's desires; the action takes place within one spatial plane, that of a single kingdom. This movement of the heroine from a more realistic space (her father's kingdom) to a marvellous one (the Ram's and the Green Serpent's Versailles-like palaces) implies different spatial planes that eventually take new shape in 'Beauty and the Beast' tales.

As we can see, 'The Ram' and 'The Green Serpent' represent the filter through which 'Cupid and Psyche' is transformed into 'Beauty and the Beast'. 'The Ram' provides the cause of the hero's metamorphosis – the prince rejecting the fairy's proposal of marriage

– which we also find in Villeneuve's 'Beauty and the Beast', a motivation that is subsequently removed by Leprince de Beaumont, who reframes her version of the tale for young readers. The relation between Merveilleuse and her father may also serve as a model for Villeneuve and later Leprince de Beaumont, whose Beauty is particularly attached to her father. The doubling of the hero in 'The Green Serpent', the prince being both the monstrous serpent and the beloved invisible husband, takes new form in Villeneuve, who establishes a contrast between the Beast and the *bel inconnu* of Beauty's dreams, a doubling that eases the heroine into the love relation with the monstrous bridegroom by hinting at a more beautiful and satisfying reality that lies beneath the surface. Leprince de Beaumont eliminates this doubling in her tale, in some ways creating a more dramatic situation for the heroine, who is simply faced with the possibility of living out her life with a beast; no hint that he may be a more physically attractive mate is presented to the heroine in Leprince de Beaumont's text.[9]

Although 'The Ram' and 'The Green Serpent' are hardly known to readers today, they did not simply disappear after the appearance of Villeneuve's and Leprince de Beaumont's versions of 'Beauty and the Beast'. D'Aulnoy's legacy resides both in her contribution to the formation of 'Beauty and the Beast' tales and in the continued enjoyment of her foundational tales within the domain of English and French adult and children's literature, English pantomime and French classical music. The fairy-tale canons of times past were quite different from the post-Disney notion of 'classic' fairy tales, and the tragic story of d'Aulnoy's Ram coexisted for generations with Villeneuve's and Leprince de Beaumont's rescued Beast.

Legacy 1: The English ram

On the French side of things, 'The Ram' was republished at least twelve times over the course of the eighteenth century in collections of d'Aulnoy's tales, including the celebrated 41-volume *Cabinet des fées* (1785–9). It also appeared in chapbook form in 1790 and was published a second time as a stand-alone tale in 1833. Each of these editions reproduced the language of d'Aulnoy's original, with little or no modification of the text. Although 'The Ram' remained in circulation in France throughout the nineteenth century, it was on the decline and proved to be more popular on the other side of the Channel.

At least 28 editions of d'Aulnoy's tales in which 'The Ram' appeared were published in English over the course of the eighteenth century. My focus here will be on late eighteenth- and nineteenth-century editions of the tale, which provide insights into how a French aristocratic tale was transformed for both adult and child readers in England.[10] The relatively new attention paid to children's literature as an emerging book market in England might lead us to speculate that 'The Ram' was increasingly adapted to child readers; however, translations and adaptations by James Robinson Planché (1855), Andrew Lang (1889) and Annie Macdonell (1892, with introduction by Anne Thackeray Ritchie) also show that d'Aulnoy's tales continued to appeal to adult audiences. Children's versions of 'The Ram' and of d'Aulnoy's tales more generally did not simply take the place of versions targeting adult readers, but coexisted with them throughout the century. Interestingly, whereas the versions targeting an adult readership remain close to the original French, we see more important modifications in versions aimed at children, owing to several factors, including considerations of what was deemed appropriate for children.

In English editions, the tale was typically titled 'The Royal Ram' or, integrating the English name of the heroine prevalent in children's versions of the tale, 'Miranda and the Royal Ram'. One might assume that an educated adult in the period would know enough French for translators and adapters, such as Planché and Macdonell, to retain the French name, 'Merveilleuse', which they use in their versions of the tale. The name 'Miranda', however, was used for more popular, chapbook formats, such as *Mother Bunch's Fairy Tales: Published for the Amusement of All Those Little Masters and Misses*. 'Mother Bunch' served as a marketing label under which editors in England published d'Aulnoy's tales from roughly 1773 to 1830, a label that also effaced d'Aulnoy's authorship of the tales.

Another significant distinction between these different adaptations of the tale concerns the ending. In adaptations aimed explicitly at children, the heroine and hero either both die, or both live. By contrast, Lang, Macdonell and an edition of d'Aulnoy's tales illustrated by Gustaf Tenggren (a key animator for Walt Disney Studios and illustrator for the Little Golden Books series) in 1923 all retain d'Aulnoy's original and troubling ending. In such collections as *Mother Bunch* (1773, 1795, 1802, 1830), *Fairy Tales: Translated from the French of the Countess d'Anois* (1817), *History of Little Jack ... Tales for Children* (1840) and the Philadelphia-published *The Child's Own Book of Standard Fairy Tales* (1868), upon seeing the deceased Ram, Miranda swoons and meets the same fate as her beloved. In two other adaptations, from *The Pleasing Companion: A Collection of Fairy Tales, Calculated to Improve the Heart: The Whole Forming a System of Moral Precepts and Examples, for the Conduct of Youth through Life* (c. 1790) and *The Enchanter; or Wonderful Story Teller: In Which Is Contained a Series of Adventures ... Calculated to Amuse, Instruct, and Improve Younger Minds* (1795), both of which were published by William Lane, the adapter repairs the tragic ending by inventing the fairy Lauretina, who revives the dead hero and restores the Ram to his original human form, giving the tale a happily-ever-after. In a third variation, from *Daddy Gander's Entertaining Fairy Tales* (1815), the Ram is transformed by an unnamed 'frightful fairy' into a 'hideous beast' for twenty years, but a good fairy modifies the curse and changes him into a sheep; when he encounters Miranda, only one year remains of his metamorphosis.[11] Miranda never leaves him, he regains his handsome form, and they marry. Miranda is then reunited with her father, who begs her forgiveness; the scene of abandonment to attend her sister's wedding is completely removed, and Miranda never takes her father's throne. Although the *Daddy Gander* version never names the frightful fairy within the tale, the book's frontispiece refers to her as 'Ragoth', showing that the adapter was clearly familiar with other versions of the tale.

The idea of having Miranda or Merveilleuse die at the end of the tale could have more than one explanation. The French reads: 'Dans son désespoir elle pensa mourir elle-même,' which literally means, 'In her despair she thought she would die herself.'[12] Could some translators have misread the line and understood that the heroine herself actually died? The versions from *The Pleasing Companion* and *The Enchanter* include a mistranslation of the first wedding scene, in which Merveilleuse leaves a chest for her sister that reads 'Jewels for the Bride'; when it is opened, the narration reads, 'et que n'y trouva-t-on pas?', which means, 'and what did one not find in it?' Both *The Pleasing Companion* and *The Enchanter* mistranslate the French as 'when they opened it, there was nothing in it'; however, their tales do not conclude with Miranda's death, but rather with the restoration of the Ram to life and to human form by the fairy Lauretina.

It is also possible that translators and editors changed the ending because of notions of marriage and the romantic couple, gender norms, and proposing the story of Miranda as a warning. Only three of the adaptations I consulted resuscitate the hero or refuse to kill him off in the first place. However, the different editions of *Mother Bunch* from the eighteenth and nineteenth centuries, and other editions of d'Aulnoy's tales from 1830, 1840 and 1868, all conclude with Miranda dying upon seeing the deceased Ram. With respect to the three versions in which the Ram revives or never dies in the first place, it is possible that 'Beauty and the Beast', which was circulating in England notably via Leprince de Beaumont's the *Young Misses' Magazine* and in stand-alone publications, may have contaminated d'Aulnoy's tale.[13] Or perhaps the ending of d'Aulnoy's tale was modified for the same reasons that Villeneuve and later Leprince de Beaumont rewrote the tale: in order to save the Beast and have a happy ending.

Some critics have suggested that 'Beauty and the Beast' and other tales about animal bridegrooms, such as 'Cupid and Psyche', communicate anxiety as well as lessons about marriage and sexuality.[14] One might read 'Beauty and the Beast' as a tale about how the heroine learns what is valuable in a spouse, or how to accept an arranged marriage, or perhaps how to deal with anxiety over sexuality in marriage, with beastliness serving as a projection of the hero's sexuality. If the message of 'Beauty and the Beast' has to do with the heroine negotiating (an arranged, depending on one's reading) marriage, it would be important for the hero to survive at the conclusion of the tale. The versions of 'The Ram' in which the fairy Lauretina intervenes, then, arguably seek to stabilize relations between women and men within the context of courtship and marriage, much in the tradition of 'Beauty and the Beast'.

What do we make of the adaptations that condemn both Miranda and the Beast to death? Most versions of the tale targeting children end in this fashion, and as suggested above, one possibility is that it is simply the result of a bad translation. However, there could be more motivated explanations. The fact of the heroine dying upon seeing the deceased Ram is both more tragic and more romantic than d'Aulnoy's original; it smacks of a *Romeo and Juliet*-type conclusion and indeed strengthens the emotional bond between hero and heroine. However, if we read this as a pedagogical tale, the heroine of 'The Ram' cannot go scot-free and gain a throne after having abandoned her beloved Ram, even if that were not fully her fault. When d'Aulnoy's Merveilleuse finds the Ram, 'she ran to him, cried, moaned, knowing that her lack of exactitude had caused the death of the Royal Ram.'[15] Several English adaptations for children emphasize that she was 'seized with remorse for having neglected him', pointing to the heroine's guilt just before she expires.[16] These English adaptations, then, accentuate Merveilleuse's moral responsibility for the Ram's death.

These different endings relate different messages. D'Aulnoy's is more philosophical: 'we thus see that the most elevated people are subject, like everyone else, to the whims of fortune, and they often experience the greatest tragedies at the very moment when they believe themselves to be fulfilling all their dreams.'[17] A verse moral follows these words, but nothing is reiterated about Merveilleuse being responsible for the Ram's death. Rather, the message suggests that Merveilleuse is at the height of her hopes – she is crowned queen, inheriting her father's throne – at the very moment when she loses her beloved. The versions in *The Pleasing Companion* and *The Enchanter* that resuscitate the Ram suggest that the message of the tale is about 'virtue' and 'perseverance' despite calamity, and that 'if we are good, we shall ultimately be happy.' Miranda's negligence is de-emphasized to make way for this happy ending. The *Mother Bunch* versions do not append a moral, but, as noted above, they introduce the notion of 'remorse', heightening the heroine's guilt over the death of the Ram, after which she expires.

Another way of understanding these modifications to 'The Ram' is through the lens of gender. Either resuscitating the Ram or killing off Miranda so that both heroine and hero meet the same fate (possibly for different reasons) suggests that some translators, editors and adapters had difficulty accepting a heroine who could take the throne over her beloved's dead body. In the words of the critic Patricia Hannon, 'Merveilleuse elects female ambition, even at the tragic price of King Mouton's [Ram's] death.'[18] Whereas for male characters, abandoning one's beloved out of ambition (the subject of d'Aulnoy's first published fairy tale, 'The Island of Felicity') fits within expectations of hegemonic forms of masculinity, a female character behaving similarly marks a challenge to normative forms of femininity. Men are supposed to rule and be dedicated to the state, prioritizing their public duty over private love – a theme that recurs in early modern French literature, notably in classical tragedy and opera. It is deemed appropriate for men to sacrifice love or family for the state or even out of personal ambition. Women, however, are supposed to privilege their relation to their husbands and children (associated with the private, the domestic) over their own desires, even over their own well-being.[19]

It is for this reason – women's relation to the family and the domestic – that makes Merveilleuse's queenship problematic: she rules on her own, and fulfils her own desires and ambitions rather than meeting those of her future husband, the Ram. As such, d'Aulnoy's 'The Ram' could be said to be more feminist in nature than either Villeneuve's or Leprince de Beaumont's 'Beauty and the Beast', whose heroine returns just in time to save the Beast, only to reside in *his* castle and be grateful for *his* generosity. One of the recurring themes in both versions of 'Beauty and the Beast' is gratitude: the heroine should return to the Beast and marry him out of gratitude. What, exactly, she should be grateful for is another question: grateful he didn't kill her or her father because her father had picked one of his many roses? Grateful for the wealth he provided her and her family with in exchange for her body, for her hand in marriage? In many respects, d'Aulnoy's tale demystifies both romance and marriage precisely by *not* having the heroine die out of love for the Ram (who dies out of love for her), and yet rewarding Merveilleuse, who will rule on her own as queen. With the more philosophical moral at the end of her tale, d'Aulnoy presents us with a complex story about love and about life, which can reward with one hand and take away with the other. Perhaps the fact that this was too sophisticated a message for children or presented too much of a challenge to late eighteenth- and nineteenth-century gender norms brought about such changes to English versions of the tale.

Other modifications made in collections targeting the child reader are less ideologically motivated. D'Aulnoy sprinkles her tales with verse, which is eliminated in most English versions (Planché, more faithful to the original, brings verse back into his translation). The plot is often condensed. For instance, d'Aulnoy's sisters undergo two 'tests' by the father: the first concerning why they selected their dresses, and the second about their respective dreams, which leads to Merveilleuse's father ordering her execution. *Mother Bunch* editions, along with *Daddy Gander's Entertaining Fairy Tales, Tales for Children* and *The Child's Own Book of Standard Fairy Tales*, cut the scene with the dresses, retaining only the essential episode from the beginning of the tale. Details relating to aristocratic culture are also toned down or eliminated. When d'Aulnoy's

Merveilleuse first comes upon the Ram and the other sheep, she sees them drinking coffee and lemonade, eating sorbet, ice cream, strawberries and cream, and playing cards, all of which would have been understood as aristocratic activities. This scene is simplified in the *Mother Bunch* version, in which the heroine sees the sheep 'regaling themselves with the choicest dainties, while others diverted themselves with play'.[20] D'Aulnoy's pumpkin carriage becomes a gourd shell, while the hippogriffs that carry Merveilleuse to her eldest sister's wedding become 'half griffins' in an edition of *Mother Bunch* from 1802, and 'a very numerous train of officers' in an edition from 1830.

In 1894 the priest and scholar Sabine Baring-Gould included 'Miranda; or, The Royal Ram' in his collection *A Book of Fairy Tales Retold by S. Baring Gould*. Baring-Gould, an Anglican vicar, is perhaps best known today for having composed the lyrics for 'Onward, Christian Soldiers', but in nineteenth-century England he was recognized as a prolific novelist and folklorist. William Hyde notes that Baring-Gould was widely known for his fiction, while Andrew Wawn has documented his important contributions to northern European and especially Icelandic folklore.[21] In *A Book of Fairy Tales*, Baring-Gould clearly positions d'Aulnoy as a canonical writer, declaring that most of the tales he includes are 'known in every nursery'.[22] In his next collection, *Old English Fairy Tales* (1895), he states: 'We have had for their delectation numerous editions of the French tales of Perrault and the Countess D'Aulnoy, and the German stories of Grimm, but our own native springs have been neglected.'[23] His adaptation of 'The Ram', then, should be read within the literary field of nineteenth-century Britain, in which d'Aulnoy's tales were common currency, at the very least alongside – and certainly not below – those of Perrault and the Grimms.

Baring-Gould includes the word 'retold' in *A Book of Fairy Tales*, alerting readers to the fact that he will modify known versions of the tales he includes. It appears that he adapted his version of 'The Ram' from one of the *Mother Bunch* editions, given some of the vocabulary choices he makes to render the French. The most important stylistic changes Baring-Gould makes are in line with other versions targeted at young readers: notably, streamlining the narrative by eliminating elaborate descriptions or inessential plot elements. He furthermore makes the tale appear more realistic by, for instance, eliminating the pumpkin or gourd coach drawn by goats that takes Merveilleuse/Miranda to the Ram's domain; instead, Baring-Gould's Miranda is led there simply by chariot. He also eliminates any description of the equipage Miranda uses to go to her eldest sister's wedding; in d'Aulnoy and in other English versions, her carriage is drawn by marvellous hippogriffs. The Ram is also depicted as more fully human. In *Mother Bunch* versions, for instance, and following d'Aulnoy, the Ram begins 'skipping and bounding [like a sheep] and kissing her hands' when Merveilleuse/Miranda returns from her first sister's wedding, thus displaying both animal and human conduct. In Baring-Gould the Ram simply 'ran towards her, and gave many tokens of passionate fondness for her', which suggests more fully human behaviour.[24]

Along with increased realism, Baring-Gould modifies the ending to make it a happy one, at the same time that he disempowers the heroine more than in other versions. Upon recounting to Miranda the story of his metamorphosis, the Ram explains that the 'old hag', the fairy Ragotta, condemned him to his animal form until a king would allow him to sit upon his throne and drink from his cup. As in other versions, when the second sister's wedding ceremony is over, the king fulfils Miranda's prophetic dream by bringing her a basin to wash her hands. When Baring-Gould's

Miranda reveals her identity, rather than handing his throne over to her, the king asks her, 'What can I do to make amends for my past injustice?', to which Miranda responds, 'Suffer a Ram to sit on thy throne, and drink out of thy cup.'[25] The Ram approaches the palace gates and is forbidden entry until Miranda appears and leads him into her father's throne room, where the Ram sits upon the king's throne and drinks from his cup, bringing an end to the curse. The transformed prince is then married to Miranda. While Baring-Gould eliminates any wrongdoing on the part of Miranda, who actively saves the Ram, he also never hands the crown over to her. In d'Aulnoy and most other versions, the father crowns the daughter he nearly murdered as compensation; basically, the crown is exchanged for the heroine's forgiveness. In Baring-Gould, however, it is the life of the Ram that is the object of exchange, not the crown. Through Baring-Gould's transformation of 'The Ram', the heroine loses a kingdom and gains a husband, while her father implicitly continues to rule. A text that originated with a woman author who crowns the heroine at the end of the tale becomes, in Baring-Gould's hands, a story about female self-sacrifice, about a heroine whose wishes and desires relate not to herself, but to the beastly hero.

That d'Aulnoy's 'The Ram' was well known becomes evident when we examine the very clever anonymous poem *Miranda and the Royal Ram* (1844), whose humour can fully be appreciated only if one is already familiar with the fairy tale.[26] This version opens with a king with a penchant for drink, and a queen with a penchant for mutton, who lectures her husband on temperance. This household disorder leads them to forsake their parental duty to educate their daughter, the princess Miranda, who is beautiful but ignorant. Because she does not know how to read, when a letter arrives, Miranda takes it to her aunt, who happens to be a witch, in order to understand its contents. It turns out that the letter is from Prince Fleecy, Miranda's beloved, and the aunt realizes that the prince prefers Miranda to her own daughter. Angry, the aunt takes her wand and, wanting to reform our 'guzzling king', turns him into a Royal Ram, 'For sheep from getting tipsy shrink,/ And very seldom want to drink.'[27] The witch-aunt then transforms Miranda, '*this* vixen', into a lamb, hoping that her mother, who 'used to beat her', will now '*eat* her'.[28]

Suddenly a fairy appears and modifies the spell. Miranda must find a 'certain' Royal Ram, 'without horns,/ Of no mother born,/ With spots black and pale,/ And a very long tail/ With a singular end./ At first, alone, penned,/ But now in a fold./ Its back marked with gold'. She can then regain her original form. The fairy and witch vanish just as Prince Fleecy – who is not a ram, but whose name associates him with one – appears. He vows to stay with Miranda and realizes that the special Royal Ram in question is not Miranda's father, but rather a book, in fact, the very book we are reading: *The Royal Ram* has no horns, is black and pale (ink and paper), it is a long 'tail/tale' (a pun noted by the prince), first penned then in a fold (the poem is an eight-fold book). With help from the fairies the 'book the Prince wanted was found! And Miranda, un-lambed, will be locked in his arms/ When *this* volume is lettered and bound.'[29] The poem shifts to the future tense to predict when Miranda will learn how to read, and the king will be restored.

The humour of this anonymous version of 'The Ram' relies on previous knowledge of the fairy tale, which suggests that d'Aulnoy's tale was well known in England in this period. In 'The Ram' d'Aulnoy arguably parodies such pastoral texts as the popular novel by Honoré d'Urfé *L'Astrée*, peopled with beautiful shepherds and shepherd-esses who are nobles in disguise, by having the hero literally turn into a sheep.[30] In the anonymous poem, the parody is pushed even further by having the characters 'baa' upon their transformation, and by having the heroine fear that her mutton-loving mother will devour her. Connections are also made with 'Beauty and the Beast' when the narrator exclaims, upon Miranda's transformation, 'Only think! so much Beauty transformed to a Beast,' which also suggests that the anonymous author saw connections between 'The Ram' and 'Beauty and the Beast'. In this version, however, the roles are reversed, with Miranda rather than the prince being transformed into an animal. Yet, interestingly, traces of the prince's beastly history are embedded in his name: although he doesn't take the form of a ram, his name, 'Prince Fleecy', retains something of his ovine origins. The idea that 'The Royal Ram' is also a book is part of the humour, with its long tail/tale, and the poem currently being read is a 'certain' Royal Ram, suggesting that there could be others.

Others, indeed, there were. D'Aulnoy's 'Le Mouton' enjoyed popularity in the nursery as well as in the parlour, having been adapted for British child and adult readers. Each adaptation reveals the choices translators and editors made to accommodate their respective audiences and conform to British middle-class gender norms. It seems that the idea of the heroine governing on her own after the death of her beloved was particularly problematic for writers targeting child readers, although at the end of the Victorian period Baring-Gould similarly modified his adaptation. One thing is clear: the tale of 'The Ram' did not die after the success of 'Beauty and the Beast', but continued to be printed and transformed.

Legacy 2: Literary and musical serpents

Whereas 'The Ram' was popular in British print culture, 'The Green Serpent' made its mark on French literary culture, British pantomime and French classical music. As did many of d'Aulnoy's tales, 'The Green Serpent' circulated in the widely popular collections of tales by d'Aulnoy in French and in English, as well as in chapbook form in France as an individual tale.[31] Honoré de Balzac, Gustave Flaubert and the lesser-known poet Robert de Bonnières all reference 'The Green Serpent' in their correspondence and works. Adapted for the British stage in pantomime form, which combines theatre, music and ballet, the tale's musical legacy culminated in the work of Maurice Ravel in the early twentieth century.

While critics, among them Jennifer Schacker, have observed the influence d'Aulnoy had on such writers as Ann Radcliffe, Maria Edgeworth and Anne Thackeray Ritchie, few have pointed out d'Aulnoy's mark on French literature beyond the domain of fairy tales.[32] However, with a little digging, there are some notable examples, and more excavation could very well reveal a broader impact than I am suggesting here. Balzac, for instance, punctuates an early work, *La Dernière Fée* (The Last Fairy, 1823), with references to *Le Cabinet des fées*, with a particular emphasis on d'Aulnoy's fairy tales. The young nature child Abel 'admired *The Green Serpent*, *Gracieuse and Percinet* [and] *The Blue Bird*', among other d'Aulnoy tales; his mother fabricates for him an outfit based on a print of Prince Charming, and he was 'a thousand times handsomer than *Percinet*, *Gracieuse*'s beloved'.[33]

In his short story 'A Prince of Bohemia' (1846), which was integrated into his larger opus *La Comédie humaine*, Balzac draws specifically from 'The Green Serpent' as a framing device. He has the character Nathan declare, as he listens attentively to Madame de La Baudraye's account of an affair between a count and an opera dancer: 'I am listening to you like a child whose mother is telling him the story of *The Great Green Serpent*.'[34] Allan Pasco remarks that d'Aulnoy's tale 'had recently been re-edited (1835)', then makes the connection between the fairy tale and the short story, which also concerns 'broken marriages, which will shortly be reconciled', and 'the benefits gained from the difficulties afflicting the wives while they were separated from their husbands'.[35] For Pasco, Balzac deploys this marvellous fairy tale to frame the message of his realistic short story, which speaks to Balzac's familiarity with d'Aulnoy's *oeuvre*. Stylistically, d'Aulnoy framed her fairy tales with realistic novellas, and she played on the relation between the 'realistic' frame narrative and the 'marvellous' fairy tale.[36] Here Balzac seems to take the opposite approach, whereby the reference to the marvellous tale about the trials of Laideronnette that eventually lead to her success and (re)union with her husband frames the realistic story, in which the opera dancer Claudine succeeds in the trials put to her by her lover, the comte de La Palférine.

Balzac was not alone among nineteenth-century authors who appreciated d'Aulnoy, and although it is not as integral to their works as in the case of 'A Prince of Bohemia', other writers indirectly or directly reference 'The Green Serpent' as well. In her autobiography *Histoire de ma vie* (1854), George Sand recalls the hours she spent reading tales by Perrault as well as 'The Blue Bird', 'Belle-Belle; or, The Chevalier Fortuné', 'The Green Serpent', 'Babiole' and 'The Good Little Mouse' by d'Aulnoy.[37] In 1853, while Flaubert was working on *Madame Bovary*, the novelist wrote a letter to his friend the poet Louis Bouilhet in which he seems to distract himself from this apparently dreary work by reading d'Aulnoy's fairy tales: 'I read *The Blue Bird* [by d'Aulnoy] the day before yesterday. It is so pretty! What a shame one cannot grasp all of this! This would be more amusing to write than the discourse of a pharmacist. The bourgeois foulness in which I'm trudging fills me with gloom.'[38] Three days earlier, in a letter to his muse and lover Louise Colet, Flaubert had already expressed his fondness for d'Aulnoy's fairy tales: 'Presently I'm reading the children's tales of Mme d'Aulnoy in an old edition whose pages I coloured when I was six or seven. The dragons are pink and the trees blue; there's one page where everything is coloured red, even the sea. They really amuse me, these tales.'[39] The tale he reminisced about colouring all in red is very probably 'The Green Serpent', a digitized image of which can be found, along with four other images from d'Aulnoy's tales that Flaubert coloured as a child, on Danielle Girard's University of Rouen website.[40] His correspondence shows that d'Aulnoy's tales, including 'The Green Serpent', play an interesting role in the creative process of *Madame Bovary*: the marvellous, aristocratic world of Madame d'Aulnoy served as a counterpart to and refuge from the dreary, bourgeois world of Madame Bovary.

Whereas Flaubert reflects on his childhood attachment to d'Aulnoy's fairy tales in a gesture of personal nostalgia, the Goncourt brothers express a more general cultural nostalgia for her pre-revolutionary tales. In *Histoire de la société française pendant la Révolution* (History of French Society during the Revolution), first published in 1854, the celebrated critics, novelists and historians Edmond and Jules de Goncourt discuss the ways in which the tales of d'Aulnoy became targets of the revolutionaries' reaction to aristocratic society. After lamenting the revolutionary rejection of opera, the brothers turn to a similar reaction to fairy tales, declaring: 'It was in a royalist joke of 1792 that fairy tales were "un-ennobled". No more kings, queens, beautiful princesses, or valorous knights! *The Green Serpent* is now *The Tricolored Serpent*, green being the colour of aristocrats.'[41] *Tricolored*, of course, refers to the blue, white and red of

Flaubert's childhood colouring of 'The Green Serpent'.

the revolutionary flag. That the tale of 'The Green Serpent' is singled out, among a few others, speaks to its popularity in eighteenth- and nineteenth-century French culture.[42]

Later in the century, the novelist, journalist and poet Robert de Bonnières opened his collection of fairy poems in 1881 with a short 'Introduction', which assumes his readers' familiarity with the tales he mentions:

> At that time lived King Charming,
> The Green Serpent and my dear Florine,
> And, in her tower asleep for a hundred years,
> Was still sleeping Sleeping Beauty.
> It was the time of fairy palaces,
> Of Blue Birds, of Glass Slippers,
> Long tales during the long winter eves.

'King Charming' and 'Florine' are characters from d'Aulnoy's 'The Blue Bird', and with the reference to 'The Green Serpent', Bonnières clearly puts d'Aulnoy's tales on a par with those of Perrault. The original poems that follow are influenced by both d'Aulnoy and Perrault, with strong female figures appearing throughout. Although not well known today, Bonnières was a lifelong friend of Guy de Maupassant and associated with Impressionist artists and writers, including Anatole France and André Gide. These references to 'The Green Serpent' in particular and to d'Aulnoy's tales in general by nineteenth-century writers clearly demonstrate that those tales were common currency. The fact that 'The Green Serpent' was eventually set to music, then, should come as no surprise.

The earliest record I have found of d'Aulnoy's 'The Green Serpent' being adapted to music occurs in England, in the work of Planché, 'one of the most significant figures in the history of nineteenth-century stage', best known for his fairy extravaganzas, which blended theatre, music and dance.[43] Planché, notably, was fluent in French, being of French Huguenot extraction. In 1856 he produced a translation of 22 tales by d'Aulnoy. Along with tales by Charles Perrault, such as 'Puss in Boots' and 'Bluebeard', Planché adapted several d'Aulnoy tales for the stage, including 'The White Cat' (1842), 'Belle-Belle; or, The Chevalier Fortuné' (1843), 'The Fair One with the Golden Locks' (1843), 'Gracieuse and Percinet' (1844) and 'The Green Serpent' (1849). Based on 'The Green Serpent' and starring Laideronnetta, his fairy extravaganza *The Island of Jewels* was first performed at the Royal Lyceum Theatre, London, on 26 December 1849. It ran for 135 nights, being 'among the most famous' of his fairy musical plays – a fact that speaks to the degree to which Victorian audiences were familiar with this particular tale by d'Aulnoy.[44]

As in the tradition of British pantomime and French vaudeville *féerie*, Planché takes a playful approach to his material, which is set in verse and punctuated by musical airs, at the same time that Planché grounds the extravaganza in British culture. For instance, in lyrics set to the music of the aria 'In questo semplice' from the recent opera *Betly; or, The Swiss Chalet* (1836) by Gaetano Donizetti, Planché compares the situation of Laideronnetta (aka Laideron-nette) to that of Robinson Crusoe; references in the script are also made to *King Lear*, as well as to the English nursery rhyme 'Jack and Jill'. Interpolated into the extravaganza is a ballet based on 'Cupid and Psyche'; thus, instead of having his heroine simply read a version of the story (as in d'Aulnoy), Planché sets it to music and dance as a play within the play.

Planché's rendition of 'The Green Serpent' may have been con-taminated by d'Aulnoy's 'The Ram' and Villeneuve's 'Beauty and the Beast' (which he translated and published in *Four and Twenty*

The Island of Jewels, extravaganza at the Lyceum Theatre, from *The Illustrated London News*, 29 December 1849.

Fairy Tales in 1858), given that he allows Magotine a motive for turning the prince into a green serpent, which is not part of d'Aulnoy's tale. Like the fairy in d'Aulnoy's 'The Ram' and Villeneuve's 'Beauty and the Beast', Planché's Magotine is in love with the hero and transforms him in order to punish him for having rejected her. Planché also removes the battle scene between Laideronnetta's pagods and Magotine's marionettes, has the Green Serpent assist Laideronnetta in her final quest, and then has Laideronnetta choose between making herself beautiful or imparting happiness to the prince (of course, she chooses the latter), all of which diminishes the heroine's agency.

The relation of 'The Green Serpent' to music history is quite different in its home country. Although there were vaudeville *féeries* performed in nineteenth-century Paris that drew from tales by d'Aulnoy, the most popular being *The White Cat* (1852) by the Cogniard brothers, to my knowledge 'The Green Serpent' was not adapted for the French musical stage. Yet it inspired several musical pieces. In 1860 René Baillot, a professor at the Paris Conservatoire, published a score entitled 'The Green Serpent: Dance Air for the Piano'. However, the most famous musical adaptation of the tale is undoubtedly that of Maurice Ravel, whose *Ma Mère l'Oye* (*Mother Goose Suite*, 1910) includes scenes from Perrault's 'Sleeping Beauty' and 'Little Thumbling', d'Aulnoy's 'The Green Serpent' and Leprince de Beaumont's 'Beauty and the Beast'. Following in the footsteps of Ravel, the composer and pianist Jean-Michel Damase recorded *Féeries* (1958), which included a piece called 'Green Serpent' among seven others inspired by d'Aulnoy's tales, out of a total of sixteen French fairy tales set to music (with eight based on Perrault and one on Leprince de Beaumont).

The evolution of Ravel's suite is interesting. In the early autumn of 1908, the composer spent several days in Valvins, south of Paris, babysitting two young children, Mimi and Jean Godebski.[45] They were the children of Ravel's close friends Ida and Cipa, a Polish couple whose salon at the rue d'Athènes gathered well-known musicians of the period, including the composers Claude Debussy, Manuel de Falla and Igor Stravinsky. Ravel read the Godebski children fairy tales, as Mimi later recollected:

> Of all my parents' friends I had a predilection for Ravel because he used to tell me stories that I loved. I used to climb on his knee and indefatigably he would begin, 'Once upon a time ...' And it would be *Laideronnette* or *La Belle et la Bête* or, especially, the adventures of a poor mouse that he made up for me. I used to laugh uproariously at these and then feel guilty because they were really very sad.[46]

Between 1908 and 1910 Ravel composed five piano duets forming *Mother Goose Suite*, based on Mimi and Jean's favourite fairy tales, and they were first performed in Paris in April 1910. In 1911 he adapted the piano pieces to create a suite for orchestra entitled *Mother Goose: Five Children's Pieces*. The work opens with a scene from the first part of Perrault's tale, 'Petit Poucet'; the episode adapted from 'The Green Serpent' concerns Laideronnette, who, upon arriving at the Green Serpent's domain, takes a bath accompanied by 'an orchestra of *pagodes* and *pagodines*' ('some had theorbos made of walnut shells, others had viols made of almond shells, for it was necessary to proportion the instruments to their sizes'); and concluding with the ending of 'Beauty and the Beast', with 'the Beast's seeming death and his magical transformation into a handsome prince'.[47] The suite found its final incarnation as a ballet, *Mother Goose, One-Act Ballet: Five Tableaux and an Apotheosis*, first performed at the Théâtre des Arts in Paris on 29 January 1912, in collaboration with the theatre director Jacques Rouché, stage designer Jacques Drésa and choreographer Jeanne Hugard. In producing the ballet, Ravel integrated a prelude and four interludes that frame the tale vignettes. Moreover, the narrative arc was modified, with the 'Beauty and the Beast' vignette coming before the one based on the 'Green Serpent'; the work concludes with a marvellous apotheosis.

While d'Aulnoy certainly plays on the exoticism of the East in her tale by making the pagods – which her readers would have associated with Chinese culture – form the court around Laideron-nette, Ravel and his team accentuate it. This is evident in Désa's design for Laideronnette's costume, as well as in the music itself. Ravel incorporates elements drawn from Chinese and Javanese trad-itions, including the use of the pentatonic scale, typical of Asian music, and the integration of rhythms inspired by the Javanese percussion tradition of gamelan.[48] D'Aulnoy's French tale with a dash of Asian flavour becomes more fully 'Oriental' in Ravel's hands.

That the suite in general and the ballet in particular focus on a scene in which Laideronnette unrobes to bathe (the quotation from d'Aulnoy's tale around which the vignette is built begins with 'She undressed and climbed into the bath') elicits an erotic tone, which is particularly striking in what is originally a tale about an ugly princess. Is it this infusion of Orientalism – an artistic movement that often objectified Eastern women for the consumption of West-ern men – that leads to the eroticization of the heroine? Besides that of the design of Laideronnette's costume, there are no known images of the performances. However, in the piano score Ravel describes Laideronnette as being 'dressed as a Chinese woman in the style of Boucher, a black velour mask concealing her face, a tulip in her hand'.[49] The evocation of the paintings of François Boucher, an artist known for his voluptuous nudes, only foregrounds the erotic nature of the scene, suggesting that it is only Laideronnette's face

Costume for Laideronnette, empress of the pagods, by Jacques Drésa for Maurice
Ravel's ballet *Mother Goose* (1912).

that is ugly; her body can be pleasurably contemplated as though it is a figure in a Boucher painting. Such an idea only takes on more meaning when we imagine that during the performance the audience gazes upon the body of the ballet dancer incarnating a bathing Laideronnette.

In 1910, some two years before the appearance of the ballet, René Chalupt, an important music critic of the period, wrote a poem directly inspired by Ravel's 'Green Serpent' vignette, also titled, after Ravel, 'Laideronnette, Empress of the Pagods'. The poem fully exploits the implicit eroticism of the original suite. Indeed, the first section reads like a striptease:

> Laideronnette, Empress of the Pagods,
> Undresses and climbs into the bath;
> She first removes her dress,
> Her beautiful satin dress
> Whose long train
> Trails behind
> On the stairs and the bushy paths
> So far behind her
> That the *negrillon* [a young Black servant] who carries it
> Is nothing but a dot in the horizon.
> She then removes her velour corset,
> Her brocatelle petticoat
> And her lace day shirt,
> Then, shivering from being naked,
> With her bare foot, pink as a flower,
> She touches
> The water contained
> In the crystal bathing tub
> And plunges herself into the sudden freshness.[50]

As depicted by Ravel and Chalupt, it is hard to imagine that the heroine was so horribly ugly that her family would have removed her from her sister's wedding. Moreover, in her tale, d'Aulnoy pairs an ugly heroine and hero, both of whom become beautiful as well as good together over the course of the tale, creating equality between women and men when it comes to ugliness, goodness and the pleasurable contemplation of a beautiful person. Both composer and poet, however, refocus the tale exclusively on female beauty within a more fully Orientalist setting; as such, their adaptations of 'The Green Serpent' recall such Orientalist paintings as Jean-Auguste-Dominique Ingres's *The Turkish Bath* (1852–9) and Jean-Léon Gérôme's *The Great Bath at Bursa* (1885), complete with nudes and the enslaved Black people who serve them. In the ballet score it is noted that 'Green Serpent comes crawling lovingly beside her [Laideronnette].'[51] Given the Orientalist setting – Gérôme also painted *The Snake Charmer* (*c.*1880), which some critics (among them Joseph Boone) have qualified as homoerotic – the snake in Ravel is further suggestive of sexual imagery that is not emphasized in the original tale by d'Aulnoy. Ravel's suite and Chalupt's poem both honour d'Aulnoy's legacy at the same time that they undermine her conception of gender relations, given their objectification of the female body through the sexualization of Laideronnette.

A final musical iteration of 'The Green Serpent' can be found in the work of the French composer Jean-Michel Damase. Damase was well known in the mid-twentieth century, having collaborated with Raymond Queneau on his ballet *La Croqueuse de diamants* (The Diamond Cruncher, 1950; later included in the film *Black Tights*, 1960); with Orson Welles on the ballet *The Lady in the Ice* (1953); and with Jean Anouilh, who wrote the libretto for Damase's opera *Eurydice* (1972). Following in Ravel's footsteps, in 1958 Damase recorded *Féeries*, which brings together sixteen songs based on

French fairy tales, as noted above, mostly by Perrault and d'Aulnoy. Damase's 'Green Serpent' in particular and *Féeries* in general is a tribute to Ravel's 'Laideronnette, Empress of the Pagodas' and his *Mother Goose Suite*.

From Balzac to Damase, 'The Green Serpent' has left its traces on French literature, British pantomime and classical music. D'Aulnoy's fairy tale has been used to frame a realistic short story, to console Flaubert as he writes *Madame Bovary*, and to inspire music and poetry. While some of these adaptations are problematic in their representations not only of gender but – in the Age of Imperialism – of race and the Oriental Other, they also speak to the enduring legacy of 'The Green Serpent' and its adaptability to different sociohistorical and ideological contexts and to different artistic mediums. An important influence in the creation of 'Beauty and the Beast' tales, as well as of the history of adaptations of 'Cupid and Psyche', 'The Green Serpent', like 'The Ram', enjoys its own longstanding legacy within fairy-tale history.

As this history makes clear, without d'Aulnoy's 'The Green Serpent' and especially without 'The Ram' we would never have had 'Beauty and the Beast'. 'The Ram' provides the overall plot – the relation to the father figure, and the idea that the hero's life depends on the timely return of the heroine – for 'Beauty and the Beast', while 'The Green Serpent' models the doubling of the hero and provides other details for Villeneuve's version in particular. Although predominant in the twentieth- and twenty-first-century European and Euro-American cultural field, 'Beauty and the Beast' did not eclipse 'The Ram' and 'The Serpent' until the twentieth century. 'The Ram' enjoyed a second life in England, while 'The Green Serpent' left traces in works by Balzac and Ravel.

In the many different adaptations of these two tales, there is a tendency on the part of (mostly male) editors and artists to lessen the agency of d'Aulnoy's heroines. Sometimes Merveilleuse dies with the Ram and never takes the throne, while Laideronnette never gets to lead an army. But through these adaptations, d'Aulnoy's legacy lives on.[52] D'Aulnoy's tales were by no means 'obscure' in this period, as some critics have suggested; such a remark is based on a twenty-first-century notion of the fairy-tale canon, largely shaped by the hegemonic hold Disney has had on the field of fairy tales.[53] D'Aulnoy's tales were indeed widely considered classics in the nineteenth and early twentieth century.

The White Cat

Illustration of the White Cat by E. MacKinstry from *The White Cat, and Other Old French Fairy Tales, by Mme. la comtesse d'Aulnoy* (1928).

3
The Other Famous Cat Tale

W hen we think of tales about clever cats, Puss-in-Boots, a character that regained acclaim through the *Shrek* franchise in the 2000s, immediately comes to mind. Based on a tale by Charles Perrault, *Shrek*'s Puss-in-Boots is decidedly male, an identity that is solidified by the cat's identification with the Hollywood icon Antonio Banderas, who voiced the character for the film series. However, the history of this cat tale leads us to many a clever female cat, the most famous being the heroine of Marie-Catherine d'Aulnoy's 'The White Cat', which was so popular that it was adapted to everything from the stage and trading cards to comic books.

James Robinson Planché, the prolific writer of fairy extravaganzas, described d'Aulnoy's 'The White Cat' as 'one of the best known, and most popular of all Madame d'Aulnoy's stories' and stated that 'few collections of Fairy Tales are to be found without a version of it'.[1] D'Aulnoy's famous cat tale appeared in numerous print editions, many beautifully illustrated, from the late seventeenth to the twentieth century, and famous theatrical adaptations made it to the British and French stage in the nineteenth century. In the twentieth century it was also adapted to comic-book form, not only in France but in Mexico, and as late as 1965. Indeed, 'The White Cat' circulated alongside Perrault's 'Puss-in-Boots' for generations, enjoying as much recognition as the cat tale by her male counterpart.

D'Aulnoy's 'The White Cat' brings together what we think of today as two distinct tales: 'Rapunzel', which folklorists refer to as a 'maiden in the tower' tale; and 'Puss-in-Boots', a tale about a clever cat who helps his master. The version of 'Rapunzel' included in Jacob and Wilhelm Grimm's *Children's and Household Tales* (1812), which is today the best-known version in Europe and North America, was not collected from an oral source but based on a literary tale, 'Rapunzel' (1790) by Friedrich Schulz. Schulz's text was in turn a German translation and adaptation of the French fairy tale 'Persinette' (1698) by the French *conteuse* Charlotte-Rose de La Force, who in turn adapted it from Giambattista Basile's Rapunzel tale 'Petrosinella' (1634). D'Aulnoy and La Force were friends, and d'Aulnoy was also familiar with Basile's tales, as is evident, for instance, in 'The Blue Bird', in which she very clearly rewrites the frame narrative of Basile's *Pentamerone*.[2] D'Aulnoy and La Force published their tales about pregnancy cravings and a maiden in a tower in the same year, 1698, both based on Basile and perhaps both knowing each other's adaptation; in the case of d'Aulnoy, it was to become one of her most famous fairy tales.

'The White Cat' also draws on cat tales. In the sixteenth century Giovanni Francesco Straparola published the earliest known version of 'Puss-in-Boots', titled 'Constantino Fortunato'. What makes this version of the tale so striking to contemporary readers is that, rather than a father leaving to his youngest son a male cat, which we have come to accept as the 'official' version of the tale, it is about a mother leaving to her youngest son an enterprising female cat, who helps him to gain the hand of a princess. Basile subsequently reworked Straparola's tale in 'Cagliuso', retaining the gender of the clever cat but replacing the dying mother with a dying father. With

Perrault we have the final elimination of an active female agent. In his version, a dying father leaves his son a resourceful *male* cat, who assists the hero in his social elevation. This masculinization of 'Puss-in-Boots' epitomizes the politics of gender in tales by Perrault, who tends to reduce the agency of female characters when rewriting Italian fairy tales by Straparola and Basile. D'Aulnoy's choice of title plays on all these cat tales. However, rather than have her clever cat play the role of simple helper – one who is taken for granted by Basile's hero, for which he is reprimanded – d'Aulnoy's female cat is a sovereign of many kingdoms and could be said to help the hero 'from above' (from the position of a patron) rather than 'from below' (from the position of a servant). As such, her female and sovereign cat presents important contrasts to the cat tales by her male counterparts.

This chapter follows the emergence of d'Aulnoy's most celebrated fairy tale and traces its legacy, with a particular emphasis on its impact within theatrical and visual culture. Grounded in early modern conceptions of and taboos about sexuality and pregnancy, 'The White Cat' evolves to symbolize the epitome of the fairy extravaganza in nineteenth-century Paris. The fact that it continued to be printed and even adapted to comic-book form in French as well as in Spanish in the twentieth century speaks to its enduring qualities and its appeal within different mediums and traditions of visual culture.

From parsley to Rapunzel

D'Aulnoy integrates several motifs from 'Puss-in-Boots' tales into 'The White Cat', but she takes much of her inspiration from Basile's 'Petrosinella' and possibly 'Persinette' by La Force, both titles meaning 'little parsley'. Basile's suggestive tale is far from a story about chaste women, an aspect that La Force tempers in her rendition. In 'Petrosinella', the mother of the heroine, Pascadozia, craves parsley while pregnant and steals some from the garden of an ogress. As we might expect, the ogress catches Pascadozia and demands the fruit of her loins. However, it isn't until Petrosinella is a well-developed child that the ogress takes her away and encloses her in a tower, accessible only through an upper window by climbing up the heroine's legendary long hair. Beautiful as a siren, Petrosinella attracts the attention of a prince, who falls in love with her; she gives the ogress a sleeping potion so that she can haul her lover up into the tower. The couple are discovered thanks to a gossipy neighbour, but Petrosinella and the prince together outwit the ogress, escape to the prince's land and marry.

In this earliest literary version of 'Rapunzel', Pascadozia appears to be a single mother; no father is mentioned in the tale. At first she refuses to give up her daughter to the ogress, and raises her until after the age of seven, when the ogress begins to harass Petrosinella on her way to and from her teacher's house, saying 'Tell your mother to remember the promise.'[3] Eventually Pascadozia gives up her daughter, more out of exasperation than out of fear: 'If you run into the old woman again and she asks you about that damned promise, you answer her, "Take her!"'[4] Petrosinella is then locked up in the magical tower without doors. Later versions are much more suggestive of an Eve-like plot, in which the daughter is punished for the 'sins' of her mother early on; here, with the delay of the transfer of the child to the ogress, this single mother suffers the least among her peers, having given up her daughter more out of annoyance than as a debt incurred as a result of her unruly desire.

Like mother like daughter: Petrosinella herself risks becoming a single mother, taking a lover from the perch of her tower. Betrayed by a gossipy neighbour, who informs the ogress that she 'was making love with a certain young man and she suspected that things might have gone even farther because she could see the buzz of activity and trafficking', Petrosinella prepares to take action and, thanks to her own cunning, escapes with the prince to his kingdom.[5] Despite her flaunting of social mores and respectability, she is rewarded in the end with the hand of a prince. Basile's 'Petrosinella' comes off as the least moralizing of the different versions of 'Rapunzel', and the heroines – both mother and daughter – suffer significantly less than their descendants. Was it easier for a male writer who didn't have to worry about his sexual reputation to create heroines who tread on the margins of respectability and still come out on top, than for a woman writer – such as La Force – to do so?

La Force experienced first hand what it meant for a woman in 'real life' to transgress norms of female respectability. Although she was from a powerful family and served as the *fille d'honneur* to the dauphine (the wife of the heir apparent of Louis xiv), she was the subject of gossip and eventually exiled from court. As Lewis Seifert notes, 'she was accused of misconduct, including possession of a pornographic novel. She was also rumoured to have had love affairs.'[6] Against prevailing laws, La Force married without parental consent in 1687 (it was annulled), and ten years later she was banished from court for writing 'satirical songs'.[7] She was certainly no prude. We might attribute the ways in which she reshaped Basile's tale to her need to negotiate the treatment of subjects that were particularly taboo in the hands of a woman writer whose own reputation was constantly being questioned, ultimately leading to her exile. La Force's characters must tread more carefully when it comes to sexual matters than those of her male counterpart, Basile.

Whereas Basile's tale opens with 'There once was a pregnant woman named Pascadozia,' focusing on the pregnant woman and her cravings, La Force's tale foregrounds the love between the heroine's mother and father: 'Two young Lovers had got married after a long courtship: nothing could surpass their ardour: they were living content and happy, when, to top off their happiness, the young wife became pregnant.'[8] The tale opens on a passionate note of love, which frames the pregnancy. At the same time that La Force makes the future heroine's mother more respectable than Basile's by having her be married, the *conteuse* also infuses her tale with (properly channelled) sexual desire. When the future mother craves a fairy's parsley to the point of dying from it, her loving husband is prepared to do anything to retrieve it for her and save her life, for 'nothing seems difficult in love.'[9] In other words, he does anything to satisfy his wife's desires, even if it means giving up his future child. When Persinette is born, the fairy comes immediately to take her away. The mother and father are no longer mentioned in the tale. Can we assume that they will continue their lives as the two lovers we met in the opening lines?

La Force's fairy does not lock the heroine in a tower until she reaches her twelfth birthday, the point in a young woman's life at which she enters reproductive age.[10] Enclosing the heroine in the tower, then, is a way for the fairy to attempt to control her destiny and avoid for her charge the fate of Persinette's mother. As such, we can read the tower as a figure for the heroine's chastity, a common trope in early modern literary and religious culture. In his sixteenth-century *Les Propos memorables et illustres hommes de la Chrestienté* (Memorable Sayings and Illustrious Men of Christianity, 1560), Gilles Corrozet writes: 'Chastity in a woman, it is the fortress of her beauty.'[11] Often attributed to Jacques Olivier and republished several times in the seventeenth century, the misogynistic essay *Le Tableau des piperies des femmes mondaines* (The Portrait of Worldly Women's Ruses, 1632) puts forth the notion that 'a well-founded and supported chastity is safer than the best fortress in the world.'[12] Early modern readers would readily have made the connection between chastity and the tower; breaching the tower, then, is symbolic of sexual penetration, a fate the fairy hopes to spare her adoptive daughter: 'she was resolved to conceal her from her [sexual] destiny' by enclosing her in the tower.[13]

In Basile, the prince discovers the heroine when Petrosinella spreads her hair out in the sun, and he finds that she has the face of a siren, those legendary beings renowned for their beauty. La Force picks up on the reference to the siren and has her hero, who is hunting in the woods, follow the beautiful singing coming from the tower. Approaching Persinette, this young prince is not only 'touched' by her beauty, but 'charmed' by her voice, in true siren fashion, and, like their victims, he at least momentarily meets a terrible fate. At first charmed herself by the handsome prince, Persinette subsequently fears that he is a monster who may kill her with his eyes. Trying to find a way into the tower, he finally imitates the voice of the fairy, who would call upon Persinette to let her hair down, and penetrates the tower window. Persinette experiences both desire and fear – she cries and trembles – then marries the prince on the spot.

Seeing the prince every day, Persinette becomes pregnant in no time at all and eventually the fairy – not a neighbourhood gossip – discovers the truth. She cuts off Persinette's hair and carries her charge away to a solitary but agreeable place by the sea – later referred to as *son désert* (her desert), a term used in the period to refer to an isolated place – where the heroine gives birth to a young prince and princess. Whereas earlier, in order to gain entry into the tower, the prince tricked Persinette by imitating the fairy's voice, now the fairy imitates Persinette's song and uses her hair to lure the prince into the tower, so that she can take 'revenge' and punish the prince for his 'crime'. The prince falls out of the tower and is

Persinette.

The prince preparing to climb up the tower using Persinette's
hair from *Les fées, contes des contes* (Paris, 1707).

blinded; as such, the fairy takes away those eyes that can kill. After years of wandering sightless through the world, the prince hears a charming voice and, realizing it is Persinette, follows it to her cabin in the wilderness. Upon seeing her 'dear husband', Persinette sheds tears that heal his blindness. The family is thus reunited, but the fairy prevents them from being able to eat or drink, until she finally takes pity on them and transports them to the palace of the prince's father.

La Force's version of 'Rapunzel' might be read as a tale about lovers as much as about childbirth. Persinette's parents are specifically described as 'lovers' – a term not commonly used in the context of marriage in early modern texts – who are happy together. Persinette, however, is forcibly separated from her lover by the fairy, an episode of the plot that recalls La Force's own biography. Like Persinette, La Force married without parental consent; her marriage was annulled, and she was forcibly separated from her lover. Unlike Persinette, La Force was never reunited with her lover, and was later exiled from the capital, the same year her collection of tales appeared. In early modern France, the term *désert* was often used to qualify one's place of exile, a solitary and uninhabited site outside the capital. In her memoirs, for instance, Anne Marie Louise de Montpensier describes her exile from the court and Paris as *le plus grand désert*, the greatest desert.[14] La Force uses the same term to refer to the place where the prince finds Persinette and their children; contemporary readers would have readily made the connection between 'desert' and 'exile', possibly making further associations between La Force's heroine and La Force herself. Perhaps La Force's retelling of Basile's tale was a way for her to imagine an alternative ending to her own story.

Before we turn to d'Aulnoy's reworking of this material to achieve her masterful 'The White Cat', it is worth mentioning the illustrious and too often unattributed legacy of La Force's tale.[15] Her 'Persinette' was translated into German by Friedrich Schulz in 1790; there is much textual evidence to support this, despite Schulz's minor changes to adapt the tale to a late eighteenth-century German readership. In La Force, the fairy brings parsley from the Indies, whereas in Schulz she orders rapunzel 'from overseas'.[16] La Force describes the heroine's wardrobe as being 'as magnificent as those of the queens of Asia' – Orientalism was in fashion in early modern France – while in Schulz the wardrobe would be worthy of 'the empress of Russia'.[17] Both tales mention that the heroine has a view of the sea and of the forest, and that the prince might be a monster, who kills with his eyes. It is Schulz's version of 'Rapunzel' that Jacob and Wilhelm Grimm adapted for their *Children's and Household Tales* of 1812, using it 'as the primary source for their own retelling, assuming (mistakenly) that Schulz had, himself, called upon German sources'.[18]

Despite these minor changes to La Force's tale, Schulz's adaptation is close to the original, maintaining the passionate relationship between Rapunzel's parents. Rather than simply stating that the heroine was pregnant, as in the case of La Force, whose fairy intuits that her charge is expecting a baby, Schulz's heroine asks the fairy why her clothes have become so tight, which reveals the pregnancy within the narrative, a detail that appeared in the Grimms' version. Over time, however, in response to critics, Wilhelm Grimm purged 'Rapunzel' of its sexual overtones. Maria Tatar explains that 'A. L. Grimm and [the historian] Friedrich Rühs singled out "Rapunzel" as a tale particularly inappropriate to include in a collection of tales that children could get their hands on. "What proper mother or nanny could tell the fairy tale about Rapunzel to an innocent daughter without blushing?" Rühs gasped.'[19] As the *Children's and Household Tales* increasingly became redefined as a children's and not a scholarly text, Wilhelm Grimm reshaped many of the tales, toning down the sexuality present in what were originally fairy tales for adults, an editorial process exemplified by the history of 'Rapunzel'.

D'Aulnoy's 'The White Cat'

Fusing cat and Rapunzel stories, d'Aulnoy's 'The White Cat' is a complex tale characteristic of the style of the *conteuses* and especially of d'Aulnoy. Such tales 'work to reveal the stories behind other stories, the unvoiced possibilities that tell a different tale. They are determinedly and openly "intertextual" and "stereophonic", evoking other tales and invoking more than one voice.'[20] D'Aulnoy's cat tale embodies these complexities. The tale opens into a plot that, albeit in cat style, anticipates Hannā Diyāb and Antoine Galland's 'The Prince Ahmed and the Fairy Pari Banou', then integrates a Rapunzel-like narrative relating White Cat's backstory.[21] 'The White Cat' concerns a king who sends his three sons on three quests: first, for the most beautiful miniature dog; second, for a delicate cloth that can pass through the eye of a needle; and third, for the most beautiful princess. During his first quest, during a storm, the youngest son comes upon a marvellous castle in a forest, illuminated by brilliant carbuncles. Its porcelain walls call attention to the text's status as tale, with representations of fairy tales by Perrault ('Donkey Skin', 'Sleeping Beauty'), Marie-Jeanne L'Héritier ('Finette') and d'Aulnoy herself ('The Bee and the Orange Tree', 'Gracieuse and Percinet', 'The Green Serpent' and 'The Sprite Prince'). At the same time that d'Aulnoy embeds intertextual references to other fairy tales within these porcelain walls, she also embeds the prince himself within a fairy genealogy by positioning him as being related to the title character of d'Aulnoy's tale 'The Sprite Prince', who had magical abilities: 'He [the youngest prince] was charmed to see the Sprite Prince, who was a relative of his.'[22]

Disembodied hands lead the prince into the castle, remove his wet clothing, powder him, curl his hair and make him 'more beautiful than Adonis', before leading him into a room that further grounds the tale within cat tales.[23] The walls are filled with 'the history of the most famous cats: Rodilardus, hung by his feet at the council of rats; Puss-in-Boots, the marquis of Carabas; the Cat who writes; the Cat transformed into a woman; witches transformed into cats'.[24] The intertextual references invoke cat tales by Jean de La Fontaine and Perrault, suggesting the many possible routes this tale might take. Then appears the beautiful White Cat, dressed in mourning, with a portrait attached to her paw of a handsome young man who perfectly resembles the prince, adding further mystery to the story. She helps the prince find the dog, the cloth and eventually the most beautiful woman, all of which occurs in Russian-doll style: the miniature dog is enclosed in an acorn; the cloth is found within a grain of millet within a grain of wheat within a cherry stone within a nut; and the princess (the White Cat) is presented to the king emerging from a crystal rock, shortly after she emerges from her cat body.[25] In fact, just when we believe we have nearly reached the end of the story, with the White Cat regaining human form after the prince very reluctantly cuts off his beloved cat's head and tail, she begins to relate to him a lengthy backstory, a maiden in the tower tale, which is also about encasement. Indeed, the interpolated backstory represents nearly half of the overall tale.

It is difficult to determine whether d'Aulnoy and La Force communicated with each other about their adaptations of Basile's 'Petrosinella', since both tales were published in 1698; we currently do not have sufficient biographical knowledge about either author to determine the frequency with which they saw each other or the precise nature of their relationship. There are definite connections between the two versions in the choices the authors make in transforming Basile's tale. For instance, both La Force and d'Aulnoy depict the heroine's mother and father as happily married. With respect to La Force, the garden in which the parsley grows is seemingly impenetrable, the height of the walls making it impossible for the husband to enter. D'Aulnoy greatly exaggerates the scene in ways that suggest that she may have been familiar with her friend's tale: the pregnant queen sends her men to fetch the fruit from the enclosed, impenetrable garden with ladders to climb its high walls, which grow taller and taller as the men climb, resulting in the maiming and death of many of them. The scene could be read as a humorous play on La Force's conception of the fairy garden. However, d'Aulnoy takes Basile's lead in having the mother be the person who manages to get the delicacies from the fairy garden and make the Faustian deal; in La Force, it is the husband who gathers the herb for his wife and negotiates with the fairy.

D'Aulnoy also exaggerates the scene in which the queen consumes the precious fruit after making the deal with the fairies, who wish to marry off the princess to someone of their choosing. First, the oldest of the fairies 'put her fingers in her mouth and whistled three times, then cried out: "Apricots, peaches, nectarines, cherries, plums, pears, melons, grapes, apples, oranges, lemons, currants, strawberries, raspberries, run towards my voice!"'[26] As they come rolling and crawling towards the fairy and the pregnant queen, the latter, 'impatient to satisfy her craving, pounced on them and grabbed with her hands the first ones that offered themselves to her; she devoured them more than she ate them.'[27] Spending three days and three nights consuming and gathering fruit, the queen then has four thousand mules loaded with fruit to take back to her kingdom.

In d'Aulnoy, the pregnant queen becomes a grotesque figure in her ferocious and insatiable desire for the fairy fruit.

By having her king at first refuse to turn his child over to the fairies, d'Aulnoy again takes cues from Basile. In La Force, the fairy takes the heroine away immediately after her birth and the parents do not protest. In d'Aulnoy, the angry king, who was not part of the deal with the fairies, locks his pregnant wife in a tower; after the heroine's birth, he removes his daughter from the tower and refuses to hand her over to the fairies. But the latter send a dragon to ravage the kingdom until the king relinquishes his heir. The father realizes the power of the bargain his wife has made and frees the queen, who also initially refuses to give her daughter to the fairies; in the end they concede, in order to save the kingdom. Whereas Basile's mother appears flippant when abandoning her daughter to the ogress, d'Aulnoy's king and queen are truly forced into a situation where they must choose between the inhabitants and welfare of their kingdom, on the one hand, and the life of their daughter – who is destined to be taken care of and exchanged in marriage by the fairies – on the other. As such, the heroine becomes a sacrificial victim as much as she functions as a token of exchange.

Given her enterprising ways, d'Aulnoy's heroine also recalls that of Basile. One day the princess in the tower sees a handsome knight, and she takes pleasure in gazing upon him before he returns her gaze. The next time she sees him, she notices that he appears to have dressed in his best clothes in order to please her. She even uses a spyglass to contemplate his beauty. Through her parrot, the king (as we learn) sends the imprisoned princess a heart-shaped diamond ring and his portrait. She eventually builds a ladder (in d'Aulnoy's version the fairies visit the princess in the tower by dragon, rather than climbing her hair), the king climbs into her tower and they marry, with her parrot and her dog Toutou as witnesses. However,

The White Cat.—p. 405.

The princess in the tower, illustrated by John Gilbert for James Robinson Planché's translation, *Fairy Tales by the Countess d'Aulnoy* (London, 1855).

the fairies wish to marry the princess to the ugly dwarf Migonnet. Eventually the fairies catch the princess with the king, who is, in the blink of an eye, devoured by the fairies' dragon, the same one that ravaged the princess's homeland. Devastated, the heroine refuses the marriage arranged by the fairies and as punishment is transformed into a white cat, condemned to remain in that form until she can find a prince who perfectly resembles the husband the fairies took from her; at this moment she also learns her own history and that both of her parents are dead. Unlike La Force's heroine, d'Aulnoy's White Cat – like Basile's Petrosinella – never becomes pregnant in the tale.

D'Aulnoy's tale concludes by emphasizing White Cat's power. After she is restored to her human self and presented to the prince's father, knowing that he sent his three sons on quests to divert them from demanding his throne, she states, somewhat ironically: 'Lord . . . I did not come to take from you a throne that you fill with such dignity; I was born with six kingdoms, let me offer you one and I give as much to each one of your sons. I request as compensation only your friendship and this young prince as my spouse. We will have enough with three kingdoms.'[28] In this Rapunzel/Puss-in-Boots tale, the independent heroine negotiates a new trade: three kingdoms for the hand of the prince (instead of fruit for a princess to marry off eventually). Whereas the initial trade between White Cat's mother and the fairies was also about others arranging her marriage, the conclusion of the tale has White Cat arrange her own marriage to the prince, who is less powerful than his wife, being a kingdomless prince and not a king (like White Cat's first husband). In Basile and La Force, the reunited couple end up in the kingdom of the prince's father; in d'Aulnoy, the prince ends up in White Cat's kingdom, which she rules independently. And, unlike Perrault's cat tale – in which the cat supports the hero's conquest of land, marriage to a princess and overall rise to power – d'Aulnoy's cat is a powerful princess who assists a less powerful prince, the latter eventually becoming her husband and joining her in her queendom.

Blending motifs from earlier cat tales and from Basile's 'Petrosinella', d'Aulnoy created a complex tale about a powerful female ruler. Like Basile's 'Petrosinella' and La Force's 'Persinette', d'Aulnoy plays on conceptions of maternal cravings at the same time that she makes her tale very much about lack of female agency when it comes to arranged marriages. Just as we might read the happy ending of La Force's tale as a compensatory narrative that repairs her own life story, we might similarly read the White Cat's agency in her own marriage arrangements as a way for d'Aulnoy to reimagine her own life story, projected into an imaginary universe where noblewomen and princesses can negotiate their own future. D'Aulnoy's cat tale also contrasts significantly with that of Perrault, in which the male cat is a subservient helper to the hero. Instead, d'Aulnoy's female cat assists the hero more from the position of patron than of servant, and the Rapunzel backstory furthermore endows her with her own narrative in which she is the main – and not a supporting – character.

While 'The White Cat' can be situated within a history of naratives that explore gender and sexual norms and female agency, it also elicits playful and sometimes shocking visual cues with its wrathful dragon, disembodied hands, flying wooden horse, decapitation and many metamorphoses. Drawing from these visual cues, d'Aulnoy's cat tale would enjoy another nine lives on the nineteenth-century British and French stage. As David Blamires notes, 'The nineteenth-century popularity of "The White Cat" was not confined to print: the story was utilized as the basis of theatrical entertainment as early as 1811, when the new comic pantomime *The White Cat: or, Harlequin in the Fairy Wood* was presented at the Lyceum

Theatre in London.'[29] Performed on 23 December by the Drury Lane company, this 'new Comic Pantomime' was apparently received 'with unbounded applause', as the title page of the published prospectus by James Kirby claims; it was followed by other theatrical adaptations, among the most celebrated of which were James Robinson Planché's extravaganza of 1842 and Théodore and Hippolyte Cogniard's vaudeville *féerie* of 1852.

'The White Cat' in British pantomime

British pantomime grew out of Italian *commedia dell'arte* and the eighteenth-century British harlequinade, coming fully into its own and attaining great popularity by the mid-nineteenth century.[30] Like *commedia dell'arte*, British harlequinades centre on the stock characters Harlequin and Columbine, the lovers whose plans are contravened by Pantaloon, Columbine's greedy father, who tries to separate them, all to comic effect. Jeffrey Richards characterizes the standard harlequinade plot as follows: 'young lovers, aided by ingenious servants, thwarting the plans of the father or guardian to marry the heroine to a wealthy older man'.[31] Harlequinades could take the form of plays or scenes in plays, and early pantomime includes more harlequinades than those produced later in the century. The history of theatrical representations of 'The White Cat' follows these developments; the early work of Kirby is more closely related to the harlequinade than is that of Planché later in the century.

According to his published prospectus, Kirby's *White Cat* is grounded in d'Aulnoy's fairy tale, but it quickly dissolves into a harlequinade when such stock characters as Harlequin and Pantaloon replace the characters from the tale through fairy magic. The highly abbreviated plot concerns Prince Paladore, who is caught in a storm and spies a castle guarded by a dragon, which he kills. Upon entering the castle, the prince finds a salon filled with cats, whose leader is the White Cat. In this version, the White Cat informs the prince that she is in fact the fairy Arborella, and that he must decapitate her in order for her and her courtiers to regain their original form. If he does so, she will reward him with 'unequalled Beauty' after he overcomes a rival. She then transforms the prince into Harlequin and gives him a magic sword. The prince (now Harlequin) goes to the abode of Sir Toby, who wishes to marry his daughter Columbine to the wealthy Dionisius Dazzle, Esquire. Columbine is disgusted by the proposal and prefers Harlequin. Arborella appears and accuses Sir Toby of avarice, then transforms Sir Toby into Pantaloon – the greedy father of Columbine in the *commedia* and harlequinade tradition – and Dazzle into the rejected lover. The pantomime concludes with the union of the two lovers and a grand ballet.

In effect, d'Aulnoy's fairy tale is stripped to a minimum and fitted into the structure of the harlequinade. Kirby borrows the motif of the dragon from her tale, but deploys it in a different context: to guard the cat castle instead of the maiden in the tower. He also retains the decapitation, but then transforms the White Cat into a helper fairy instead of the marriageable princess, after which Prince Paladore is turned into Harlequin, who goes to find his Columbine. Instead of the hero's rival being an ugly, powerful dwarf, he is a repulsive (at least to Columbine), wealthy older man. In this theatrical adaptation, d'Aulnoy's tale is a pretext for the harlequinade.

It is possible that the composer Adolphe Adam, who is best known for his ballet *Giselle* (1841), adapted Kirby's pantomime to the French stage in 1830. In his *Souvenirs d'un musicien* (Memories of a Musician, 1857), Adam remarks: 'I had done, in collaboration with [the composer Casimir] Gide, the music for an English pantomime,

The White Cat, for the Théâtre des Nouveautés.'[32] Before its official premiere, Adam describes a performance of the pantomime before the young French princes at Saint-Cloud, who were 'enchanted by the good kicks exchanged between the clowns and Pantaloon'.[33] Adam had connections to London theatre; he had married the Parisian actress Sara Lescot, sister of Pierre François Laporte, who served as actor and manager at the Haymarket theatre (1828–31; 1833–41) and Covent Garden (1832–3). In his documentation of British plays based on d'Aulnoy's tales, Philip H. Bolton lists only Kirby's adaptation of *The White Cat* on the British stage before Planché's popular and more faithful adaptation of 1842, *The White Cat: A Grand Comic, Romantic, Operatic, Melo-Dramatic Fairy Extravaganza*, making the fact of Adam's possible adaptation of Kirby's play quite likely.[34]

Another harlequinade version of 'The White Cat', *Harlequin and a Happy New Year! or, The White Cat and the King and His Three Sons* by Thomas Longden Greenwood, appeared at Sadler's Wells Theatre in 1846. Here the tale of the White Cat is inserted into a frame narrative that concerns the year 1846 personified, whom Time helps to usher out to bring about the new year. Then Year 1847 appears onstage and informs the audience that 'Dame Bunch' (Mother Bunch, that is, the tales of d'Aulnoy) 'shall lend a hand' in the festivities for the new year. What follows is a highly abbreviated version of 'The White Cat' in which Prince Formoso and his squire come upon the princess's castle and her court of cats; they enter the palace, guided by hands holding torches to light their way; Formoso meets the White Cat and shortly thereafter is instructed to cut off her head and tail with an axe; he does so, returns with her to his father's kingdom, and the pantomime concludes with Formoso being transformed into Harlequin, White Cat into Columbine, the king into Pantaloon, and the squire into a clown. The script contains minimal song and no dialogue, the focus of this adaptation residing in dance, slapstick and spectacle. The context of the contest between the three princes is evoked only quickly and briefly at the end, immediately before the characters' final harlequinade transformations, and most of the plot goes unexplained, which suggests that the pantomime audience was already familiar with the tale and could simply enjoy references to it.

Moving from Kirby and Greenwood to Planché, we witness the ways in which mid-nineteenth-century pantomime was coming into its own, becoming distinct from the *commedia dell'arte* and the harlequinade. This change can be attributed to numerous factors, including the new social mores that emerged with the Victorian age.[35] Planché calls his play an 'extravaganza', distancing it from pantomime tradition, at the same time that his work inevitably grows out of it. As in d'Aulnoy's tale, the action is launched when the king – here King Wunsuponatyme of Neverminditsnamia – establishes a contest between his three sons, Prince Paragon, Prince Precious and Prince Placid, to find a dog that can fit through a thumb ring, and, later, the most beautiful princess. Planché creates a stronger logic for the king to send the three sons on these quests: they are triplets, and the absence of an eldest son thus demands such a trial. Planché invents the character Jingo, who plays the role of servant and sidekick to Paragon, playing on earlier *commedia dell'arte* and harlequinade traditions.

We learn early on – well before they find themselves at White Cat's isolated fairy palace – that Jingo, comically, is afraid of cats. Planché truly capitalizes on the visual cues of d'Aulnoy's tale with the incorporation of the disembodied hands that welcome the prince and Jingo into the White Cat's chateau. Jingo declares: 'We've fallen into friendly hands,' after which Paragon quips, 'This show of hands is clearly in our favour.'[36] When they enter, Jingo is strangely attracted to a pair of soft hands, which he speculates belong to a 'hand-some' creature, while Paragon dines with the White Cat and sees a miniature portrait attached to her paw. White Cat delivers the tiny dog the prince offers to his father, and upon Paragon and Jingo's return to White Cat's chateau, Jingo asks for the hands in marriage; he marries them just as White Cat explains to Paragon that the prince must cut off her head and tail in order to save her, which the prince succeeds in doing. This releases Princess *Cat*arina from her feline form, while Jingo finds himself holding the hands of *Palm*yra, Catarina's lady-in-waiting. Catarina recounts her back-story, which is significantly streamlined: her father was a king who died and left her in the hands of an old fairy, who wished to marry her to a 'vile dwarf'; she was courted by a prince, whom they killed, then they transformed Catarina and her friends into cats or just hands. Catarina proposes that they return to the prince's land by train via the 'fairy railroad', and rather than have the White Cat offer the prince's father and brothers each a kingdom, Paragon does so, stating: 'Great sir, your crown I shall no longer need,/ For to her royal father's I succeed.'[37] The finale includes a wink to another cat tale, 'Puss-in-Boots': 'Come, let us dance and sing,/ While all the City bells shall ring,/ Long life to everything!/ and our 'White Cat' to boot!'[38]

Planché makes some interesting changes to conform to the genre of the extravaganza – the addition of the character Jingo, for instance – and modifies the class and gender dynamics found in d'Aulnoy's tale to suit nineteenth-century London audiences. According to Planché, one of the particularly successful features of *The White Cat* was

> the very ingenious realization of the description in the story of the attendance of hands without bodies. They appeared

in all parts of the stage bearing flambeaux, moving chairs, and executing various other orders in the most natural and graceful manner without its being possible for the audience to detect the *modus operandi*. It was certainly the *chef d'oeuvre* of that unequalled machinist, Mr W. Bradwell, and the effect was as picturesque as it was puzzling.[39]

In the tale, the disembodied hands represent the servant class, who within the early modern social hierarchy are all but invisible, reduced to their essential function.[40] Planché's extravaganza both reproduces this invisibility, to spectacular ends, and challenges it by having Jingo – himself of lower social status – fall in love with the set of hands, as if he somehow sensed that he didn't actually marry 'nobody' ('I've married nobody, and would introduce her'), realizing after the many transformations that he in fact married 'somebody' ('I've married somebody, then, after all').[41] Jingo's attachment to the hands comically and in visually stunning ways points to the hands' 'humanity', their agency (for they consent to marry him), thus challenging the invisibility and objectification of the servant class found in d'Aulnoy's aristocratic tale. Appealing to a broad range of social classes who flocked to pantomimes and extravaganzas in a post-French Revolution Europe, Planché necessarily plays with and undermines the static social structures found in d'Aulnoy's tales. The genre itself demanded it.

When it comes to gender, things become more complicated. On the one hand, Planché removes the Eve-like episode of the tempting fruit, making the princess an orphan who is taken in by a fairy who – as in d'Aulnoy's tale – wishes to marry her against her will; neither mother nor father is culpable in any way. On the other, he seems to reinstate a patriarchal regime; whereas d'Aulnoy's heroine is the one who offers the kingdoms to the prince's father, here Paragon claims Catarina's realms as if he were the true heir, stating, 'For to her royal father's I succeed.' It would seem, then, that the sovereignty of d'Aulnoy's White Cat is undermined in Planché's version.

Yet what happens when we realize that the famous actress Lucia Vestris was playing the role of Paragon, and that the two other princes were also played by women? It was indeed common in English pantomime and extravaganza for the 'principal boy' – the main hero – to be played by a woman, and Vestris was one of the best known among them.[42] She had become famous in 1820 for playing the principal role in *Giovanni in London*, and was believed to be 'one of the most beautiful and charismatic women in the kingdom'; she 'was also powerful, assertive and independent, and invaded a traditional male preserve by becoming a successful theatre manager later in her career'.[43] By the time Vestris performed in *The White Cat* in 1842, she had already managed the Olympic Theatre and was running Covent Garden. Vestris being a well-known celebrity and theatre manager, it is quite possible that audiences saw behind the character of Paragon the successful and independent woman who incarnated him. The principal-boy role blurs, transcends and challenges gender boundaries, being perceived as both feminine (a ballad was written celebrating Vestris's legs) and masculine (she also demonstrated manly, swashbuckling mannerisms onstage). The principal boy in general and Vestris in particular troubled gender and sexual norms. Rereading Planché's ending within the context of the extravaganza's first performances, with the complex figure of Vestris playing Prince Paragon, perhaps the ending isn't quite as patriarchal as it might appear on paper.

Planché's *White Cat* was performed throughout the 1840s in London, Bath and New York City.[44] The tale took another life on the British stage with F. C. Burnand's production *The White Cat! of*

Scenes from 'Finette; or, The Clever Princess', depicted on chromolithographs for the Paris department store Le Bon Marché, *c.* 1890–1900. They highlight Finette's ability to overcome her aggressor through violence.

Print of 'Finette-Cendron' from Basset Marchand d'Estampes, *c.* 1810.

Poster for the 1830 *Singspiel Finette Aschenbrödel* by August Schreiber.

Frontispiece of *Daddy Gander's Entertaining Tales* (London, 1815).

Disembodied hands open golden doors, ushering the prince into the White Cat's castle, as represented in a chromolithograph for Poulain chocolate, *c.* 1890s.

A Poulain chocolate chromolithograph of the scene when the prince first encounters the White Cat, *c.* 1890s. 'The young Prince, amazed, enters the castle . . .'.

Scene from *La Gatita Blanca* (Mexico City, 1965) in which we see the image of the prince on the ring, from the Mexican comic series 'Famous Tales Illustrated in Colour' (1961–*c.* 1965).

The White Cat transforms into a blonde bombshell in *La Gatita Blanca*.

Fortunio with Strongback, who carries the dead dragon back to Alfourite,
from *The History of Fortunio* (London, 1804).

Opposite: (*top*) Fortunio slaying the dragon. Detail from the board game *Fortunio
and His Seven Gifted Servants* (London, 1843).

(*below*) Fortunio meets the emperor Matapa. Detail from the board game
Fortunio and His Seven Gifted Servants.

Chocolat **POULAIN**
Goûtez & Comparez!

7. La Biche au Bois.

Déposé

The chocolate company Poulain used fairy tales such as Marie-Catherine d'Aulnoy's 'The Doe in the Woods' to sell their chocolate bars.

Prince Lardi-Dardi and the Radiant Rosetta: A Fairy Burlesque Extravaganza in 1870. This theatrical adaptation of the tale opens with Princess Rosetta – the maiden in the tower – being courted by Prince Lardi-Dardi, the prince of all the Handy-Dandies, who is accompanied by his men. Burnand reintegrates details that were absent from earlier theatrical adaptations of d'Aulnoy's tale, such as the heroine's dog and parrot, her companions in the tower. Lardi-Dardi learns that Rosetta is kept in the palace by the fairy Dragonetta – a name that fuses d'Aulnoy's fairy Violente with the dragon that carries out her bidding – who is planning to marry her off to the gnome king, Humpi Dumpi. Prince Lardi-Dardi's plan is to send a postcard to his fairy godmother through Rosetta's parrot to ask for her assistance in the affair. As they wait for the fairy godmother, Lardi-Dardi and his men smoke cigarettes onstage, as the prince sings: 'My friends and me,/ When we've some tea,/ Enjoy a cigarette . . . A cigarette, a cigarette,/ You want a fellow who,/ Can make a Cigarette,/ While making love – that's me.'[45] As they smoke, the fairy Dragonetta approaches, and, playing on the famous lines from 'Jack the Giant Killer', she declares, 'Fee, fi, fo, fum! I think I get a whiff,/ A sort of scent – fee, fi, fo, fum – a sniff.'[46] Here it isn't an Englishman she smells, but the cigarette smoke. The Fairy Queen of Dreamy Dell appears with her fairies and puts Lardi-Dardi to sleep for a hundred years to save him from Dragonetta's wrath (making him a male Sleeping Beauty), while Dragonetta transforms Rosetta and her friends into cats.

The next scene is said to occur a hundred years later, and the current king of the Handy-Dandies, King Dawdle the Doddler, fears the moment when Lardi-Dardi will awake and retake the kingdom. His stepson, Prince Dapper, and his son by his first wife, Prince Sprightly, both hope to inherit the throne when, upon awaking from his hundred-year sleep, Prince Lardi-Dardi makes his own claim. Burnand thus creates a new motivation behind the quests: that of resolving the three-way rivalry between the two half-brothers and Prince Sprightly's ancestor. As we might expect, Lardi-Dardi ends up at 'Katz Kastle' (this time after being captured by cats out hunting) and meets the beautiful White Cat, who helps him to acquire a dog that can fit into a nut, and later the loveliest princess. The White Cat tells her tale, reveals herself to be Rosetta and asks Lardi-Dardi to cut off her head and tail. Needing encouragement from the Fairy Queen of Dreamy Dell, who makes reference to the recent *Alice's Adventures in Wonderland* (1865) by saying 'Off with her head', the prince gives two blows, the stage goes dark and the play moves quickly to the happy ending with the union of Rosetta and Lardi-Dardi. Rosetta sings: "Tis a very old story in a rather new dress,/ And we hope it is none the worse for that.'[47]

The play is full of puns and quips. 'Mounseer' is used for 'Monsieur'; *pretending* and *persuasive* become *purr*-tending and *purr*-suasive; Bobbi and Miss McTabby dance a *paw-de-two* (or *pas-de-deux*); reference is made to Louis *Cat-orze* (Louis xiv); and Lardi-Dardi declares ironically that cats are 'such sly dogs'. The tale is a French one, but Burnand's nods to 'Jack the Giant Killer', *Alice's Adventures in Wonderland* and Shakespeare (when the fairy queen declares 'All's well that ends well') infuse it with English flavour.

Interestingly, Burnand makes his prince into a Sleeping Beauty, while the White Cat demonstrates her authority when she prevents her fellow cats from pouncing on Lardi-Dardi as he approaches Katz Castle. Although the ending suggests that sovereignty lies in the hands of Lardi-Dardi – in this version Rosetta possesses no lands – as in Planché's extravaganza, gender becomes more complex than the text itself might suggest given that the prince and his retinue are all played by women, with the well-known actress and theatre manager Emily Fowler incarnating Lardi-Dardi.

Burnand exploits gender play to humorous and transgressive
ends in the scene in which Lardi-Dardi and his 'men' smoke onstage,
an action highlighted by the prince's smoking song and Dragonetta's reaction to the smoke, all of which refocuses the audience's
attention to the smoking characters. In Victorian England smoking
in public was viewed as transgressive behaviour for women, but
represented a socially acceptable and even integral form of masculinity. While nineteenth-century caricaturists depicted smoking
women 'as ugly and immoral', smoking was 'an important element
in male bonding rituals', emblematized by the gender-segregated
smoking room.[48] Burnand's production of *The White Cat!* pokes fun
at the social taboo of women smoking by having women dressed as
men smoke onstage, in public, thus challenging Victorian gender
norms.

For most of the nineteenth century, d'Aulnoy's French tale
influenced the British stage, with one British *White Cat* crossing
back over the Channel to be adapted for the Parisian stage by Adam
and Gide. While Planché's extravaganza was the most successful
theatrical adaptation that appeared on the London stage, the
Cogniards' French adaptation of 'The White Cat' (1852) was wildly
popular in Paris for at least two decades. It is possible that Burnand
was familiar with the Parisian play – he may have been influenced
by its opening, but for the most part his play remains distinct – while
Richard Soutar directly adapted the celebrated French vaudeville
féerie for the British stage, a circumstance that speaks to its renown.

La Chatte Blanche, or the féerie of all féeries

The Cogniard brothers produced immensely popular vaudeville
féeries in nineteenth-century Paris, and among their most popular
was *La Chatte blanche* (The White Cat), first staged in 1852. The

newspaper *Le Figaro* noted that the production in 1875 of this *féerie* would be 'the 486th representation of *The White Cat* at the Gaîté [theatre]' in Paris; importantly, it was also regularly featured in other popular Parisian venues.[49] At its first staging at the Cirque-National theatre, the *féerie* was praised in Théophile Gautier's *Revue de Paris* for going well beyond the Cogniards' other popular plays: 'Let's just say that *The White Cat* surpasses what we know to be the marvellous up to this point.'[50] Writing in the weekly *Le Monde illustré*, Charles Monselet describes the Châtelet theatre production of 1869 in terms of 'a terrifying luxury', and gives us a sense of the persistent nature of stagings of *The White Cat* in nineteenth-century Parisian culture:

> You will tell me that there are always the same ballets, always the same decors ... always the same nude women suspended in the air, always the same kings given to the same pleasantries, always the same fairies chanting the same spells with the same golden wand, always the same lily-livered squire, always the same demons leaping about ... but what do you want me to say? It isn't always the same audience; spectators replace other spectators; it's my son, it's yours, who watch wide-eyed at those moments where I watched wide-eyed.[51]

Following the Châtelet theatre representation of the Cogniards' *White Cat* in 1887, the *Revue d'art dramatique* described with awe the re-creation of a river onstage using actual water: 'they practically diverted the Seine in order to have it pass through the stage [*scène*] of the Châtelet theatre.'[52] The play continued to thrill audiences into the early twentieth century. In 1908, more than fifty years after its premiere, the journalist and critic Francis Chevassu declared

Drawing from *Le Figaro* (5 November 1908) of the actor M. Claudius playing the role of King Migonnet in the Cogniards' *The White Cat*.

AU CHATELET : La Chatte blanche

M. Claudius

LA SOIRÉE

that *The White Cat* 'is not a play, it is a symbol ... renewing itself incessantly, becoming little by little the unique *féerie*, the typical *féerie*, destined to absorb all other similar creations'.[53]

This sumptuous *féerie*, which often featured the very fashionable singer Thérésa as Pierrette, was as baroque as the fairy tales by d'Aulnoy from which it drew. Much like British pantomimes, French vaudeville *féeries* interspersed song, dance and spectacle with the goal, in Marie-Françoise Christout's words, of 'fill[ing] the audience with wonder'.[54] Thanks to the elaborate use of machines and luxurious stage props, a *féerie* 'allows one to escape from the logic of facts', generates imaginary spaces in which 'fish dance the gavotte and cottages suddenly become hell or a palace'.[55] In his review from 1845 of *La Biche au bois* (The Doe in the Woods), an earlier *féerie* by the Cogniards, Gautier takes great relish in describing the dreamlike world of the play, showing appreciation for the scene featuring the kingdom of the fish, which he calls 'the most baroque fantasy', and another in which mushrooms and leeks dance the polka.[56]

Already in these descriptions of the lavish spaces of the *féerie*, we get a glimpse of the unstable universe created on stage in which different realistic and fantasy worlds – cottages and palaces, fish and human kingdoms – are incongruously juxtaposed and flow into one another via the movements through the plot of the main characters, who themselves are also transformed over the course of the play, sometimes by virtue of passing through fantastical spaces. In *The White Cat*, the heroine, Blanchette, is transformed into a knight and later into a cat; the prince Pimpondor spends nearly two out of three acts playing the role of the maiden in the tower; the inarticulate, patois-speaking peasant Petitpatapon becomes an eloquent and even snobbish squire; and the peasant Pierrette metamorphoses into a semiprecious gemstone and later into a shrimp as she moves through the Kingdom of Gems and the Kingdom of the Sea to be with her true love, Petitpatapon.[57]

The Cogniards' *The White Cat* weaves together two stories by d'Aulnoy, 'The White Cat' and 'Belle-Belle; or, The Knight Fortuné' (see Chapter Four), both of which concern female leads who metamorphose: a princess turned into a cat, a noblewoman transformed into a knight. *The White Cat* reorganizes chronologically the plotline of d'Aulnoy's 'The White Cat' – which does not proceed linearly – into which the Cogniards splice the *conteuse*'s maiden warrior tale 'Belle-Belle'. The *féerie* opens with the backstory of d'Aulnoy's tale: the fairy Violente has imprisoned the heroine, Blanchette, her adoptive daughter, in a castle that sits on a great rock in the sea. Blanchette's isolation here resides in the inaccessibility of the rock as opposed to the impenetrability of the tower. Although we do not know how Blanchette finds herself in this situation, Violente, as in d'Aulnoy's tale, wishes to marry her to the evil, ugly dwarf king Migonnet. Violente tries to assure Blanchette that, although her future spouse may not be handsome (and Blanchette has never seen a man before), he will make her a powerful queen. But, as in the tale, the heroine encounters a handsome prince, Pimpondor (who in this case washes ashore, much like the prince Aimé in d'Aulnoy's 'The Bee and the Orange Tree'), and is immediately attracted to him. When Migonnet arrives to wed Blanchette, the heroine rejects him, while Violente decries her rebellious spirit. Initially in the *féerie* Pimpondor plays the role of the chivalric knight who tries to preserve his beloved from a monstrous marriage, but he is kidnapped by Migonnet, who imprisons him and later plunders the kingdom of his father, King Matapa (which is the name of the evil emperor in d'Aulnoy's 'Belle-Belle'). Meanwhile, Violente casts Blanchette into the sea (recalling a similar scene in d'Aulnoy's 'The Princess Rosette').

Blanchette survives and is taken in by the Chiendents, a family of peasants, who make her their goatherd. However, they eventually reject her because their daughter Pierrette's fiancé, Petitpatapon, has fallen in love with her. Blanchette then encounters the good Heather Fairy (*la fée de la bruyère*), who transforms her into the knight Fidèle to help Blanchette rescue Prince Pimpondor and save Matapa's kingdom. When Petitpatapon later comes upon Fidèle, he believes that he had been in love with a man. Fidèle asks Petitpatapon to become his squire, to which he agrees, while requesting

'Some costumes from *The White Cat*, at La Gaïté theatre', from
the *Revue Parisienne*, 21 August 1869.

that the fairy grant him eloquent language to accompany his new social standing, which she does. The pair journey to find their 'extraordinary companions' to help them save the prince and Matapa's kingdom. After locating Forte-Echine (Strong Spine), Fend-l'Air (Air Splitter), Fine-Oreille (Keen Ear), Trinquefort (Drink-a-Lot), Bouffelaballe (Bail-Eater) and Bourrasque (Burst of Wind), Fidèle and Petitpatapon need one further magical thing to assist them, a sapphire ring, which they seek out in the Kingdom of Gems (*le royaume des bijoux*). With a little help from his friends, Fidèle returns to Matapa his kingdom's wealth, and frees the prince. However, Violente reappears, turns Fidèle/Blanchette into a cat-headed woman, and isolates her in another castle. These events lead to a second quest, this time carried out by Pimpondor and Petitpatapon, and eventually they save both Blanchette and Pierrette. In some ways the play gives Pimpondor, who spends most of it locked up, the role of the maiden in the tower, whereas Fidèle/Blanchette spends more than half of the play incarnating the active hero.[58]

This broad overview of the plot cannot begin to do justice to the complexity of the *féerie*, which is packed with wordplay and burlesque, along with various airs and dances. One could view it as a tribute to d'Aulnoy and her impact on the fairy-tale genre in the period, with its allusions not only to the two main source tales – 'The White Cat' and 'Belle-Belle' – but to 'The Bee and the Orange Tree', 'The Boar Prince' and 'The Princess Rosette'. Like d'Aulnoy, in many respects the Cogniards flatten gender hierarchy, positioning female characters as being just as capable if not more so than male characters, and they further challenge fixed notions of social class, notably through Petitpatapon, whose character reveals the performative and arbitrary nature of class hierarchy.

He (Fidèle) – the pronoun used throughout the section of Blanchette's transformation – never hesitates in his quest to save

Pimpondor from the evil Migonnet, and does a lot of other saving along the way, much like the knights of medieval cycles. After the Heather Fairy provides him with a chest full of luxurious clothes, the hero/heroine seeks out King Matapa, furnishing the impoverished king and queen with clothes appropriate to their rank and swearing that he will free Pimpondor and return to them the wealth of their kingdom. When travelling to the Kingdom of Gems to obtain the magical sapphire ring, Fidèle uncovers a plot to overthrow the diamond Regent, thus saving his kingdom. After successfully completing his first test – Matapa challenges Fidèle and his men to eating all the food the king has amassed in the central square, which Bouffelaballe easily does – Fidèle sets out on his second quest: he must kill the dragon that is ravaging Migonnet's kingdom. On the way he comes across many marble statues, which he discovers are princesses transformed by Migonnet for having rejected his hand in marriage. With the magic ring, which allows its possessor to undo any enchantment, Fidèle saves the women whose fate he could have shared. As in d'Aulnoy's 'Belle-Belle', here Fidèle overcomes the dragon, manages to retrieve the treasure that Migonnet stole from Matapa, and finally frees the prince. It is only with the appearance of the fairy Violente that the happy ending is postponed, with another episode of d'Aulnoy's 'The White Cat' spliced into the action.

The prince charming of the *féerie*, Pimpondor, incarnates imperfect masculinity, spending the period of the play in which Blanchette shifts from goatherd to questing knight shut up in a dungeon in Migonnet's castle. Like the princesses of Disney films, he is waiting to be saved, hoping to compensate the person who saves him. He also lacks the courage we see in Blanchette/Fidèle, who is ready to sacrifice everything to save him. While in his cell, Pimpondor laments: 'Oh Blanchette! I don't reproach you, but

making your acquaintance cost me dearly.'[59] The idea that it is Fidèle/
Blanchette who saves the prince is made explicit, and is articulated
by Fidèle himself:

> PIMPONDOR: Who are you . . . young knight? Oh, these
> traits . . . and these words that I just heard . . . am I
> dreaming?
> FIDÈLE: My dear prince, no . . . it is Blanchette who is
> before you.
> PIMPONDOR: Blanchette! . . . it is she!
> FIDÈLE: Who comes to save you . . . but let's go, let's go,
> for a thousand dangers still threaten you . . . we could be
> surprised.[60]

Fidèle succeeds in both freeing Pimpondor and returning the
riches of Matapa's kingdom; it is not a male character but a female
one, the fairy Violente, who defers the happy ending by giving
Blanchette the head of a cat and flying her off to an isolated castle.
In the meantime, Pimpondor continues to demonstrate a lack of
chivalry. When Blanchette is carried off, Matapa convinces his son
that she is dead and that it is therefore pointless to try to find her;
it is only when the Heather Fairy appears and scolds Pimpondor
for seeming to forget her so quickly that he begins his quest to find
Blanchette.

In the Cogniards' *féerie*, Blanchette and later Pierrette are not
fully transformed into cats; they have human bodies with a cat's
head. While d'Aulnoy's heroine looks like a cat but speaks and acts
human, the Cogniards' heroines, able only to purr and meow, look
part cat and part human, to comical effect. Petitpatapon observes
Pierrette, who has her eyes on a mouse, while Blanchette plays like a
cat with the feather in Pimpondor's cap. Whereas d'Aulnoy's White

Cat, in full cat appearance, conducts herself as the human queen she is, the Cogniards playfully make Blanchette and Pierrette less cat-like in appearance, but more cat-like in behaviour.

In their complex theatrical adaptation of d'Aulnoy, the Cogniards frame their *féerie* with two episodes of 'The White Cat'. Their play met with resounding success for decades in France, remaining so popular that in 1888 it entered the history of photography. The Parisian photographer George Balagny produced the first successful photographs taken of theatre actors onstage indoors at a Châtelet staging of *The White Cat*. In his coverage of this technological innovation in *La Nature*, Georges Mareschal remarks on the importance it will have for both the future of photography and documenting the history of theatre, and that history begins with the Cogniards' *White Cat*.[61]

'A ballet from *The White Cat*, fairy play at the Châtelet Theatre in Paris', from *La Nature: revue des sciences et de leurs applications aux arts et à l'industrie*, 5 December 1887.

Such success, however, was not the fate of the British adaptations of the Cogniards' play. Although their influence goes unattributed in the printed text, Richard Soutar very clearly adapted the Cogniards' *féerie* in 1870, significantly streamlining the plot, including cutting the episodes that take place in the Kingdom of Gems and the Kingdom of the Sea. Acknowledging his debt to the Cogniards, Henry Leigh wrote the script for another British adaptation of the French *féerie*, which was performed at the Queen's Theatre in December 1875. Jeffrey Richards quotes *The Era*, which described the performance as a 'dismal failure', and notes that the French play, which 'had run for some 500 nights in Paris . . . closed at the Queen's after only eight days'.[62] However, this did not mean the end to White Cat productions on the London stage. In 1877 the writer E. L. Blanchard produced another successful pantomime adaptation of d'Aulnoy's fairy tale. The fact that playwrights continued to produce theatrical adaptations of this tale speaks to its enduring public appeal. *The White Cat* was a title that brought people in droves to the theatre in both France and Great Britain for much of the nineteenth century. D'Aulnoy's cultural impact was far from dead in the Victorian era, and her 'White Cat' was given new manifestations in visual culture in the twentieth century in, among other forms, the comic book.

The White Cat in comics

Along with other tales by d'Aulnoy, 'The White Cat' continued to circulate in various forms in the twentieth century in French, English, Italian and Spanish.[63] The tale's popularity led to at least two comic-book adaptations: first, a French adaptation in 1935, from the collection *Les Merveilleuses histoires racontées par l'image* (Marvellous Stories Told through Images); and second, a Mexican adaptation from 1965, 'La Gatita blanca', from the collection *Cuentos famosos ilustrados a colores* (Famous Tales Illustrated in Colour). Each adaptation modifies the tale to suit its respective audience, taking into account child versus young adult readers, and each is marked by different cultural influences that shape its visual representation. Produced in social contexts in which arranged marriage was no longer the rule, these adaptations necessarily modify the story, but sometimes in ways that undermine the model of female agency proposed in d'Aulnoy's source tale.

The comic from 1935 was not the tale's first adaptation to a visual medium. In the 1880s and 1890s the French chocolate company Chocolat Poulain serialized several fairy tales by d'Aulnoy, including 'The White Cat', by including in their chocolate bars chromolithographs or 'chromos' with colour images illustrating the tale on the recto, and the narrative of the tale on the verso. In order to reconstitute the tale, chromos could be collected by purchasing enough chocolate bars, making it a sort of comic-book form itself, with each chromo functioning as a comic panel. The earliest comic books emerged in this same period – the 1890s – and typically the narrative was placed outside the comic panel, as is the case with one of the first French comics, *La Famille Fenouillard* (1889–93), and with other comics that appeared in the French children's periodical *Le Petit Français illustré*.[64]

As a full-fledged comic, 'The White Cat' appeared in 1935 in the 26th of 34 'albums' of the comic-book series 'Marvellous Stories Told through Images', which included tales by Perrault, Sophie de Ségur and Antoine Galland, and others by d'Aulnoy. Known later for his 'Petit-Riquet Reporter' series, Gaston Niezab served as the series illustrator. The narrative structure of the series, which claims to relate the tale 'through images', feels a little disjointed, although it is the same structure as that later used for the 'Petit-Riquet

LE SERPENT

M. Boule, de passage dans une petite ville, fit porter sa malle dans un hôtel et sortit en recommandant à Mlle Félicie, la bonne...

...de ne pas l'ouvrir pendant son absence. La bonne, une fois seule, ne put résister au désir de savoir ce qu'elle contenait.

Elle fut bien punie de sa curiosité en voyant apparaître devant elle un grand serpent à sonnettes que M. Boule exhibait dans les foires.

— Au secours! A moi! Je suis morte! se mit à crier la bonne épouvantée en détalant à toutes jambes.

Le reptile saivit ses traces. Il arriva dans le couloir du rez-de-chaussée. Une boîte à lait attira ses regards. Les serpents aiment le lait.

Celui-ci se régala. Il en but même un peu plus qu'il n'aurait voulu.

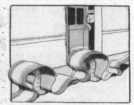

Il alla ensuite faire un tour dans la cour de l'immeuble, histoire de dire un petit bonjour à Fix le chien de garde.

Le serpent songea même un instant à visiter l'intérieur de la cabane de Fix qu'il trouva fort bien aménagée.

Le reptile, histoire de s'amuser, fit ensuite une petite promenade entre le sol et le tapis du couloir au grand désespoir de la concierge.

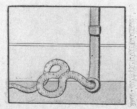

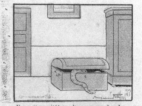

Puis il songea à rentrer, par le plus court chemin. Il prit même l'ascenseur qui se présenta à lui sous la forme d'un tuyau de descente.

Il rentra par la fenêtre, en quittant la gouttière et se dirigea incontinent vers la malle.

Il reprit aussitôt sa place sur ses chaudes couvertures. Son maître n'y vit que du feu et Félicie, la bonne, fut guérie du péché de curiosité.

A serpent tale about female curiosity in *La jeunesse illustrée* (1903), with the narrative located outside the comic panel.

Il y avait une fois un vieux roi qui, fatigué de régner, appela ses trois fils pour leur faire connaître ses intentions...

... Après leur avoir dit qu'il était disposé à prendre du repos, il promit son trône à celui de ses garçons qui lui rapporterait le chien...

... le plus minuscule. C'était évidemment une idée bizarre, mais les princes n'eurent garde de discuter. Ils s'inclinèrent devant...

... leur auguste papa, et se mirent en route aussitôt pour essayer de réussir, tout en se souhaitant à chacun, sincèrement...

... de parvenir au but. Le plus jeune qui était parti à pied ne tarda pas à se trouver, le soir venu, dans un bois où l'averse...

... le surprit. Elle se mit même à tomber avec une telle violence que le jeune homme dut chercher un refuge...

Opening of *The White Cat* (Paris, 1935) from the comic series 'Marvellous Stories Told through Images' (1930-38).

Reporter' series. While earlier comics include narrative and speech below the panel, by the 1930s speech balloons were integrated into it. In the case of *The White Cat*, each panel contains only speech balloons, with context provided by the narrative below the panel. For instance, in the first panel of the comic, the speech balloon relates the words of the king: 'My dear sons, I bring you together to inform you of my desire to give up my throne to one of you! I feel I am becoming old, and I am looking forward to rest!' Then, below the panel, one finds the narrative, which provides the context for these words: 'Once upon a time an old king, tired of reigning, called his three sons before him to inform them of his intentions.'

The disjointed nature of the narrative structure is even clearer in subsequent panels:

SPEECH BALLOON: King: 'Which one of you three will inherit the throne? You are going to find out! Don't be surprised by the strangeness of my will. My throne will go to he who brings back for me the prettiest little dog!'
NARRATIVE: ' ... After having told them that he was inclined to lead a more restful life, he promised the throne to the son who would bring back to him the most miniscule ... '
SPEECH BALLOON: King: 'Go on, my children, be quick about it and come back tomorrow with the animal you judge to be the most perfect!'
Princes: 'It will be done as you desire, father!'
NARRATIVE: ' ... dog. This evidently was a strange idea, but the princes did not dare discuss it, and bowed before ... '

As these examples illustrate, the relation between the narrative context provided below the panel and the speech balloons does not always proceed in smooth, linear fashion. Moreover, the addition of the narrative below each panel ironically suggests that the images themselves do not suffice to relate the story, harking back to the structure of the chromos, where the image illustrates the narrative more than it tells the story in picture-book style.

This comic-book adaptation streamlines the story significantly, including modifying the three one-year quests into three one-day quests. The most significant modifications, however, are made in relation to the White Cat's backstory. As in d'Aulnoy's original, the queen craves fruit from a fairy garden, and promises her unborn daughter in exchange. But later she refuses to give up her daughter, and instead of sending a dragon to ravage the kingdom, the fairy sends an ogre. When the princess spies the gallant prince who wishes to wed her, we learn that the fairy kills him, but this is not represented visually. One wonders if this might be owing to the desire to avoid violence in a comic book ostensibly targeting children, although that did not stop the illustrator from depicting White Cat's decapitation; perhaps representing the killing of an animal that doesn't actually die was considered less disturbing than portraying the killing of the human king, who does not transform or revive. As in d'Aulnoy, White Cat explains to the prince's father that she possesses six kingdoms, and grants one to each of her beloved's brothers. While the princess remains powerful in this version, a more domestic tone is introduced when, at the tale's conclusion, White Cat explains to the king, 'As for me, my most beautiful kingdom is the heart of my spouse, my greatest treasure,' while the narrative below the panel explains: 'As for her, her happiness would be to dedicate herself to her husband.' Such an ending resituates d'Aulnoy's powerful princess, who leads a state, within the context of bourgeois domestic bliss in which the wife dedicates herself to her husband.

While it might not be surprising to see d'Aulnoy's tale adapted to comic-book form in France in the 1930s, its later Mexican appearance is perhaps more unexpected. It was published by Editora Sol, which also published such American comics as Buck Rogers in Spanish. The series consisted of 46 issues, each recounting a fairy tale, among them 'Snow White', 'Little Red Riding Hood', 'Ali Baba' and 'The White Cat'. In this period, d'Aulnoy's tales were in the air. Her cat tale was circulating in Spain and Mexico in the 1950s and 1960s, published as a stand-alone book in Barcelona in 1958 and in the Mexican collection *Pulgarcito y otros cuentos* (Little Thumbling and Other Tales, 1959), alongside Perrault's 'Riquet with the Tuft', 'The Fairies' and 'Little Red Riding Hood'; Jeanne-Marie Leprince de Beaumont's 'Beauty and the Beast'; and two other tales by d'Aulnoy, 'The Doe in the Woods' and 'Beauty with the Golden Hair'. This collection was popular enough to see a second edition in 1962, three years before 'The White Cat' was adapted by Editora Sol to comic-book form.

The Mexican comic is structured more linearly than the French one, and does a better job of letting the images tell the story, a circumstance that can also be attributed to developments in the comic-book genre. The comic opens with 'once upon a time' in the narrative box within the panel (instead of below it, as in the earlier French comic), which introduces and contextualizes the speech balloon. The title of the comic is rendered in a style that resembles the titles of superhero comics, such as *Superman* and *Titans*, both of which were adapted to Spanish and published by Editorial Novaro. Not surprisingly, Editora Sol was founded by Antonio Gascón, the ex-director of Editorial Novaro.

The Mexican comic appears to return to the original text, or a very close translation of it, and it appeals to an older age group than the French comic does. It streamlines the main action less, lingering on the leisure activities that occupy the prince at White Cat's palace, such as the hunting party, a banquet and the theatre. Produced thirty years after the French one, the Mexican comic uses image effectively to relate story. A striking example is when the prince notices White Cat's wooden ring bearing the portrait of a handsome man. While d'Aulnoy's tale explains that the portrait resembles the prince perfectly, and the French comic leaves this out altogether, in the Mexican comic it is the image that informs the reader that the man in the portrait exactly resembles the prince. However, by the time the comic gets to the White Cat's backstory, the tale is rewritten in such a way that the portrait on the ring either was a mistake – the Mexican backstory does not include a former lover who was killed by the fairies – or is supposed to take on new meaning: the portrait does not refer to a first love, but rather anticipates White Cat's rescue by this particular prince. I lean towards the first option, since the heroine loses her appetite and becomes saddened at the specific moment when the prince sees the portrait. It is as if the Mexican adaptation follows the structure of d'Aulnoy's tale, then, when the creators get to adapting the backstory – which should have shed light on the significance of the portrait in the ring – they streamline it so much that the portrait loses its original meaning.

Indeed, as with the French comic, the biggest modification to the source text in the Mexican comic also occurs with respect to White Cat's backstory. After regaining her beautiful human form, White Cat relates her story, which is greatly simplified: her father was a king, who died before she was born, and her mother took refuge upon her husband's death in the fairies' castle. The queen has no pregnancy cravings and there is no trade with the fairies. Upon her own death, the queen simply leaves her daughter in the care of the fairies, who transform the princess into a cat only because she tried to run away on several occasions, the reasons for which are not illuminated in the comic. Metamorphosis thus does not serve as a punishment for rejecting an arranged marriage – which might not make sense in a 1960s comic produced in Mexico City – but it is meant to prevent the princess from running away. Moreover, the antidote to her animal transformation is never revealed, unless we are to understand that the ring with the portrait hints at how she might regain her human form. The ending is also modified: it is the prince who asks White Cat for her hand in marriage, whereas d'Aulnoy's heroine asks the king for his son's hand and, as such, challenges gender norms. Yet the Mexican adaptation does have the heroine grant kingdoms to the prince's two brothers, thus maintaining her economic power.

The Mexican comic tones down the violence and ramps up the sex appeal and romance. In the scene in which the prince must cut off White Cat's head and tail and burn them, we see only what happens after the prince kills her; with tears in his eyes, he throws her head and tail into the fire. Then, when she transforms, she becomes a blonde bombshell in the tradition of Jayne Mansfield and Lana Turner. Anne Rubenstein has observed 'a strong demand for the modernist melodrama that has characterized *historietas* [Mexican comics] for the past forty years', and 'The White Cat' is no exception.[65] After the prince's first year with White Cat, we learn that 'the kitty wrote verses so passionate that it could be judged that she had a burning and loving heart.'[66] This passion originates in d'Aulnoy's text, in which the narrator, perhaps not as emphatically, remarks: 'Often the beautiful cat composed verses and little songs in such a passionate style that it seemed she had a tender heart.'[67] The Mexican comic retained those moments of passion found in the source text, and exemplifies that passion in its images. After she regains her human form, the princess thanks the prince, who has 'saved' her. While the text in the speech bubble isn't particularly romantic – the princess declares 'Thanks to you I have recovered my original form and that

Sexual tension in *La Gatita Blanca*.

of my subjects, and my misfortunes are over' – the image certainly is; she gazes longingly at the prince, and the proximity of their lips creates a sexual tension we don't see in the French comic, which targets a younger audience.[68] Interestingly, in the 1960s Editora Sol published Spanish translations of the 1950s American comic 'My Romantic Adventures' under the title 'Cortejos Románticos' (Romantic Courtships) and 'Aventuras Románticas' (Romantic Adventures). It is possible that the editors were playing on the romance market, in which they already had a foothold, when adapting d'Aulnoy's tale.

D'Aulnoy's 'The White Cat' examined the problem of arranged marriage, and d'Aulnoy positioned her heroine in such a way as to grant her the ability to negotiate her own marriage, on her own terms. The Mexican comic removes any reference to arranged marriage and instead emphasizes romance and passion, which is reflected in the way d'Aulnoy's conclusion is reworked. Her conclusion reads: 'The beautiful White Cat immortalized herself here [in her kingdom] as much for her kindness and generosity as for her rare merit and beauty.'[69] D'Aulnoy's conclusion suggests a broad context for her heroine's renown, based on her position as sovereign. In the Mexican adaptation, White Cat is taken out of a governing, public function, and the focus instead is on love: 'And that is how the white kitty was immortalized, both for her beauty and her intelligence. Of course, she fulfilled her dream of love and married the prince, and they were both very happy.'[70] Here, the royal sovereign proposed by d'Aulnoy is transformed into a 1960s blonde bombshell who dreams of love, modelled on many a Hollywood romance.

Both the French and the Mexican comic-book adaptations of 'The White Cat' show the continued legacy of d'Aulnoy's tales within the domain of the comic book in the twentieth century. They are clearly written for different age groups; the French targets a younger audience and the Mexican – with its infusion of sex appeal – is geared towards young adult readers. They also represent distinct moments in the history of the comic book, the French produced just as the comic was coming into its own, the Mexican when the comic was more established as an independent art form. However, they come together in that both adaptations reduce the agency of d'Aulnoy's cat princess in different ways. Whereas the French comic circum-scribes the heroine within what feels like bourgeois domestic bliss, the Mexican comic suggests a sexier version of basically the same, playing on Hollywood-style romance tropes. In the end, however, both comics represent one of the many lives d'Aulnoy's White Cat enjoyed.

We have come a long way from d'Aulnoy's tale, which blended elements of Perrault's 'Puss-in-Boots' and La Force's 'Persinette'. Much like La Force's maiden in the tower tale (the source tale for the Grimms' 'Rapunzel'), d'Aulnoy's 'The White Cat' functioned as a compensatory narrative in a society that denied women the choice of spouse, often forcing them to marry against their will. As the tale was adapted to the pantomime and the *féerie*-vaudeville stage, it came to represent gender, class and even species fluidity, challenging all kinds of social norms at every turn. The subversive elements that were already present in the seventeenth-century source tale were exploited fully on the nineteenth-century British and French stage. However, when adapted to comic-book form in the 1930s and 1960s, in France and Mexico, female agency is curtailed to some degree, which also points to the fact that the history of gender and sexuality in fairy tales and their adaptations is never one of continual, linear progress. In the end, what all these adaptations within and across mediums reveal is that d'Aulnoy's 'White Cat' continued to thrive, even into the twentieth century. This begs us to rethink the role the *conteuses* have played in the history of fairy tales, and consequently to rethink what we believe we know about fairy-tale canons in different historical periods. 'The White Cat' indeed coexisted for a good two centuries with that other cat tale, 'Puss-in-Boots', and enjoyed her own nine lives, which she lived out across nations and across media forms.

The biblical Deborah as woman warrior in Le Moyne's *Galerie des femmes fortes* (Paris, 1647).

4
The Lost Amazon Warriors

In the previous chapters, the twentieth- and twenty-first-century notion that the classic fairy tale is synonymous with passive princesses and damsels in distress, such as Cinderella, Beauty and Rapunzel, is challenged by examining the history of the genre. This history reveals the changing nature of the fairy-tale canon and the existence of earlier, often more empowering variants of these and other tales. It also takes into account the enduring appreciation by the general public across Europe and North America for fairy tales by Marie-Catherine d'Aulnoy in particular, as well as by other women authors, such as Marie-Jeanne L'Héritier, Gabrielle-Suzanne de Villeneuve and Jeanne-Marie Leprince de Beaumont. As we have seen, since the fairy tale's early modern inception, which gave us 'our' (Euro-American and now global) classic canon, women writers – as well as countless male writers – have produced many an enterprising heroine; they regularly challenged gender norms and such customs as arranged marriage based on a conception of women as passive objects of exchange. Importantly, these tales also enjoyed a healthy legacy throughout the twentieth century in the Czech Republic, England, France, Germany, Italy, Spain, Mexico and the United States, among other countries.

Along with different variants of Cinderella, Beauty and the Beast, Rapunzel and cat tales, one type of fairy tale that emerged in the early modern period and that enjoyed popularity in the seventeenth and eighteenth centuries – with d'Aulnoy's variant remaining popular into the nineteenth century, as is evident in its stage and board-game adaptations – is what folklorists refer to as maiden warrior tales. Such tales revolve around noblewomen who cross-dress and engage in battle to preserve their family honour and the integrity of the state, much in the tradition of the Chinese legend of Mulan. Maiden warrior tales foreground the construct-edness of gender by featuring a heroine who not only passes, but excels as a male knight. Such tales also necessarily blur the bound-aries between heterosexuality and homosexuality by having both male and female characters fall in love with the cross-dressed maiden warrior.[1] These tales directly challenge any associations between

Engraving of the duchesse de Montpensier as woman warrior, reproduced in Arvède Barine's *La Grande Mademoiselle* (Paris, 1905).

the fairy-tale genre and passive princesses or damsels in distress by granting the heroine the agency to change not only her own fate, but that of entire kingdoms.

In the 1690s Henriette-Julie de Murat, Marie-Jeanne L'Héritier and Marie-Catherine d'Aulnoy each produced a maiden warrior tale. Although Amazonian heroines make appearances in other fairy tales by women writers, from d'Aulnoy's 'The Bee and the Orange Tree' and 'The Beneficent Frog' to Gabrielle-Suzanne de Villeneuve's 'Beauty and the Beast', the tales in question here make the woman warrior the main focus of the narrative. The three authors drew on themes and motifs found in tales by Giovanni Francesco Straparola and Giambattista Basile, but also, importantly, they were inspired by recent events and a prominent iconographical tradition centring on *femmes fortes*, 'strong women'. A pro-woman iconographical and textual tradition flourished in France from at least the fifteenth century, with the appearance of Christine de Pizan's *The Book of the City of Ladies* (1405), Symphorien Champier's *The Ship of Virtuous Ladies* (1503), Jehan Du Pré's *The Palace of Noble Ladies* (1534), François de Billon's *The Impregnable Fortress of Female Honour* (1555) and Madeleine and Georges de Scudéry's *The Illustrious Women* (1642), among many other texts.[2] The figure of Joan of Arc also came back into fashion in the seventeenth century, as is evident from such works as Jean Chapelain's epic poem *The Maiden; or, France Delivered* (1656), in which she is referred to as 'the Amazon from the Heavens'.[3] Although Salic law prevented women from taking the throne, there were three queen regents in early modern France, owing to the youth of French kings, and pro-woman works helped to legitimate their reign.[4]

Catherine de' Medici, wife of Henri II, was officially regent only from 1560 to 1563; however, she remained influential throughout the reigns of her young sons. Upon the death of her husband, Henri IV, Marie de' Medici became queen regent from 1610 to 1614. Nearly three decades later Anne d'Autriche, the mother of Louis XIV, served as regent from 1643 to 1651. It was under her that the civil war known as the Fronde (1648–53) broke out, which introduced further strong women to the public stage and historical memory. Aristocratic women, including Anne-Geneviève de Bourbon, duchesse de Longueville; Anne Marie Louise d'Orléans, duchesse de Montpensier; and Madame de Saint-Balmon, defended their families and their lands and challenged the regency through both diplomatic and military actions, and they were regularly referred to as 'Amazons'.[5] Indeed, as both visual and literary culture show, Amazons were in fashion from the 1640s onwards.

During the regency of Anne d'Autriche, Jean Desmarets and Stefano della Bella produced a card game, the *Jeu des reynes renommées* (Game of Famous Queens, 1644), initially for the purpose of educating a young Louis XIV and legitimating the authority of the queen regent. It also was released 'on to the commercial marketplace', representing another means of diffusing among the reading public images of strong queens, including Amazonian ones, collectively referred to as 'valiant'.[6] Given the broad diffusion through art, literature and games of strong female figures, often blending imagery from Greco-Roman mythology with medieval and contemporary female figures, it should come as no surprise that maiden warriors would provide compelling subject matter within the domain of fairy tales in this period. Twenty-first-century readers might find this more surprising than would the seventeenth-century readers of texts by Murat, L'Héritier and d'Aulnoy.

Among the three maiden warrior fairy tales that arose out of this historical context, Murat's 'Le Sauvage' (The Wild Man, 1699) remains closest to Straparola's earlier story about a cross-dressed

ALBERTE BARBE D'ERNECOVRT DAME DE SAINT BALMONT DE NEVVI,
LLE DE GIBAVMEY, DE VAVX LE GRAND ELE PETITE AGEE DE 36 ANS 1645
C'est Avecques Raison Qu'aux Sanglans Exercices Puisque Ton Coeur Par Elle a Triomphe' des Vices
Ta Vertu Ne Craint Point Les Efforts de L'enfer Ton Bras Vaincra Tousiours Les Meschans Parleser
Dedié à Madame de Haraucour Sa Fille Vnique.
Par son Tres humble Seruiteur Baltasar Moncornet avec Priuilege du Roy

Madame de Balmont, whose 'arm always vanquishes the villains', 1645, engraving.

Joan of Arc, from the frontispiece of Jean Chapelain's *La Pucelle, ou la France délivrée* (Paris, 1656).

Penthesilee
Reyne des Amazones. Elle vint
au secours des Troyens contre les
Grecs, et rendit de grandes preuues
de sa vaillance. Elle fut tuée par
Achille.

Martesie
Reyne des Amazones. Elle se
disoit fille de Mars. Elle conquit
vne partie de l'Europe, et plusieurs
Villes en Asie.

Hippolite
Amazone, sœur d'Orithie. Elle fut
rauie par Hercule et Thesée, lequel
l'espousa et la fit Reyne d'athenes,
dont jl eut le chaste Hippolite

Orithie
Reyne des Amazones . fille de
Marthesie. outre son extreme
vaillance, Elle a eu la louange d'auoir
conserué sa virginité toute sa vie.
Elle fit la guerre aux Atheniens acau=
se d'Hercule qui auoit rauy ses sœurs

Amazonian queens Penthesilea, Martesia, Hippolyta and Orithyia, from Stefano
Della Bella's card game *Jeu des reynes renommées* (Paris, 1644).

knight, and it is the tale that received the least acclaim. L'Héritier's 'Marmoisan, ou l'Innocente Tromperie' (Marmoisan; or, The Innocent Deception, 1695) enjoyed some renown and was translated into English as well as German. The maiden warrior tale that enjoyed enduring appeal, however, is d'Aulnoy's 'Belle-Belle, ou le chevalier Fortuné' (Belle-Belle; or, The Knight Fortuné, 1698). It was regularly translated and adapted into English and was popular enough that it not only hit the pantomime circuits in England, but was turned into a board game in 1846, developed by William Spooner at a time when the board-game industry in England was on the rise.

By examining these three tales together, we can consider the different ways women writers used maiden warrior tales to explore the politics of gender, challenge gender roles and criticize the patriarchal monarchy of Louis XIV. This chapter also allows us to see the broader impact of maiden warrior tales on the field of fairy tales – including literary texts, illustration, theatre and games – all of which seriously challenges any kind of essentializing associations between fairy tales on the one hand, and passive princesses and damsels in distress on the other. Because of the ambiguity of the heroine's gender identity, in the following discussion I will move back and forth – as do these different narratives – between using 'she' and 'he', and will often use the term 'hero(ine)' to foreground the gender fluidity of the maiden warrior.

From Costanzo/a to Constantin/e

Straparola's 'Costanzo/Costanza' provided the 1690s fairy-tale writers with a model for a full-fledged maiden warrior tale, although Murat, L'Héritier and d'Aulnoy each take a different approach to their reimagining of the figure. Within *The Pleasant Nights*,

Straparola's tale is recounted to a group of courtiers by Fiordiana
and concerns the king of Thebes, Ricardo, and his wife, Valeriana,
who initially have three daughters: Valenzia, Dorotea and Spinella.
Ricardo and Valeriana decide to give each of their daughters a third
of the kingdom as their dowry, and they marry them to the king
of Scardona, the king of the Goths and the king of Scythia, respectively. Later the king and queen are surprised by the arrival of a
fourth daughter, Costanza, which disturbs them only because they
cannot 'marry her properly'.[7] Costanza is gifted in the 'feminine' skills
of embroidery, singing, music and dance, as well as the study of literature and the 'masculine' skills of taming horses, wielding weapons
and jousting. In effect, the queen considers these abilities her daughter's dowry. Her parents wish her to marry a marquis (below her in
rank), which Costanza refuses; she then leaves Thebes, dressed as a
man and calling herself 'Costanzo', to undertake a voyage that would
have been typical of a young nobleman: 'she saw many countries,
heard various languages, and studied the manners and the customs
of the inhabitants.'[8] Costanzo eventually arrives in the kingdom of
Bettinia, and while the king wishes Costanzo to serve him, his wife,
the queen, 'hotly inflamed by love for him', wants the lad for herself.[9]
Costanzo rejects her many advances, and the queen's love turns to
hate, leading her to give him dangerous trials in the hope that he
will be killed.

For the first trial, Costanzo must capture a satyr, which he
accomplishes by planting wine and food to induce a group of satyrs
to sleep. He names the satyr he brings back to the king Chiappino,
but the satyr refuses to utter a word, which represents the second
trial Costanzo must overcome: to find a way to make Chiappino
speak. Costanzo succeeds by getting the satyr to reveal why he
laughed on four occasions, and this leads to the revelation that
Costanzo is in fact a woman, and that the queen's maidens are in

reality men in drag. The tale playfully uses cross-dressing to challenge gender norms by showing that Costanzo is brave and clever, and to reveal the queen's deceitful behaviour. The king marries Costanza, whose feminine and masculine skills together prove as valuable as a piece of land. One might argue that her value thus does not reside in her objectification (woman is equal to a piece of land) but rather in her abilities, her agency.

Murat takes an ironic and novelistic approach to her adaptation of Straparola's tale. She maintains the exotic location of the action (with respect to France), situating it in 'Les Isles Terceres' – the Terceira Islands, off the coast of Portugal – rather than Egyptian Thebes.[10] In so doing she plays on the use of islands often found in the French fairy-tale tradition, particularly notable in the works of her friend d'Aulnoy.[11] In Murat, Straparola's Ricardo is rendered as 'Richardin', who manages to marry his beloved, the Egyptian princess Corianthe, only after waging war against her father, who had tried to force her to marry the king of Bitter Fountains. Murat's tale thus opens with a critique of arranged marriage, then parodies the scene in which the royal couple bear three daughters. Happily married, Murat's beautiful couple manage to produce only ugly daughters, named Disgrace, Douleur (Suffering) and Desespoir (Hopelessness). After the birth of their second daughter, they attempt to influence the outcome of the pregnancy by surrounding the queen with attractive people and portraits of beautiful ones – in line with seventeenth-century notions of conception and birth – but to no avail. The Terceres is a system of islands, so the royal couple give each daughter one island, and marry them off to a hunchback named Magotin ('ugly monkey'), a one-eyed man with a limp, Gambille (which, ironically, means 'dance'), and a one-armed and one-legged man named Trottemal ('trots badly'). As in Straparola, the king and queen are later surprised by the birth of a fourth daughter, Constantine, who happens to be beautiful and talented.

When Straparola describes the heroine's talents, he begins by enumerating her womanly skills and concludes with her more masculine abilities. Murat takes the opposite approach, first relating that her heroine rode perfectly, excelled in archery, could handle a sword 'with marvellous skill' and enjoyed the sciences, and concluding her literary portrait with the more feminine occupations of embroidery, singing and dance.[12] As in the case of Straparola's Constantine, Murat's heroine 'is' her own dowry: her superior abilities, which transcend gender norms and boundaries, allow her to gain the hand of a king.

Murat elaborates on the problem of arranged marriage in her version of the tale. In Straparola the king wishes to marry his fourth daughter to a marquis, which is a *mésalliance* – a union between social unequals – but this fact is not dwelled upon. Murat exaggerates the gap in status; Constantine's father wants to marry her to an officer – not even a marquis – who furthermore lacks wit. He is unsuitable socially, owing to his low social status, as well as intellectually. Murat increases the tension between father and daughter, and between female family members and the patriarch, by having the queen assist her daughter in disguising herself as a man in order to flee this unwanted marriage. Significantly, the queen gives Constantine her father's clothes to wear, which could be read as the daughter's subversion and even usurping of her father's power, all of which is supported by the queen, her mother, who later incurs the king's rage.[13] Constantine also gains the support of another powerful woman – a fairy dressed as Diana, another Amazonian figure – who gives her a horse, Embletin. The heroine then makes her way to the city ruled by the king of Sicily.

In Murat, the episodes concerning the rivalry over the hero(ine) take on novelistic traits. Murat considerably expands on this section of Straparola's tale, integrating much more exploration of emotion and emotional tension, in line with Bronwyn Reddan's argument that the women fairy-tale writers of the 1690s were interested in developing 'a range of different perspectives that engaged with early modern intellectual debate about the nature of the passions, early feminist criticism of courtship and marriage, and ongoing conflict about the status of women and women's writing'.[14] Murat modifies the dynamic by eliminating the theme of adultery; the king of Sicily lives with his widowed sister Fleurianne, and both are charmed by this lovely gentleman – now referred to in the masculine as 'Constantin' – who makes many conquests among the ladies at court, but none greater than that of Fleurianne. The king arranges to marry his sister to the prince of the Canary Islands, Prince Carabut, a disagreeable hunchback who nevertheless possesses great wit and gallantry, only to regret it later, saying that he has consented to a 'disproportionate' marriage.[15] By including a king who wishes to marry his daughter against her will without regretting it, and a second king who arranges a disproportionate marriage for his sister and expresses remorse, Murat shows us different models of male figures who continue to implement patriarchal practices, even if they are reluctant to do so. This points to the underlying systemic nature of patriarchy: even a gentle king feels obliged to sacrifice his female family members to inappropriate suitors for the sake of political expediency.

Whereas Straparola's Costanzo is thoroughly male when disguised as a knight, Murat's Constantin proves to be more gender-fluid. Constantin not only excels at races and the hunt, but enjoys feminine pastimes, notably embroidering with Fleurianne's ladies, which – interestingly – only increases the princess's passion for him. The tale takes a novelistic turn with Fleurianne's passionate confession to Constantin of her love, which she believes is doomed because of her impending marriage to Carabut. For his part, Prince Carabut becomes jealous of Constantin, realizing that the princess is in love with the newcomer, and prepares to kill his rival. Given his superior swordsmanship, Constantin kills Carabut instead. Questions of love and passion propel the narrative forward, being the root cause of the wars that occupy the latter part of the tale. As such, Murat integrates elements of the French *nouvelle* or novella, which 'explained the mysteries of state by something that everyone could understand – love'.[16] The amorous tension found in Straparola is multiplied in Murat, who focuses our attention on the problems of forced marriage and its repercussions when love interests reside elsewhere, which can have consequences in the realm of the political.

The death of Carabut leads to Constantin's flight, when he comes upon the Fairy Obligeantine, who appeared to the hero(ine) earlier as Diana, and he reassumes his feminine appearance. The fairy leads Constantine around the world, including to Versailles, using a herb that renders them invisible. Cross-dressing and invisibility serve the same function: to conceal a feminine identity that limits women to the domestic sphere and hampers their mobility and access to public spaces. Constantine thus remains disguised through her invisibility, which provides her with the experience enjoyed by male nobles, who were expected to travel and visit courts around the world as part of their education. In the meantime, civil war explodes in her home islands, Princess Fleurianne finds herself again forced to marry against her will (this time to a satyr), and the king of Sicily is at war with the king of Canary, who is avenging his son Carabut's death. Through various trials and tribulations, a kind satyr (the eponymous *sauvage*, 'wild man') saves the king of

Sicily, and, like the captured satyr of Straparola, displays enigmatic behaviour as he tells the king to inform his people that he will soon marry, later revealing the identity of Constantine. We learn that the satyr is in fact the prince of the Aimantine Islands who was transformed into a satyr for rejecting the love of a fairy, and the tale ends with the double marriage of Constantine to the king of Sicily and Fleurianne to the Aimantine prince, an appropriate suitor at last.

In rewriting Straparola's tale, Murat has her maiden warrior fight above all against unjust, forced marriage. Straparola's Costanza dons male attire to flee a forced marriage, but the tale then revolves around the adulterous queen's vengeful behaviour towards Costanzo for having thwarted her passionate advances. The wild-man character, Chiappino, serves to reveal the truth about Costanza's identity and the queen's adulterous behaviour. Murat, on the other hand, maintains the focus on the institution of forced marriage throughout her tale: Constantine flees an unwanted marriage; Fleurianne nearly succumbs to two undesirable mates; and even the prince of the Aimantine Islands is punished for rejecting the love of a fairy. Although Constantin does not fight in the name of his king – which will be the case in L'Héritier and d'Aulnoy – he does fight, in the end, to save Fleurianne from an unwelcome marriage. Whereas Murat uses the trope of the maiden warrior to criticize arranged marriage above all, L'Héritier and d'Aulnoy send out their maiden warriors to save kingdoms. In all cases, however, these authors play on the iconography of warrior women to foreground the constructedness of gender and the agency of their heroines.

'Marmoisan' and Amazonian warriors

In *Oeuvres meslées* (Various Works, 1696), L'Héritier included a
tale, 'Marmoisan; or, The Innocent Deception', which she dedicated
to 'Mademoiselle Perrault' (Marie-Madeleine), the only daughter
of Charles Perrault. Directly addressing Marie-Madeleine in the
preface, the narrator explains that, at a recent gathering of distinguished individuals, the group began discussing the tales of her
talented father and later those of one of his young 'students' (the
publication in 1697 of *Stories or Tales from Past Times, with Morals*
was attributed to Perrault's youngest son, Pierre). The narrator
decides to recount one of her own, which she asks Mademoiselle
to share with her brother.

Both the attribution of *Stories or Tales from Past Times* and the
existence of Mademoiselle Perrault have been debated by scholars,
but we will focus only on the latter question here. Critics have
suggested that L'Héritier's dedication is more symbolic than real;
that is, it does not refer to an actual daughter, since Perrault does
not mention her in any of his works, not even in his memoirs of
1702, in which he speaks about all his male children (she was his
only daughter).[17] However, Volker Schröder has found definitive
evidence that Marie-Madeleine Perrault (1674–1701) indeed existed.
In fact, he has uncovered documents dating from 1699 revealing
that her father, Charles, and eldest brother, Charles-Samuel,
coerced her into renouncing her part of the inheritance that she
should have received from her mother's estate. She testifies that
she 'did so only because of the authority of my father, his ill treat-
ments, and the threats of my oldest brother ... I did not find the
opportunity to protest earlier since I have been detained for the
past month and have attended mass only on holy days being always
under the guard of my father who has not allowed me to see or

speak to anyone and has even had the door barred to all those who have asked for me.'[18] Given this disturbing state of affairs only three years after the publication of 'Marmoisan', one wonders if the dedication of this maiden warrior tale, in which a sister proves more noble than her despicable twin brother, is more motivated than critics had previously believed. Such a speculation was made by Catherine Velay-Vallantin in 1992: 'It isn't innocent that this story of a young woman disguised as a young man was offered specifically to this child forgotten by her father and marginalized with respect to her brothers.'[19] The new evidence uncovered by Schröder suggests that this was indeed the case. The legal case was settled in Marie-Madeleine's favour by 1700; shortly thereafter, she died in childbirth.

While the dedication of this first appearance of 'Marmoisan' could be viewed as a means for L'Héritier to validate and empower her female relative, she reframed the tale again more than twenty years later, with a different context in mind, but one that provides insights into the development of her tale. In 1717 she included a version of 'Marmoisan' in *Les Caprices du destin* (The Whims of Destiny), titling it 'L'Amazone françoise: Histoire ancienne' (The French Amazon: An Ancient Story). In the preface she makes a different kind of connection between the tale and another 'real' historical figure, this time between her heroine and Alberte-Barbe d'Erne-court, Countess of Saint-Balmon (also rendered as Saint-Baslement or Balmont). L'Héritier's revised title plays on the popularity of the account of Saint-Balmon by, among others, Jean-Marie de Vernon, 'historiographer for the Tertiary Order of St Francis, of which [Mme de] Saint-Balmon was a lay member', who published *L'Amazone chrestienne, ou les aventures de Madame de Saint-Balmon* (The Christian Amazon; or, The Adventures of Madame de Saint-Balmon) in 1678.[20] During the Thirty Years War, between 1636 and

1643, Saint-Balmon trained locals to form a cavalry and foot soldiers whom she 'led in more than two dozen distinct outings', combating different forces to protect civilians from attack, including rape, and to preserve their livestock and livelihoods. She also negotiated the exchange of prisoners, among other military and administrative duties.[21]

In her preface from 1717 to the tale that she by now refers to as 'The Story of the French Amazon', L'Héritier maintains that she learned about it through oral tradition and insists that the tale, whose origins are in ancient romances, was passed down from generation to generation. She then explains how she constructed her version by blending 'some of the adventures of a young woman of quality of this century, who, owing to the agitation caused by a violent reversal of fortune, left behind the clothes of her sex, embraced the profession of arms and distinguished herself through prodigious valour, without anyone ever knowing anything about her disguise'.[22] Of course, L'Héritier takes some liberties here; historical accounts suggest that people were well aware that Saint-Balmon was indeed a woman. On the other hand, L'Héritier notes that despite the 'conformity of her [Saint-Balmon's] destiny with that of Marmoisan-Léonore', her story concludes differently. Whereas Saint-Balmon finished her life in a convent, the fictional(ized) Amazonian warrior marries a prince – whom, it should be noted, she saves. Although it is only in this later preface that L'Héritier makes the connection between her tale and Saint-Balmon, it is possible that Saint-Balmon's story indeed shaped L'Héritier's maiden warrior tale from the beginning, and that this discussion was less of an afterthought than a revelation of the writer's sources.

The story itself is quite different from Straparola's and Murat's maiden warrior tales, most notably in the absence of a specific female suitor or seducer. It opens with the Count de Solac, a widower with

three frivolous daughters – a gambler, a coquette and a prude – twins
(a boy, Marmoisan, and his sister Léonore), and a youngest daughter
who is being raised in a convent in order to avoid the faults of her
three sisters and her brother. We learn that – unlike her twin brother,
Marmoisan, who possesses the faults of his gambling and coquettish
sisters with the male freedom to take them even further – Léonore
is endowed with modesty and common sense, and enjoys hunting,
reading and tapestry as well as horse riding and fencing. When war
breaks out in the kingdom, the count reluctantly plans to send his
only son to fight in the first battle, in exchange for settling in his
favour an affair with an enemy of his household. However, one
night, when her husband was supposed to be away, Marmoisan
pursues a married woman who had been rejecting his advances, and
he attempts to enter her chambers using a ladder. The husband suddenly appears, Marmoisan falls off the ladder, and the husband slays
him with his sword. Given their close resemblance, Léonore proposes
to take her brother's place to fight for the king, and the 'good lord,
charmed by this resolution, applauded it'.[23] Her sister Ioland, who
had been living in a convent, dresses as Léonore's – now Marmoisan's – page, in order to assist in concealing Marmoisan's real
identity.

While the narrative does not focus extensively on Marmoisan's
military exploits, he is lauded for having saved the king's son Prince
Cloderic: 'Marmoisan distinguished himself in a most heroic manner
... and had the good fortune of saving the prince's life.'[24] Marmoisan
also, importantly – much like the heroine's model, Saint-Balmon
– bravely prevents the pillage against civilians as well as the rape
of a lady, which leads to Marmoisan killing one of the perpetrators
and injuring a second. Although the king settled the Count de
Solac's affair in his favour after the first battle, as agreed, and thus
Marmoisan had the right to return to her father, 'our heroine was

too courageous to disappear before the campaign was over.'[25] Marmoisan proves committed to fighting for her family as well as for her king.

Most of the narrative concerns the hero(ine)'s gender ambiguity and efforts on the part of other characters to expose (sometimes wishfully) her potentially female identity through a series of gender tests. As such, it becomes clear that this gender ambiguity creates gender trouble in the text. For starters, the prince, who initially shows no interest in women whatsoever, is so attracted to Marmoisan that he wishes this hero were a woman; indeed, 'he couldn't live without him [Marmoisan]'.[26] In an attempt to reveal Marmoisan's female identity, the prince tries to tempt him with sweets and gifts that would normally appeal to women, but Marmoisan, realizing what the prince was doing, is able to resist. Another character, Richevol (literally 'Rich-steal'), becomes annoyed at Marmoisan for preventing him from pillaging, and starts a rumour – which he in fact does not truly believe – that Marmoisan is actually a woman, given his 'gentleness, modesty and compassion for the poor'.[27] Because of this rumour, the other soldiers start to monitor Marmoisan's behaviour to detect signs of femininity (as does the prince). The text thus reveals how social surveillance functions to enforce gender norms, which indeed works, since Marmoisan is particularly careful to adhere to them when under suspicion.

The episode concerning Richevol is only one moment among several when L'Héritier uses her hero(ine) to question the brutal norms of masculinity. Marmoisan reflects on how the men who surround him engage in negative behaviour, such as swearing, beating their valets, blaspheming and drinking excessively, and asks himself: 'why imitate the bad models?'[28] Marmoisan then laments what he refers to as the 'extravagant' behaviour of both women and men, something that is also incarnated within her family, in the behaviour of her three sisters and her brother; the narrator uses the same term when the twin brother attempts to violate a married woman. In the early modern period, 'extravagant' signified 'that which goes against good sense, against reason'.[29] Through Léonore-Marmoisan, L'Héritier proposes for her readers a model of female and male subjectivity based in reason and common sense. The double identity of Léonore-Marmoisan embodies together ideal femininity and masculinity in ways that undo the opposition between these terms, for ideal models of either gender blend qualities that are associated with the other: as a woman, Léonore trains in arms; as a man, Marmoisan cares for others. L'Héritier thus puts forth an androgynous model for both women and men to follow, whereby they can embrace the best qualities associated with both femininity and masculinity. As such, her models of femininity and masculinity are inherently gender-fluid.

The tale concludes with Marmoisan's gender reveal. Demonstrating superior skill during a tournament, the hero(ine) is injured when his competitor's lance shatters, an event that reads as an allusion to the sixteenth-century French king Henri II, who similarly was wounded (and died) after a lance splintered during a joust. Upon examining the wound, Marmoisan-Léonore's white breast is exposed, which brings the prince much joy (as well as concern for her well-being). Everyone at court subsequently refers to her as 'the beautiful, wounded woman warrior' (*la belle guerrière blessée*) and as an 'Amazon'.[30] The prince wishes to marry her, but Léonore fears the difference in rank between them; she doesn't want him to engage in a *mésalliance*, since she is not royalty. However, the wise king, complaining about his first and second wives, who did not support his kingdom and who sowed division at court, feels that the 'counsel of a cherished wife whose sentiments only aspire to virtue' would be better than 'some ambitious favourite'.[31] It is

notable that at the outset of the tale, the king expresses concern
about the influence a favourite might have over his son, implying
that the king himself believes the prince has a weaker character
for ruling than Léonore-Marmoisan. Here, just as in her tale about
Finette, L'Héritier posits the heroine as a wise advisor, suggesting that even though her heroines may marry in the end, they will
indeed play important roles in the administration of the kingdom.
As with Straparola's Costanza and Murat's Constantine, Léonore's
value resides in her physical and intellectual skill, in her agency, and
this arguably allows the heroine to determine her own value – leading to her marrying a prince – rather than to depend primarily or
exclusively on such external, superficial qualities as class, wealth
and beauty.

Although L'Héritier's 'Marmoisan' did not enjoy the same
legacy as d'Aulnoy's 'Belle-Belle; or, The Chevalier Fortuné', the
tale was translated into English and German and appeared in important British magazines. The earliest English translation I have
been able to locate dates from 1744, taking serialized form in the
Universal Spectator. This journal – founded in 1728 by Henry Baker
(under the pseudonym Henry Stonecastle) and his father-in-law
Daniel Defoe – had various contributors and published works by
such writers as Henry Fielding.[32] From 17 March to 21 April 1744
Stonecastle (the name used in the weekly) provided this preface to
'Marmoisan':

It is not long since I gave my Readers *The Adventures of
Finette, a Novel* or rather a FABLE, which I assured them was
written originally by one of the Fair-Sex: And as I have had
no Reason to think it was *disagreeable*, I shall this Day enter
on another Piece by the same Hand. The only Objection I
have heard made to the former, was the Introduction of

the *Fairy Character*, which too much deprives it of the Air of *Probability*; but this has not that Defect of *Verisimilitude*, and therefore, whether true or false, may pass, at least, for a Picture of what might have happened. I am not going to recommend the Character of my *Heroine* to *Imitation*, in the Campaign that is just approaching; because if such Virtue did now exist, and was to be carried into Action, we are not sure it would meet with the same *Reward* as our Historian has here bestow'd.[33]

In 1743 Stonecastle published a serialized version of 'Finette', a tale that circulated more broadly within British print culture (as we have seen in Chapter One). He clearly believes in the literary merit of both tales, suggesting here that 'Marmoisan', with its absence of marvellous characters, may be even more pleasing to his readers than 'Finette'. In his introduction from 1743 to 'The Wary Princess: or, The Adventures of Finette. A Novel', Stonecastle attributes the tale to 'a *young Lady* in *France*, who signs her Name *Mademoiselle L'H*****', but the printing of 'Marmoisan' only refers to the author of the earlier tale, without any more specific information. Stonecastle creates a contemporary frame for 'Marmoisan', stating ironically: 'I am not going to recommend the Character of my *Heroine* to *Imitation*, in the Campaign that is just approaching.' The first instalment of the tale appeared just two days after France declared war against Britain during the War of the Austrian Succession. The English translation of L'Héritier's tale remains quite close to the original, and it was reprinted later that year, from August to September 1744, in the *Scots Journal*, with no attribution to L'Héritier, but acknowledging that it was a reprint from the *Universal Spectator*.

Thirty years later the tale made an appearance in the *Lady's Magazine; or, Entertaining Companion for the Fair Sex, Appropriated*

Solely to their Use and Amusement. As Jennie Batchelor maintains, this 'hugely successful' magazine exaggerated its apparently exclusive focus on female contributors and readers; in reality, it was a 'mixed-sex but female-dominated community of authors'.[34] Authors of articles were not paid for their contributions, which sometimes led to the failure to complete a piece. Interestingly, it looks as though this was the case with 'Marmoisan': the narrative stops just as the heroine is about to embark on her journey as a knight. The tale is not presented as a translation or a text that comes from abroad, being instead attributed to a certain 'Theodosia M.' In this adaptation, Theodosia names the three nasty sisters Finetta (which might suggest that she was familiar with L'Héritier's other tale), Lucinda and Constansia. Besides the names of the three sisters and a few minor distinctions (using 'ugly' instead of 'homely', for example), for the most part Theodosia's 'Marmoisan' is probably based on the version found in the *Universal Spectator*, given the proximity to the earlier translation.

A final version I located of the tale was reproduced in Leipzig in 1772 in the collection *Landbibliothek zu einem angenehmen und lehrreichen Zeit vertreibe aus verschiedenen Sprachen zusammen getragen* (Regional Library Brought Together from Different Languages for a Pleasant and Instructive Pastime). The German translation is clearly based on the version of the tale published in L'Héritier's *Oeuvres meslées*; it includes the introductory and concluding remarks addressed to Mademoiselle Perrault, and the tale is attributed to 'Mademoiselle L'H***', the name under which L'Héritier published her works in France. All these versions show that L'Héritier's tale enjoyed some appeal in England and Germany, even if it never attained the status of a major hit, as was the case with d'Aulnoy's maiden warrior tale, particularly in nineteenth-century England.

'Belle-Belle; or, The Knight Fortuné' and its legacy

It would seem that by the 1860s d'Aulnoy's maiden warrior tale – rendered in English as 'The Story of Fortunio the Fortunate Knight' and 'The History of Fortunio and His Famous Companions' or simply 'The Story of Fortunio' – was popular enough that it had become part of British oral and folk memory. The Irish nationalist, novelist and participant in the suffragette movement Justin McCarthy uses his narrator's recollection of the tale to qualify the character Grace in his novel *The Waterdale Neighbours* (1867):

> Children now do not read the story of Fortunio; it is probably out of print; and this writer, though remembering the tale well enough, does not know who wrote it, or in what collection it is found, except that it is not in the *Arabian Nights*. But it is a charming story. It is about a girl whose father was dead, and whose mother and sisters were in difficulties of some kind, and who, having a spirit far too high for inactivity and starvation, resolved to pull them out of all trouble by her own unaided effort and enterprise. So she dressed herself as a man, and went out to seek her fortune; which she found in the shape of some dreadful adventures and daring exploits, whereby she won the gratitude of the king – the king of all the stories. Unhappily, however, she also won the love of the king's daughter; and this was, for some reason or other, a deadly offence, and Fortunio was doomed to die . . . But when Fortunio's white young bosom came to be uncovered, the king necessarily saw that he was dooming a girl to death, and for an offence which she could not possibly commit; and of course he pardoned her, and she triumphed, and

I think married the king's son in the end, and made all her family happy.

In these days the little fairy story may be taken as a sort of timely parable. We are told that signs are everywhere visible of a feminine revolt against petticoats.[35]

In some ways, the fact that McCarthy produces an incorrect version of d'Aulnoy's tale only exemplifies the entry of 'Belle-Belle; or, The Knight Fortuné' into Irish and English folk culture; it is – or at least was – so well known that people could recall important fragments and a general sense of the frame of the tale, which itself becomes detached from a specific collection or author or even cultural context. Moreover, McCarthy uses the figure of Fortunio to qualify Grace, a woman 'weary of her narrow, monotonous, routine life' and who wishes to become an artist, which further demonstrates the ability of this seventeenth-century fairy tale to appeal to nineteenth-century readers.[36] It continues to express notions of female liberation from what McCarthy condemns in a later essay as women's 'condition of dependency and domestic vassalage'.[37]

At the same time, 'Belle-Belle' was redeployed in the service of British imperialism, a fact that is evident in the ways theatrical and board game adaptors played up the hints of Orientalism found in d'Aulnoy's original tale. While they do maintain the agency of the hero(ine), William Spooner and Henry J. Byron reframe the tale in line with British imperialist ideology. From a story that challenges early modern notions of women in power, 'Belle-Belle' could also be deployed to legitimate British imperialism, which expanded significantly during the reign of Queen Victoria (1837–1901).

In some ways, we might read d'Aulnoy's tale as one that sets into play 'two "opposing" images of women': the king's troublesome widowed sister, who threatens to destroy the hero(ine), without whom the kingdom is doomed; and Belle-Belle, the Knight Fortuné, who saves her family's honour as well as the kingdom.[38] Although France enjoyed the reign of three queen regents in the early modern period, and numerous writers and artists produced works that supported the political, social and cultural roles women could play, there were always those, including Charles Perrault and the writer and critic Nicolas Boileau, who were wary of women and their access to any form of public power or authority.[39] In such works as Boileau's *Satire* X (1694) against women and Perrault's supposed *Apology of Women* (1694), antifeminist male writers represented women who roamed the public sphere as excessively passionate and unable to control themselves, wreaking public havoc and endangering both family and state; these men did so in order to de-legitimate women's active public roles.

In her maiden warrior tale, d'Aulnoy takes this stereotype of the out-of-control woman and places her within a broader context of political upheaval. In the tale, political turmoil is initially caused by a king who is, effectively, 'castrated': he is 'despoiled' of his soldiers and his wealth; that is, he has lost his political potency.[40] It is the male ruler who is responsible for the fall of the kingdom, and his sister – embodying the negative female stereotype – risks the possibility that the kingdom will not regain its earlier position of power. However, it is another woman, Belle-Belle, cross-dressed as the Knight Fortuné, who saves the day, showing that women are as capable as men are of establishing and maintaining the stability of kingdoms – or of destroying them.

To create 'Belle-Belle; or, The Knight Fortuné', d'Aulnoy draws not only from Straparola's 'Costanzo-Costanza' in creating a rivalry between the king and queen over the hero(ine), with both d'Aulnoy and Murat making the queen the king's sister and not his wife. She also borrows motifs from Basile's 'The Ignoramus' and 'The Three Crowns'. In 'The Ignoramus', a good-for-nothing son of a merchant, Moscione, is sent away by his father to help sharpen his mind; as he makes his way to Cairo he meets five men with extraordinary running, hearing, shooting, blowing and carrying abilities, who join him on his adventures. As is the case with Basile, tales concerning extraordinary companions typically cast a male lead, while d'Aulnoy changes the gender of the character who will assemble the team of gifted men. From Basile's 'The Three Crowns', a cross-dressing tale in which the queen falls madly in love with the hero(ine), d'Aulnoy incorporates the theme of the queen who not only sends the hero(ine) out on dangerous deeds, as in Straparola and Murat, but furthermore accuses the hero(ine) of trying to seduce or rape her, for which the hero(ine) is sentenced to death. In both Basile and d'Aulnoy the hero(ine)'s 'true' gender identity is revealed as she is about to be executed, and she marries the king.

D'Aulnoy's tale opens in a situation of political instability. The powerful emperor, Matapa, defeats a king who has lost much of his army, his wealth and his people, and rules over a depleted kingdom with his sister, the dowager queen, beside him. In order to reconstitute his power, the king calls upon all the nobles of his kingdom to serve him themselves, to send one of their sons to serve him, or to help finance the war. We are then introduced to a second impotent man, an eighty-year-old lord, who no longer has the physical or financial capacity to contribute to the war effort himself, and who has three daughters but no sons. One by one, beginning with the eldest, the three daughters propose that they can pass as his son at court and in battle. The eldest makes the first attempt, and sets out on horseback for the king's court. However, when she comes upon what appears to be an old shepherdess, whose sheep have fallen into a ditch and are drowning, the sister fails to come to her aid; as

A cross-dressed Belle-Belle assists the old shepherdess, who is in reality a
fairy. From *Le Cabinet des fées*, vol. IV (Geneva, 1785).

she distances herself from the distressing scene, the old woman cries out: 'Adieu, beautiful disguised woman.' Believing she cannot pass as a man, the girl returns to her father's home.[41] The second sister follows suit in all respects, failing to assist the old shepherdess, being called out as a woman, and returning to the paternal home. Finally, the youngest daughter, Belle-Belle, who is taller than her sisters and who hunts daily – an exercise 'that does not fail to give talent for war' – leaps over a hedge and into the ditch to save the sheep, and is rewarded for her kindness by the old shepherdess, who turns out to be a good fairy.[42]

The fairy gives her a faithful, wise horse named Camarade (Comrade), who serves as her counsellor; a magical chest covered with Moroccan leather and filled with luxurious clothes, the key to which is hidden in Comrade's ear; and a new name, the Knight Fortuné. When Fortuné stops for the night with Comrade in a beautiful city on his way to court, everyone finds 'him' to be the most handsome and richly dressed knight. As Fortuné makes his way to see the king, Comrade advises him to bring on board seven gifted men, each endowed with special abilities by the fairies. Fortuné first comes upon a woodcutter so strong that he can carry trees, called Fort Echine ('Strong Back' – literally 'strong spine'); Léger ('Light-foot') runs faster than the deer and hare he hunts; Bon Tireur ('Marks-man') has such a keen eye that he can clear a forest of partridges in no time at all; Fine Oreille ('Fine Ear') is capable of hearing grass grow; Impétueux ('Violent Wind') can uproot trees with a sigh; Trin-quet ('The Toaster') can drink a pond in a single gulp; and Grugeon ('The Cruncher', from early modern French *gruger*, to crunch, bite or nibble) is capable of devouring more than sixty thousand loaves of bread. Each man swears to be faithful to Fortuné's orders, and for his part, Fortuné endows them with rich clothing and horses, and promises to reward them generously.

When Fortuné, his seven gifted companions and Comrade reach the king, everyone who sees the knight is impressed, including the king, his sister the dowager queen and her lady-in-waiting Floride, all of whom vie for Fortuné's attention. D'Aulnoy's narrative momentarily dwells on the hero(ine)'s experiences at court, a novelistic interlude in line with what we have seen in Murat's maiden warrior tale. Both king and queen wish to have Fortuné serve them, and the queen furthermore dreams of contracting a secret marriage with the young knight, despite the inequality of their stations. Fortuné proves to be exemplary among all the men at court, for he 'took first prize at tournaments, he killed more game than all the others during hunting parties, he danced with more grace and finesse than any other courtier at the ball', and this leads to him receiving love letters and gifts from women at court.[43] For 'his' part, Fortuné is in love with the king and becomes melancholic; this leads the queen to believe that he is in love with another woman, which enrages her. It is her attempt at vengeance that sets the narrative action back in motion.[44]

In many respects, the role of the dowager queen recalls that of the king in mythological narratives about such heroes as Perseus and Jason. In *Oedipe philosophe* (1990), Jean-Joseph Goux maintains that the typical myth of the hero in Greco-Roman culture revolves around a king who fears that a younger male rival will take his place; instead of simply killing him, however, the king gives him perilous tasks that puts the hero's life at risk. When the hero manages to kill the monster and stave off his own death (often with the assistance of gods or other helpers), the king is reconciled to him and marries the hero to his daughter.[45] D'Aulnoy's tale seems to draw from and modify this structure. Here, it is the queen who seeks the death of the hero(ine) not out of rivalry but out of revenge, sending Fortuné out first to kill a dragon that is ravaging the kingdom, then to the

emperor Matapa to retrieve the king's wealth without the support
of the king's newly reconstituted army – which never engages in
battle in the tale. Despite his efforts to raise troops, the king
continues to be represented as passive and impotent. It is thus the
tension between the dowager queen and the hero(ine) that propels
the series of heroic actions.

For his part, Matapa gives the hero(ine) – who is described on
several occasions as the 'young ambassador' – three seemingly impossible tasks (upon pain of death) as conditions for returning the riches
the emperor took from the king. Fortuné must bring before him:
first, a man who can consume all of the hot bread in his city (which
happens to be bigger than Paris, Constantinople and Rome com-
bined); second, a man who can drink all of the water from the fountains, aqueducts and reservoirs of the city and all of the wine in the
city's wine cellars; and third, a man who can beat his so far undefeated daughter in a foot race. Of course, with the help of his seven
merry men, Fortuné succeeds in all these trials and is able – with
further help from Strong Back and Violent Wind – to return all the
kingdom's treasures and defeat Matapa's army. Coming back to the
parallel with such stories as that of Perseus, we could consider each
of Fortuné's seven gifted companions as serving a similar function
to Athena's shield, or Hermes' sword, which helps the mythical hero
defeat Medusa; even Perseus does not defeat the Gorgon on his
own but relies on the magical assistance of the gods. Here, Fortuné
relies on the magical help of the fairies, who function much like
the gods of Greco-Roman mythology.

After successfully completing these trials, our hero(ine) marries
not the prince, but the king himself. In some respects, if the dowager queen fulfils the function of the king who sends the hero out
on perilous quests, we might read the figure of the king in d'Aulnoy
as playing the role of the princess, who is the reward for the hero(ine)'s

successful exploits. As such, the king plays a conventionally feminine role in the tale. Charlotte Trinquet du Lys observes that 'the king laments his [Fortuné's] departure like a mistress who would see her lover leave for the battlefield.'[46] And, like the knight regretting having to abandon his true love to engage in battle, Fortuné requests his lover the king's portrait before leaving to confront Matapa, receiving it 'with extraordinary joy'.[47] Throughout the tale, the king plays a passive role with respect to both his sister, who dominates at court, and Fortuné, who, with the support of his seven gifted companions and the fairies, successfully restabilizes the kingdom.

Although Fortuné is counselled by his horse, Comrade, and assisted by his seven companions (all of whom are gifts from the female fairies), he remains a figure of authority. When the fairy presents Comrade to Fortuné, she says: 'he will give you such good advice that sovereigns would be fortunate to have counsellors that resemble him.'[48] Through this analogy, the fairy positions Fortuné as a sort of sovereign himself. Throughout the trials put to him and his men by Matapa, Fortuné is referred to on several occasions as 'ambassador', meaning that he is the representative of the king before Matapa; even if our hero(ine) does not carry out all the actions of the tale himself, like a king, he is counselled and delegates tasks to the men who have pledged their allegiance to him. Less than a traditional Amazonian warrior, which the text suggests Fortuné is perfectly capable of incarnating given his skill at hunting and jousting, he is more like a king or sovereign in his own right.[49] When the seven gifted men squabble over their compensation after having carried away the treasure Matapa looted from the kingdom, each claiming that he deserves a larger share of the reward than the others, Fortuné declares, 'with an absolute air':

'My friends . . . you have all carried out marvels, but we must leave to the king the care of recognizing our services. I would be very sorry to be compensated by a hand other than his own. Believe me, leave everything to his will, he sent us to bring back his treasures and not to steal them. This thought is even so shameful that I am of the opinion that we must never speak of it again, and I assure you that, for my part, I will make it such that you will have nothing to regret even if it were possible that the king would neglect you.' The Seven gifted ones felt penetrated by the remonstrance of their master; they threw themselves at his feet, and promised never to have a will other than his own.[50]

Fortuné indeed exercises more authority than we see in the character of the king whose kingdom he seeks to re-establish; the hero(ine) can rein in the passions of his gifted companions, essential in restoring order to the kingdom.

The narrative returns to the preoccupation with, and danger relating to, affairs of the heart. Upon Fortuné's return, the love rivalries retake centre stage from heroic action, and this time the queen directly proposes marriage to Fortuné. As we have seen in 'The White Cat', a female character proposing marriage to a man is not problematic in and of itself in d'Aulnoy's tales, but the author does condemn all forms of coerced marriage, whether that concerns a powerful woman (a fairy or queen) pressurizing a less powerful man (a king or knight), or a powerful man (a king, prince or magical dwarf) pressurizing a less powerful woman (a princess or noblewoman) into marriage. Fortuné resorts to invoking a patriarchal custom – the legal right of the king to approve or not of his sister's marriage – in order to avoid having to answer the queen and incur her wrath, but to no avail. The queen subsequently beats and scratches him, then scratches her own face and tears her clothes to make her brother believe that Fortuné tried to take her by force. Because his sister is 'capable of overturning the kingdom', the king does not dare to oppose her wish to have Fortuné condemned to death, and corrupt judges side with her in Fortuné's case.[51] In the meantime, Floride, who is still in love with Fortuné, decides to poison the queen to punish her for his impending execution, and plans to poison herself as well out of love for the hero(ine). Then, as the executioner prepares to stab the hero(ine) in the heart, Fortuné's chest is exposed, and the queen, in an excess of emotion, dies quickly from the poison administered by Floride (who survives). In the end, Belle-Belle's family and fairy godmother share in the joy of her marriage to the king. The tale concludes with 'and this charming adventure was passed down from century to century until our own.'[52] Like L'Héritier, at least in her edition of 'Marmoisan' from 1717, d'Aulnoy suggests that this tale has circulated for centuries.

Although d'Aulnoy's Belle-Belle is not specifically described as an 'Amazon' – the narrator refers only to the second sister as 'our Amazon' – she does pass as a male courtier and as a knight, demonstrating physical prowess in court tournaments, and above all displaying the diplomatic skill necessary to oversee a kingdom in ways that the king in the tale does not. Opposing the dowager queen to Belle-Belle/Fortuné in a family and kingdom led by impotent men (Belle-Belle's father and the king), d'Aulnoy essentially puts the fate of this fairy-tale world in the hands of women. Even Matapa's daughter, undefeated until her encounter with Lightfoot, plays an important role as a strong woman in the tale. D'Aulnoy stages the stereotype of the destabilizing female ruler to challenge it with the figure of Belle-Belle/Fortuné, who knows how to manage people – as is evident in her ability to rein in the emotions of her seven companions – and can stabilize the kingdom both politically and financially. Although at the end of the tale Belle-Belle is not explicitly designated counsellor of her husband, as in the case of L'Héritier, she has certainly displayed more diplomatic skill than the king, and we can safely assume that she will rule at his side, just as Léonore does in 'Marmoisan'.

Eventually adapted to British pantomime and even board-game form, 'Belle-Belle; or, The Knight Fortuné' was reprinted in several English collections of tales. As we saw in Chapter Three, many of d'Aulnoy's tales were published in the collection *Mother Bunch*, and 'Belle-Belle; or, The Knight Fortuné' is no exception. Along with adaptations of d'Aulnoy's 'The Yellow Dwarf', 'Pigeon and Dove', 'Miranda and the Royal Ram' and 'The Story of Finetta; or, The Cinder-Girl', the edition of *Mother Bunch's Fairy Tales* from 1773 also includes 'The Story of Fortunio'. Parts of the narrative are stream-lined – the test of the second sister, for instance, is not described in detail – and other details are modified. For instance, the Moroccan leather chest becomes one of Turkish leather. As in d'Aulnoy, Comrade assists the hero(ine) in engaging the seven gifted companions – here named Strongback, Lightfoot, Marksman, Fine-Ear, Boisterer, Tipler and Grugeon/Gabrugeon – but in abbreviated form. Although this collection was aimed at young readers, it retains the queen's accusation that Fortunio 'had attempted to use her ill', as well as the exposure of the hero(ine)'s chest.[53] This streamlined version also eliminates the character Florine, so that it is the queen who poisons herself after Fortunio's triumph, and the tale concludes with the knighting of the seven companions. Some twenty years later an unattributed translation opens *The Fairiest; or Surprising and Entertaining Adventures of the Aerial Beings . . . The Whole Selected to Amuse and Improve Juvenile Minds* (1795), published by the popular Minerva Press. This version follows the French original more closely than the *Mother Bunch* edition does. The publisher, William

Lane, used an illustration of 'The Story of Fortunio, the Fortunate Knight' as the frontispiece for the collection, suggesting that the image and tale would have had an appeal within the English book market.

It is with the stand-alone edition of 1804 by Benjamin Tabart, *The History of Fortunio*, that we see modifications to d'Aulnoy's (unattributed) original that will persist in later English adaptations.[54] In Tabart's version, the king is given a name, Alfourite, which becomes a feature of the English tradition of the tale. Along with the publisher John Harris, Tabart produced 'retellings of both the French and indigenous British stories, revised, and now marketed directly at children'; the changes he made to the tale clearly reflect this target audience.[55] The narrative is streamlined, with the elimination of details concerning the plundering of Alfourite's kingdom and minimal descriptions of the companions (who are referred to as Strongback, Lightfoot, Marksman, Fine-Ear, Boisterer, Gormand and Tippler). Yet the situation of the dowager queen is qualified; we learn that she had been married to a neighbouring prince, who died. While the rivalry over Fortunio among Alfourite, the queen and Florida (Floride) remains, the lingering on romantic details, such as Fortunio looking melancholic or relishing the receipt of the king's portrait, is minimized (as was the case in the earlier *Mother Bunch* version, which targets a younger audience). When it comes to the dragon, Tabart leaves all the glory to the hero(ine), who 'with a single blow cut off his head'.[56]

Tabart makes a final important change to d'Aulnoy's tale. Rather than have the queen accuse Fortunio of assault or attempted rape, she basically accuses him of rapt,[57] claiming that Fortunio sent Strongback to forcibly carry her off, possibly with the intent of marrying her. The violence of the ending is somewhat minimized, as well. Florida does not poison the queen; Fortunio nearly receives

Fortunio combating the dragon. Frontispiece from *The Fairiest; or, Surprising and Entertaining Adventures of the Aerial Beings* (London, 1795).

three 'darts' and not stabs to the heart, but the queen does plunge a knife into her heart to kill herself. The tale concludes with the wedding and with the new queen rewarding Comrade with 'a magnificent stable', and the seven companions with 'a handsome pension', while they promise to remain in her service should she ever require them again.[58] This conclusion de-emphasizes the romantic part of d'Aulnoy's tale, given its focus on the bond between Fortunio-now-queen and the seven gifted men. The complicated, queer love story gives way to a tale about friendship.

All these adaptations, which also reached the early nineteenth-century American book market, reveal the popularity of
this tale about a cross-dressed noblewoman who slays dragons and
organizes her men to preserve the kingdom.[59] It should come as
no surprise, then, that the tale was adapted to the pantomime stage,

Belle-Belle preparing to depart to join the king's army in Planché's
Fairy Tales, by the Countess d'Aulnoy (London, 1856),
illustrated by John Gilbert.

the most popular stage performance being that of James Robinson Planché, *Fortunio and his Seven Gifted Servants: A Fairy Extravaganza*, which was first performed at the Theatre Royal, Drury Lane, on Easter Monday 1843. Although in 1856 Planché produced a fairly accurate translation of the tale, which he called 'Belle-Belle or, the Chevalier Fortuné', his pantomime also draws from the other English adaptations that were circulating within the British book market.

Planché's extravaganza opens with a herald, who announces King Alfourite's decree that every man must 'Turn out, or fork out – fight or pay you must!'[60] The play then turns to the impoverished Baron Dunover, who has three daughters named Miss Pertina, Miss Flirtina and Miss Myrtina (Fortunio). The play exaggerates the impotence of male characters. We learn that the baron has never drawn his sword in his life; he gives it, looking all shiny and new, to his daughter, and she later uses it to decapitate the dragon. The situation of King Alfourite is even more dire than in the tale. Just before Fortunio's arrival at court, the minister informs the king that no one has responded to his proclamation: 'Not a soul/ Has yet appeared who will his name enrol.'[61] For her part, the queen is represented as being more wicked and bloodthirsty than in d'Aulnoy, as is expressed at the outset of the play when she suggests that the king (here, her half-brother) should hang all those who refuse to acknowledge the proclamation. Rather than Comrade, it is the fairy queen who advises Fortunio to engage the seven companions as they make their way to court. Planché maintains the rivalry among the king ('That he [Fortunio] is not a girl 'tis quite a pity'), Florida and the queen, and emphasizes the sexual desire of the queen for Fortunio, whom she wishes to make 'Groom of the Bedchamber'.[62]

Filled with puns playing on homonyms, such as (military) 'breaches' and (vestimentary) 'breeches', and a 'horse' who does not speak 'hoarser', the extravaganza also makes numerous references to contemporary British culture. Upon meeting Fortunio, the king offers him a pinch of snuff. The play includes a drinking song that is critical of teetotallers, as the king sings, 'A plague upon such sober times.'[63] Since the 1820s, attitudes toward alcohol consumption in Britain were 'hardening' and temperance societies were on the rise; the play thus mocks this new trend.[64] After killing the dragon (it is Fortunio who deals the final blow and cuts off his head, as in the Tabart version) and preparing to confront Matapa, all of which is orchestrated by the resentful queen, Fortunio laments:

> Is she determined to make me a martyr?
> Does she suppose me Van Amburgh or Carter?
> First fight a dragon, then go catch a Tartar,
> Is out of the frying-pan into the fire.[65]

Here Fortunio is comparing himself to 'lion king' Isaac Van Amburgh, an American lion tamer who became quite popular in Victorian England and performed at Drury Lane, the same venue as Planché's *Fortunio and his Seven Gifted Servants*; and to Van Amburgh's 'successor and competitor', James (John) Carter.[66] Fortunio's lines here are cleverly self-referential, given the fact that some of the audience members may have sat in that very same theatre to see Van Amburgh's lion-taming performance.

We can also identify in the passage the ways in which d'Aulnoy's tale becomes 'Orientalized' in Planché's hands. While d'Aulnoy's invention of the name 'Matapa' could invoke an Orientalist setting, suggested by his (for French readers) exotic name, she does not explicitly qualify Matapa's empire in Orientalist terms. Planché plays on the Orientalist potential of the tale, specifically identifying Matapa as being 'a Tartar'. Moreover, comparing Fortunio to these two famous lion tamers further situates the action within Orientalist narratives. As Peta Tait observes, such '[c]age acts were theatrical presentations, and integrated into Orientalist narratives about geographical exploration that had been widely presented in theatre from the late eighteenth century.'[67] This 'exoticizing' of the tale arguably paved the way for its adaptation to a British board game, a genre that was inextricably linked to both geography and empire, as we shall see.

Like Tabart, Planché chooses to eliminate any implication of rape in his rendition of the story. Whereas Tabart attenuates the situation by having the queen accuse Fortunio of attempted rapt and not rape, Planché has her accuse the hero(ine) of treason. She claims that Fortunio wishes to marry her and murder the king in order to usurp his throne, and demands the hero(ine)'s arrest. But instead of revealing her identity through the revelation of her bosom – not a practical move on the Victorian stage – Planché has Fortunio declare that she is the daughter and not son of the Baron Dunover, without the need for further evidence. Instead of being killed or killing herself, the queen simply faints, and Alfourite and Fortunio (identified as such in the play) decide that they will rule together:

> King: (*to* Fortunio): A crown you merit.
> Fortunio: Half a one, I'd rather.
> King: Will you share mine?[68]

Fortunio insists she needs the permission of her father to marry the king, which is immediately granted. Planché explicitly concludes with the hero(ine) sharing the throne with the king, perhaps not such a bold move during the reign of Queen Victoria. In some respects, the play is produced in a context that recalls that of d'Aulnoy, in which the circulation of images of strong women supported and was supported by 'real' women in positions of power. The play was popular enough to see some forty performances, and it made its way to New York, with performances in 1844, 1845 and 1846.[69] It was also adapted to board-game form some three years later, a circumstance that speaks to the popularity of Planché's extravaganza.

William Spooner, an 'active game manufacturer from the 1830s through the early 1850s', produced a board-game version of *Fortunio and his Seven Gifted Servants* in 1846, based on Planché's extravaganza.[70] Spooner uses Planché's names: the three sisters are called Pertina, Flirtina and Myrtina, with Alfourite as the king. Players spin a teetotum spinner, which is marked with an F to move a space forward and a B to move a space back; if the spinner lands on its blank side, the player cannot move at all. Players begin at a point that reads 'The Proclamation of King Alfourite'. Interestingly, in the rules of the game, nothing is said about the story itself, which presupposes that the players were familiar with Planché's extravaganza, or another version of the tale. Players would have understood that this unqualified proclamation concerned the need to send a man or funds to support the king's efforts against Matapa, none of which is explained anywhere in the game materials. We then see the two scenes with the fairy disguised as a shepherdess, and Pertina and Flirtina failing the test (as a player familiar with the tale would understand). After these failures, the stopping bubbles planted near the scenes read, respectively, 'Pay 2 [tokens] for Pertness' and 'Pay 2 [tokens] for vain pride.' When Myrtina passes the test of goodness, the fairy retakes her original form, resembling a white ballerina (a familiar figure on the *féerie* and pantomime stage), and the reward is four tokens 'for a good Deed'.

The next image that follows the winding path of the game is the fairy introducing Fortunio to the seven gifted servants, after which players must pay three tokens for an introduction at King Alfourite's court. The game itself, again, does not provide the backstory – that is, the events that lead to Fortunio battling the dragon – but we do see the cross-dressed Fortunio bravely confront the beast, and the player is rewarded with four tokens 'for slaying the dragon'. The narrative of the game then takes us to Matapa's kingdom, where the dark-skinned, fez-wearing Matapa greets the cross-dressed knight. Reaching the end of the game, Fortunio and his men succeed in their tests, bring the (implicitly) stolen treasures back to Alfourite's court, leading to the final image of the game, which recalls the apotheoses of vaudeville *féeries* and British pantomimes and extravaganzas. The narrative of the game removes the love intrigues – it does not conclude in marriage – to focus on the hero(ine)'s actions moving across space, conquering monsters and enemy kingdoms populated by dark-skinned people wearing turbans and fezzes.

Nineteenth-century board games focused on historical and geographic material that fed into British nationalism, and basically encouraged identification with the British imperial project by positioning players as potential conquerors of often foreign, 'exotic' lands.[71] Spooner himself produced *The Journey; or, Cross Roads to Conqueror's Castle: A New and Interesting Game* between 1831 and 1837, and *An Eccentric Excursion to the Chinese Empire* in 1843, among other games that were grounded in the culture of empire.[72] In these game texts, Spooner blends fictional and realistic geographies, but they all concern, in one manner or another, the conquest of a space. *Fortunio* is a fully imaginary space, but, more than d'Aulnoy, Tabart or Planché before him, Spooner creates a distinct opposition between the 'good' light-skinned European agents making their way across the board, and the 'bad' dark-skinned,

The final stopping image concluding the game *Fortunio and His Seven Gifted Servants*, resembling the theatrical apotheosis.

Oriental people of Matapa's empire. The game legitimates the right of Fortunio and his men to carry away the (albeit stolen) treasures of Matapa. In fact, the lack of information provided by the game – players again supposedly know that Matapa had pillaged Alfourite's kingdom, but that is not emphasized in the game itself – makes the taking of Matapa's treasures appear more problematic and, one might say, more imperialistic. D'Aulnoy's hint of exoticism plays out much more fully in Spooner's adaptation of Planché. At the same time that Spooner retains the agency of the maiden warrior – Fortunio here looks quite courageous in her slaying of the dragon – he uses d'Aulnoy's tale to legitimate imperialistic desires whereby white Europeans have a right to confiscate wealth from dark-skinned Middle Eastern or Asian people.

Board game *Fortunio and His Seven Gifted Servants* (London, 1843).

Nearly twenty years after Spooner released the imperialist game version of 'Belle-Belle; or, The Knight Fortuné', Henry J. Byron produced another staged version integrating further Orientalist and imperialist tropes. While the other versions, from d'Aulnoy to Planché, suggest that Matapa is a bad emperor, in Byron's *Lady Belle Belle: Fortunio and His Seven Magic Men* (1864) he is emphatically represented as a despot. Matapa is described as an unkind 'despotic monarch', and at one point Byron even has the character declare himself: 'Yes, I'm a despot.'[73] Examples of his despotism include the fact that this khan of Tartary enslaves his people (the serfs complain that they are not free) and has created a 'double income tax', to which his subjects object. Whereas the Matapa of the other versions pillages the kingdom of Belle-Belle, it is not suggested at all that he exploits his own people, as is the case in Byron. One of the recurring features of European Orientalism – which persists to this day – is the idea that the despotic leader enslaves his own people, which serves as legitimation for European intervention, taking the form of colonization and imperialism. From Spooner's game to Byron's play, 'Belle-Belle; or, The Knight Fortuné' was repeatedly used to support imperialist ideology in the Victorian era.

Byron seems to want to break from – at the same time that he plays on – earlier incarnations of the tale. He does away with the name 'Alfourite' and calls the main king of the tale 'King Courtly'; this could be a way to sharpen the divide between the 'European' kingdom of Belle-Belle (Alfourite could sound like an Arab name) and Mataypa's 'Oriental' realm of Tartary. Perhaps in a nod to Planché's reference to famous lion tamers, Byron uses images of lions to represent different threats to Fortunio. When the hero(ine) takes leave of the palpitating queen who pines over him to present himself to Mataypa ('rushing into the lion's jaws', as the king

remarks), Fortunio says that he is escaping 'the lioness'.[74] Byron
later has the khan threaten Fortunio: 'You'll lose your *head*, with
none to tell your *tale*./ You thrust your head into the lion's jaw,/
There's the hand on it of King Mata-*paw*.'[75] At one point Planché
compares his Fortunio to St George the dragon slayer, a reference
that Byron plays on as well, when King Courtly declares that they
will display the dead dragon 'at St George's Hall'.[76]

Belle/Fortunio was incarnated by Carry Nelson, who often
played the leading male role. In 1842 she incarnated Prince Amabel,
and in another Byron extravaganza of 1863 she played Manrico, a
wandering minstrel. *Lady Belle* alludes to Nelson's success at playing the male lead when the hero(ine) announces that she would
like to serve as her father's substitute, declaring: 'They'll not know
I'm a woman in male dress,/ I've played a man so often with success.'[77] When Fortunio is at court, he flirts with Florida, and even
kisses her three times, fully embracing his heterosexual male identity in a gesture that also elicits queer desire. After Fortunio returns
from conquering Mataypa, Florida learns that the hero(ine) does
not actually love her, but he promises not to marry another woman,
and eventually confesses: 'this fella's a lady.'[78] The queen, who has
been pursuing him, is actually quite relieved by this revelation,
believing that she was not in fact slighted by him, while the king
then proposes to the hero(ine) and the extravaganza ends without
further bloodshed or death.

Interestingly, whereas d'Aulnoy's fairy tale represented a way to
display the abilities of a woman in the areas of fighting and diplo-
macy in the wake of literary trends celebrating powerful women,
her tale was later reimagined to celebrate the imperial age of Queen
Victoria. The tale of an able, ambiguously gendered hero(ine) who
stabilizes monarchies and conquers non-European empires is a fit-
ting allegory for the period. Maeve Adams and Adrienne Munich

have documented the Amazonian imagery as it relates to Queen Victoria, Munich remarking on the complex blending of 'fierce warrior and sheltering mother' as part of her representational strategy.[79] Arguably, each of the three maiden warrior tales discussed in this chapter could fit the bill, but it was d'Aulnoy's 'Belle-Belle', particularly evident in Spooner's board game and Byron's extravaganza, that came to convey simultaneously female strength and authority, and imperial might.

Both L'Héritier and d'Aulnoy claim that their maiden warrior tales were passed down from generation to generation. If this was not quite true at the time they wrote their tales – although it surely could have been – it certainly was the case by the 1860s. Murat, L'Héritier and d'Aulnoy use the figure of the maiden warrior to address the practice of arranged marriage, the construct of gender, and the ability of women to fight and govern. Riding the tide of early modern imagery of Amazons and *femmes fortes*, these tales about strong women did not represent an exception or bizarre occurrence within the French literary field; indeed, they drew from popular literary and artistic trends that had been in place for decades. The fact that these tales were translated into English and German, serialized in magazines, staged and even served as the storyline behind a board game speaks to the continued relatability of this type of tale in later periods, in which the hero(ine) of a fairy tale could fight dragons and save kings during battle. D'Aulnoy's tale in particular was widespread and well known, reaching thousands of readers, theatregoers and board-game players through the different forms it took. Such a history should give pause to anyone who generalizes about the relation between damsels in distress and fairy tales. That might be 'our' twentieth- and twenty-first-century notion of the genre, but it certainly does not reflect the history of the fairy tale in the sixteenth, seventeenth, eighteenth and nineteenth centuries.

Popularized by French women writers, Amazonian warriors proved to be an integral feature of European 'classic' fairy tales for at least two centuries.

The actress Madame Marie Daubrun as Beauty with the Golden Hair, 1847.

Epilogue

The previous chapters have explored the seminal contributions made by early modern French women writers to the histories of Cinderella, Beauty and the Beast, cat, Rapunzel and maiden warrior tales, and how these stories fed into literary and oral cultures, theatre, music, comic books and board games, among other art forms. Evident in these histories is the fact that women writers of fairy tales had an impact on both elite and popular culture across media, historical periods and national boundaries. Yet there is much more to explore; *The Lost Princess* represents only the tip of the iceberg. I could have written an entire book on the history of theatrical adaptations of 'Beauty and the Beast' in eighteenth- and nineteenth-century Paris and London, based on Gabrielle-Suzanne de Villeneuve's and Jeanne-Marie Leprince de Beaumont's versions of the tale; or one that looked at a cross-section of stage adaptations of tales not only by Marie-Catherine d'Aulnoy, whose works dominated the field, but by the cousins Charlotte-Rose Caumont de La Force and Henriette-Julie de Murat, whose 'The Good Woman' and 'Young and Handsome', respectively, were transformed into extravaganzas by James Robinson Planché in the 1850s.

A study could be carried out into the legacy of the *conteuses* in eighteenth-century France. In a posthumously published work, the eighteenth-century antiquarian and fairy-tale writer Anne Claude de Caylus maintains, 'in my youth one read hardly anything else [except fairy tales]. Madame la Comtesse de Murat and Madame d'Aulnoy created charming pieces in this genre'; he later remarks: 'I would find in works by these Illustrious Ladies of whom I spoke, and in the *Arabian Nights*, an infinity of moral lessons that made their way into one's heart under the mask of pleasure.'[1] While the writer Antoine Hamilton parodied d'Aulnoy's tales earlier in the century, Marie-Antoinette included in her library at the Petit Trianon palace collections of tales by d'Aulnoy, La Force and Murat, which continued to be published throughout the century.[2] In Enlightenment France, tales by the *conteuses* remained as popular within the literary scene as the more recent appearance of *The Arabian Nights*.

Much more could be written about the popularity of d'Aulnoy's tales 'Beauty with the Golden Hair' and 'The Doe in the Woods', which also saw numerous stage adaptations in Paris and London, made their way into the work of Charles Baudelaire and Théodore de Banville, and were deployed commercially. In an edition of his *Flowers of Evil* published in the *Revue des deux mondes* in 1855, Baudelaire included a poem bearing the title 'To Beauty with the Golden Hair', which later appeared as 'Irreparable'.[3] In it, the Beauty with the Golden Hair is a reference to the actress Marie Daubrun, with whom Baudelaire had a brief affair, and who played the leading role in the Cogniard brothers' *féerie* adaptation of the tale in 1847.[4] Baudelaire implicitly compares the 'fairy illuminating a miraculous aurora in an infernal sky' to Marie, bringing d'Aulnoy's tale – via its theatrical adaptation – to bear on his renowned poetry collection. Banville, another celebrated poet from the period, composed 'To the Stuffed Doe, Which Was in *The Doe in the Woods* at the [Theatre] Porte-Saint-Martin', playing comically on the Cogniard *féerie* from 1853.[5] The cultural capital of these two tales was so great that they – along

Scene from Marie-Catherine d'Aulnoy's 'Beauty with the Golden
Hair', used in a chromolithograph to promote one of the first Parisian
department stores, Le Bon Marché.

with other tales by d'Aulnoy, Marie-Jeanne L'Héritier and Charles
Perrault – were used in the nineteenth century to promote such
products as chocolate and the newly rising department store.

D'Aulnoy in particular inspired late eighteenth- and nineteenth-
century German women tellers and writers of fairy tales, as well as

British women writers. Elizabeth Wanning Harries has pointed to the influence of d'Aulnoy and the *conteuses* of the 1690s on the work of the eighteenth-century writer Sarah Fielding.[6] In a dissertation in 2020, Caitlin Lawrence furthers our understanding of d'Aulnoy's impact on Fielding, Sara Coleridge and Anne Thackeray Ritchie, evident in such works as Fielding's 'Princess Hebe' (1749), Coleridge's *Phantasmion* (1837) and Thackeray Ritchie's novella 'The White Cat', which was included in *Bluebeard's Keys and Other Stories* (1874).[7] While most critics have focused on Angela Carter's interest in Perrault's and Leprince de Beaumont's fairy tales, Andrew Teverson foregrounds Carter's appreciation for d'Aulnoy's tales as well.[8] Of course, the *conteuses* also inspired male authors, as we have seen in previous chapters and as is clear from such studies as that of Veronica Bonanni, who has demonstrated d'Aulnoy's significant impact on the creator of Pinocchio, Carlo Collodi.[9]

After taking these journeys through fairy-tale pasts in the previous chapters, the reader should come away with several insights into the history of 'classic' fairy tales as it relates to women writers. First, the fairy tales that are familiar to us today were shaped by women writers, whose names and contributions have been buried under the dominance of the Perrault-Grimms-Andersen triumvirate and of Walt Disney, a dominance that began to emerge only in the twentieth century. Second, fairy tales by women writers have often enjoyed and continue to enjoy the status of 'classic', which is a concept that changes from generation to generation; 'Finette-Cinders' and 'The White Cat', along with maiden warrior tales, were 'classic' in different periods and places, and women writers shaped tales, such as 'Beauty and the Beast' and 'Rapunzel', that are today considered 'classic'. Fairy tales by these women were incredibly popular, particularly those by d'Aulnoy, entering the folklore, theatrical tradition and popular culture of many European countries. Third, fairy tales are not inherently disempowering to women, and in fact one can see feminist tendencies in French early modern fairy tales, which may explain why German and British women writers later drew from them to explore questions relating to women and gender, and to legitimate women's lives and experiences. Fourth, when it comes to representations of female characters and conceptions of their abilities and rights in fairy tales, we cannot assume that things only get better, that Disney must somehow give more agency to female characters than writers from the sixteenth, seventeenth, eighteenth and nineteenth centuries.

In fact, the notion of the damsel in distress associated with the genre today would not have been quite so obvious before the twentieth century. Giambattista Basile's Zezolla kills her first stepmother; L'Héritier's Finette fatally wounds the man who seeks to abuse her; d'Aulnoy's Merveilleuse survives the death of her Beast to rule a kingdom, while her White Cat is a powerful sovereign who gives kingdoms to men; and L'Héritier's Léonore and d'Aulnoy's Belle-Belle prove to be adept saviours of kingdoms. As these tales were transformed through literary, theatrical, visual and musical adaptations across the centuries, the agency of their heroines not always but quite often remained intact. Illustrations, film, staged adaptations and board games represent female characters demonstrating bravery, killing dragons, ruling kingdoms and challenging gender norms in many different ways. Reading the history of the fairy tale through the lens of Perrault-Grimms-Andersen and Disney offers a scope that is much too narrow, and does not reflect the vibrant and often feminist history of the genre and the non-negligible role that women writers played in its constitution and its history.

This is the story of one group of lost princesses, whose threads were severed, whose ashes blew away, arguably influenced by Disney Studios, which reshaped Euro-American and even global conceptions about which names we associate with fairy tales, and what a fairy tale was, is and can be. As one might suspect, there are other lost princesses, other stories to be told, many more female voices that shaped wonder tales around the world, begging to be recovered. We need more fairy godmothers and godfathers to restore the threads and reveal the full tapestry of texts that constitute fairy-tale cultures, cultures that owe a great debt to many a woman writer.

References

Introduction

1 On the American oral adaptation of d'Aulnoy, see Charlotte
Trinquet du Lys, 'On the Literary Origins of Folkloric Fairy Tales:
A Comparison between Madame d'Aulnoy's "Finette Cendron" and
Frank Bourisaw's "Belle-Finette"', *Marvels and Tales*, xxi/1 (2007),
pp. 34–49.

2 See for example Mary Elizabeth Storer, *Un Épisode littéraire de la
fin du xviie siècle: La Mode des contes de fées (1685–1700)* (Paris, 1928);
Raymonde Robert, *Le Conte de fées littéraire en France de la fin du
xviie à la fin du xviiie siècle* (Nancy, 1982); Lewis Seifert, *Fairy
Tales, Sexuality, and Gender in France, 1690–1715: Nostalgic Utopias*
(Cambridge, 1996); Patricia Hannon, *Fabulous Identities: Women's Fairy
Tales in Seventeenth-Century France* (Amsterdam and Atlanta, GA,
1998); Anne Defrance, *Les Contes et les nouvelles de Madame d'Aulnoy
(1690–1698)* (Geneva, 1998); Sophie Raynard, *La Seconde Préciosité:
Floriason des conteuses de 1690 à 1756* (Tübingen, 2002); Holly Tucker,
Pregnant Fictions: Childbirth and the Fairy Tale in Early Modern France
(Detroit, MI, 2003); Charlotte Trinquet du Lys, *Le Conte de fées français
(1690–1700): Traditions italiennes et origines aristocratiques* (Tübingen,
2012); and, more recently, Bronwyn Reddan, *Love, Power, and Gender
in Seventeenth-Century French Fairy Tales* (Lincoln, NE, 2020), and Rori
Bloom, *Making the Marvelous: Marie-Catherine d'Aulnoy, Henriette-
Julie de Murat, and the Literary Representation of the Decorative Arts*
(Lincoln, NE, 2022). Much of the biographical information on the
conteuses presented here is taken from Sophie Raynard, ed., *The Teller's
Tale: Lives of the Classic Fairy Tale Writers* (Albany, NY, 2012).

3 For the most accurate information on d'Aulnoy's biography, see
Volker Schröder, 'Madame d'Aulnoy's Productive Confinement',

Anecdota blog, 2 May 2020, https://anecdota.princeton.edu. See also Nadine Jasmin's biography in Raynard, ed., *The Teller's Tale*, pp. 61–8.

4 On La Force, see Lewis Seifert's biography in Raynard, ed., *The Teller's Tale*, pp. 89–93.

5 Allison Stedman, 'Introduction', in *A Trip to the Country: By Henriette-Julie de Castelnau, comtesse de Murat*, ed. and trans. Perry Gethner and Allison Stedman (Detroit, MI, 2011), p. 8. See also Geneviève Patard's biography of Murat in Raynard, ed., *The Teller's Tale*, pp. 81–8.

6 On Scudéry's feminism, see Anne E. Duggan, Chapters 2 and 3 of *Salonnières, Furies and Fairies: The Politics of Gender and Cultural Change in Absolutist France*, 2nd revd edn (Newark, NJ, 2021); '*Les Femmes Illustres*, or the Book as Triumphal Arch', *Papers on French Seventeenth-Century Literature*, XLIV/87 (2017), pp. 1–20; and 'Madeleine de Scudéry's Animal Sublime; or, Of Chameleons', *Ecozon*, VII/1 (2016), pp. 28–42.

7 Marie-Jeanne L'Héritier, *Oeuvres meslées* (Paris, 1696), p. 229. Unless otherwise noted, all translations from the French are mine.

8 Henriette-Julie de Murat, *Journal pour Mademoiselle de Menou* (Paris, 2016), pp. 180–81.

9 Reddan, *Love, Power, and Gender*, pp. 30–31.

10 Ibid., p. 31.

11 For a non-exhaustive list of French salons, see Duggan, *Salonnières*, p. 16. For a wonderful history of the salon, see Faith E. Beasley, *Salons, History, and the Creation of 17th-Century France: Mastering Memory* (New York, 2006).

12 Volker Schröder has documented the earliest German translation of d'Aulnoy in 'The First German Translation of *Les Contes des fées*', *Anecdota* blog, 20 February 2022, https://anecdota.princeton.edu.

13 Julie L. J. Koehler, 'Navigating the Patriarchy in Variants of "The Bee and the Orange Tree" by German Women', New Directions in d'Aulnoy Studies, *Marvels and Tales*, XXXV/2 (2021), p. 252.

14 Shawn Jarvis, 'Monkey Tails: D'Aulnoy and Unger Explore Descartes, Rousseau, and the Animal-Human Divide', New Directions in d'Aulnoy Studies, *Marvels and Tales*, XXXV/2 (2021), p. 279.

15 See Julie Koehler's introduction to Stahl's tale in Julie L. J. Koehler et al., eds and trans., *Women Writing Wonder: An Anthology of Subversive Nineteenth-Century British, French, and German Fairy Tales* (Detroit, MI, 2021), pp. 203–204.

16 Koehler et al., *Women Writing Wonder*, an anthology of nineteenth-century British, French and German fairy tales by women writers, does some of this transnational and transhistorical work to begin to

bring to the fore influences across national and historical boundaries that connected women writers of fairy tales.

17 Francesco Giovan Straparola, *The Pleasant Nights*, ed. and trans. Suzanne Magnanini (Toronto, 2015), pp. 95–6.

18 Jennifer Schacker discusses this event in her *Staging Fairyland: Folklore, Children's Entertainment, and Nineteenth-Century Pantomime* (Detroit, MI, 2018), pp. 47–50. See also 'Fancy-Dress Ball at Marlborough House', *London Illustrated News*, 1 August 1874, p. 114.

1 A Not-So-Passive Cinderella

1 Simone de Beauvoir, *The Second Sex* (New York, 1989), p. 291.

2 Marcia R. Lieberman, '"Some Day My Prince Will Come": Female Acculturation through the Fairy Tale', *College English*, XXXIV/3 (1972), p. 389.

3 Charles Perrault, *Contes* (Paris, 1981), p. 172.

4 Ruth Bottigheimer maintains that Perrault's 'Cinderella' was circulating at court by 1695 and was published several months before d'Aulnoy's 'Finette-Cendron'. See her chapter 'Cinderella: The People's Princess', in *Cinderella across Cultures: New Directions and Interdisciplinary Perspectives*, ed. Martine Hennard Dutheil de La Rochère et al. (Detroit, MI, 2016), p. 36. Even if it was circulating only in manuscript form, it is quite possible that d'Aulnoy had heard a version of the tale before it appeared in print.

5 Marie-Jeanne L'Héritier, *Les Caprices du destin* [1717] (Paris, 1718), p. 265.

6 Marie-Catherine d'Aulnoy, *Contes I* [1697], intro. Jacques Barchilon, ed. Philippe Hourcade (Paris, 1997), p. 378.

7 Ibid., pp. 382–3.

8 Ibid., p. 384.

9 Tatiana Korneeva, 'Rival Sisters and Vengeance Motifs in the *Contes de fées* of d'Aulnoy, Lhéritier and Perrault', *Modern Language Notes*, CXXVII/4 (2012), p. 735.

10 Rebecca-Anne C. Do Rozario, *Fashion in the Fairy Tale Tradition: What Cinderella Wore* (New York, 2018), p. 19.

11 Volker Schröder, 'The Birth and Beginnings of Madame d'Aulnoy', *Anecdota* blog, 29 March 2019, https://anecdota.princeton.edu.

12 Korneeva, 'Rival Sisters', p. 747.

13 D'Aulnoy, *Contes I*, p. 379.

14 Korneeva, 'Rival Sisters', p. 745.

15 See Charlotte Trinquet du Lys, 'On the Literary Origins of Folkloric Fairy Tales: A Comparison between Madame d'Aulnoy's "Finette

Cendron" and Frank Bourisaw's "Belle-Finette"', *Marvels and Tales*,
XXI/I (2007), p. 38.

16 In *Le Conte populaire* (Paris, 1984), Michèle Simonsen also noted
similarities between 'La Cendrouse', and d'Aulnoy's and Perrault's
Cinderella tales.

17 Léon Pineau, *Les Contes populaires du Poitou* (Paris, 1891), p. 199.
Perrault's Cinderella also makes the comment, 'She was thus quite
beautiful?', but without hinting as directly as d'Aulnoy or the Poitou
narrator that she, indeed, is the mystery princess. See Perrault, *Contes*,
p. 175.

18 On the Nova Scotia version, see France Martineau, 'Perspectives sur le
changement linguistique: aux sources du français canadien', *Canadian
Journal of Linguistics/ La revue canadienne de linguistique*, L/I–4 (2005),
p. 206.

19 See Volker Schröder, 'The First German Translation of *Les Contes des
fées*', *Anecdota* blog, 20 February 2022, https://anecdota.princeton.edu.

20 Jack Zipes, *Why Fairy Tales Stick: The Evolution and Relevance of a
Genre* (New York, 2006), p. 79.

21 On this history of German editions in which we find tales by
d'Aulnoy, see Bottigheimer, 'The People's Princess', *Cinderella across
Cultures*, p. 38; and Manfred Grätz, *Das Märchen in der deutschen
Aufklärung: Vom Feenmärchen zum Volksmärchen* (Stuttgart, 1988), p. 19.

22 Jeannine Blackwell, 'German Fairy Tales: A User's Manual.
Translations of Six Frames and Fragments by Romantic Women', in
Fairy Tales and Feminism: New Approaches (Detroit, MI, 2004), p. 85.

23 On Hassenpflug and the background to her tale 'Okerlo', see
Introduction, above; Jack Zipes, ed., *The Golden Age of Folk and Fairy
Tales: From the Brothers Grimm to Andrew Lang* (Indianapolis, IN,
2013), p. xxiv; and Julie L. J. Koehler, 'Navigating the Patriarchy in
Variants of "The Bee and the Orange Tree" by German Women', New
Directions in d'Aulnoy Studies, *Marvels and Tales*, XXXV/2 (2021), pp.
252–70. On the connections between 'Finette-Cendron' and 'Hansel
and Gretel', as well as the informants for the latter, see Zipes, *Golden
Age*, p. 121; Zipes (p. 453) also notes the similarities between 'How Six
Made their Way through the World', related by Dorothea Viehmann,
and d'Aulnoy's 'Belle-Belle', with which the Grimms were familiar.

24 Julie Koehler remarks: 'Although the Grimms saw d'Aulnoy's
influence as a corruption of German and oral traditions, we now
know that many of the tales in their collection were the result
of a reintegration of French literary fairy tales into German oral
storytelling' ('Navigating the Patriarchy', p. 188).

25 Hermann Kletke, *Märchensaal: Märchen aller Völker für Jung und Alt* (Berlin, 1845), p. 361.

26 Margaret Ross Griffel, *Operas in German: A Dictionary* (New York, 2018), p. 153.

27 Jan Máchal, 'Počátky zábavné prosy novočeské', in *Literatura česká devatenáctého století* (Prague, 1902), p. 328.

28 Václav Tille, 'Les Contes français dans la tradition populaire tchèque', in *Mélanges d'histoire littéraire générale et comparée offerts à Fernand Baldensperger* [1930] (Geneva, 1972), p. 285.

29 Zuzana Raková, *La Traduction tchèque du français* (Brno, 2014), p. 15.

30 Jiřina Šmejkalová, 'Němcová, Božena (born Barbora Panklová) (1820?–1862)', in *Biographical Dictionary of Women's Movements and Feminisms: Central, Eastern, and South Eastern Europe, Nineteenth and Twentieth Centuries*, ed. Francisca de Haan, Krassimira Daskalova and Anna Loutfi (Budapest, 2006), pp. 366–7.

31 Alfred Thomas, 'Form, Gender and Ethnicity in the Work of Three Nineteenth-Century Czech Women Writers', *Bohemia*, XXXVIII (13 December 1997), p. 281.

32 See Francis Gregor, 'Biographical Sketch of the Author', in Božena Němcová, *The Grandmother: A Story of Country Life in Bohemia* (Chicago, IL, 1891), p. 5.

33 Božena Němcová, '"Cinderella" by Božena Němcová', trans. Rebecca Cravens, New Directions in d'Aulnoy Studies, *Marvels and Tales*, XXXV/2 (2021), p. 368.

34 Tille, 'Les Contes', p. 293.

35 On the broadcast history of the film, see Claudia Schwabe, 'The Legacy of DEFA's *Three Hazelnuts for Cinderella* in Post-Wall Germany: Tracing the Popularity of a Binational Fairy-Tale Film on Television', *Marvels and Tales*, XXXI/1 (2017), pp. 81, 86–7.

36 On the fortieth anniversary, see Qinna Shen, *The Politics of Magic: DEFA Fairy-Tale Films* (Detroit, MI, 2015), p. 158; on the restoration, see Schwabe, 'The Legacy', p. 89. I wish to thank Nicole Thesz, who informed me that exhibits date from as early as 2009; see www.dreihaselnuessefueraschenbroedel.de/ausstellungen/dauerausstellung-in-moritzburg.

37 According to Pavel Skopal, 'In 1962 Pavlíček wrote a script for a biopic of Němcová, *Horoucí srdce* (An Ardent Heart, 1962); and just two years before *Three Wishes for Cinderella* he authored a script for a TV adaptation of the most famous work by Němcová', *The Grandmother*. See 'The Czechoslovak–East German Co-Production *Tři oříšky pro Popelku/Drei Haselnüsse für Aschenbrödel/Three Wishes for*

Cinderella: A Transnational Tale', in *Popular Cinemas in East Central Europe: Film Cultures and Histories*, ed. Dorota Ostrowska, Francesco Pitassio and Zsuzsanna Varga (London and New York, 2017), p. 193.

38 See Pavel Skopal, 'Příběh úspěšné koprodukce: Národní, mezinárodní a transnârodní prvky *Tři oříšky pro Popelku*', in *Tři oříšky pro Popelku*, ed. Pavel Skopal (Prague, 2016), pp. 36–55; and Adéla Ficová's discussion of how Pavlíček drew from all three Cinderella tales for his screenplay in 'To Whom the Shoe Fits: Cinderella as a Cultural Phenomenon in the Czech and Norwegian Context', MA diss., Masaryk University, Brno, 2020, pp. 42–4.

39 Skopal, 'Czechoslovak–East German Co-Production', p. 189. Skopal clarified for me in email correspondence that he is indeed speaking of Němcová's 'O Popelce' with respect to the active heroine.

40 Quoted in Skopal, 'Czechoslovak–East German Co-Production', p. 190.

41 Shen, *Politics of Magic*, pp. 155, 216.

2 Beauties, Beasts and d'Aulnoy's Legacy

1 I am using 'Rococo' in Allison Stedman's sense of the term, relating to 'heterogeneous literary creations'; see Allison Stedman, *Rococo Fiction in France, 1600–1715: Seditious Frivolity* (Lewisburg, PA, 2013), p. 8.

2 Jack Zipes, *Fairy Tale as Myth/Myth as Fairy Tale* (Lexington, KY, 1994), p. 25.

3 The episode concerning the Moor is clearly racist, manifest in the subordinate position of the Moor as pet through her association with the monkey and dog, and in the idea expressed in the tale that her tongue is black and therefore could not be taken to be that of Merveilleuse.

4 Marie-Catherine d'Aulnoy, *Contes 1* [1697], intro. Jacques Barchilon, ed. Philippe Hourcade (Paris, 1997), pp. 345–6.

5 D'Aulnoy's 'The Boar Prince' is closely related to Straparola's 'The Pig Prince', but the heroine is noble, not a commoner, a class switch that d'Aulnoy makes frequently when adapting tales by Straparola and Basile.

6 On inscriptions of Versailles in d'Aulnoy's tales, see Anne E. Duggan, *Salonnières, Furies and Fairies: The Politics of Gender and Cultural Change in Absolutist France*, 2nd revd edn (Newark, NJ, 2021), pp. 210–13. Also notable is La Fontaine's influence via d'Aulnoy; his version of 'Cupid and Psyche' is couched in a frame narrative in which three friends listen to a fourth friend's adaptation of the Latin text

in the gardens of Versailles, and the text is punctuated by numerous references to Louis XIV's palace.

7 On d'Aulnoy's confinement, see Volker Schröder's excellent blog post, 'Madame d'Aulnoy's Productive Confinement', *Anecdota* blog, 2 May 2020, https://anecdota.princeton.edu.

8 Gabrielle-Suzanne de Villeneuve, *Beauty and the Beast: The Original Story*, ed. and trans. Aurora Wolfgang (Toronto, 2020), p. 116.

9 Adrion Dula suggested in our exchanges about the chapter that we could look at the husbands of Beauty's sisters in Leprince de Beaumont as functioning similarly to the doubling of the hero, although there is no rivalry over the heroine herself, but rather a split between positive and negative models of masculinity as it relates to marriage.

10 On the publishing history of d'Aulnoy and Charles Perrault in England in the eighteenth century, see the tables on pp. 4–6 of Anne E. Duggan, 'Introduction: The Emergence of the Classic Fairy-Tale Tradition', in *A Cultural History of Fairy Tales in the Long Eighteenth Century* (London, 2021).

11 *Daddy Gander's Entertaining Fairy Tales* (London, 1815), pp. 31, 23.

12 D'Aulnoy, *Contes 1*, p. 345.

13 The *Young Misses' Magazine* was regularly published in England in the eighteenth century. The British Library holds the following English editions published in London, Dublin and Edinburgh: 1760, 1780, 1781, 1783 and 1800. In *Beauty and the Beast: Visions and Revisions of an Old Tale* (Chicago, 1989), Betsy Hearne includes 'A Sampling of Nineteenth-Century Editions' of the tale, pp. 207–12.

14 On approaches that have posited the Beast as embodying sexuality, see Jerry Grisold, *The Meanings of 'Beauty and the Beast': A Handbook* (Toronto, 2004), pp. 55–7.

15 D'Aulnoy, *Contes 1*, p. 345.

16 The versions that use 'seized with remorse' include *Mother Bunch's Fairy Tales* (1802, 1830), *History of Little Jack* (1840) and *The Child's Own Book of Standard Fairy Tales* (1868).

17 D'Aulnoy, *Contes 1*, p. 346.

18 Patricia Hannon, *Fabulous Identities: Women's Fairy Tales in Seventeenth-Century France* (Amsterdam and Atlanta, 1998), p. 119.

19 I want to thank Adrion Dula for bringing up notions of state versus family, and public versus private, when I was discussing the chapter with her.

20 *Mother Bunch's Fairy Tales* (London, 1830), p. 49.

21 See William Hyde, 'The Stature of Baring-Gould as a Novelist', *Nineteenth-Century Fiction*, XV/1 (1960): pp. 1–2; and Andrew

Warn, 'The Grimms, the Kirk-Grims, and Sabine Baring-Gould', *Constructing Nations, Reconstructing Myth: Essays in Honour of T. A. Shippey* (Turnhout, 2007), pp. 219 and 227–8.

22 Sabine Baring-Gould, *A Book of Fairy Tales* (London, 1894), p. vii.
23 Sabine Baring-Gould, *Old English Fairy Tales* (London, 1895), p. 5.
24 Baring-Gould, *A Book of Fairy Tales*, p. 157.
25 Ibid., p. 158.
26 After consulting WCAT and the National Library of Scotland, the book is listed as possibly issuing from London, from the publisher Puck & Co., for which I have not found any information. Online booksellers, such as 'Antiquates: Fine and Rare Books', advertise the poem as a 'separate and unillustrated edition of the satirical fairy-tale poem that first appeared in George Cruikshank's *Daddy Gander's Entertaining Fairy Tales* (London, 1821)'. Although I have not been able to consult *Daddy Gander*, the British Museum has a print by Cruikshank from the book with two scenes from his version of 'The Royal Ram', which do not correspond at all to the anonymous verse parody of 1844. It is perhaps the subject of temperance, treated in the poem, that led to this attribution, given that Cruikshank was involved in the temperance movement, although that did not happen until the 1840s, years after the publication of *Daddy Gander*.
27 *Miranda and the Royal Ram* (London, 1844), p. 5.
28 Ibid.
29 Ibid., p. 8.
30 This is asserted by Hannon, *Fabulous Identities*, p. 117.
31 Cheap chapbook versions include Milan 1782, Troyes 1807, Toulouse *c.* 1809 and 1816, and Montbéliard 1834. An illustrated version by Marcel Bloch appeared in Marcq-en-Barouel (near Lille) in 1936, re-edited in 1953.
32 Jennifer Schacker, 'Fluid Identities: Madame d'Aulnoy, Mother Bunch and Fairy-Tale History', in *The Individual and Tradition: Folkloristic Perspectives*, ed. Ray Cashman et al. (Bloomington, IN, 2011), pp. 249–64.
33 Honoré de Balzac, *La Dernière Fée* [1823] (Paris, 1876), pp. 18, 24.
34 Honoré de Balzac, 'Un Prince de la Bohème', in *Oeuvres complètes* (Paris, 1879), vol. IV, p. 22.
35 Allan H. Pasco, *Balzacian Montage* (Toronto, 1991), pp. 112–13.
36 See, for instance, Stedman's examination of the relation between frame and fairy tale in d'Aulnoy in *Rococo Fiction*, pp. 164–5.
37 George Sand, *Histoire de ma vie* (Paris, 1856), vol. IV, p. 222.
38 Gustave Flaubert, *Correspondance*, vol. II: *1853–63* (Paris, 1923), p. 71.
39 Ibid., p. 68.

40 The coloured engraving can be found at https://flaubert-vɪ.
univ-rouen.fr/bovary/bovary_6/albumɪ/a-serpen.html.
41 Edmond and Jules de Goncourt, *Histoire de la société française pendant
la révolution*, 3rd edn (Paris, 1864), p. 309.
42 The Goncourts also mention revolutionary changes made to d'Aulnoy's
'Beauty with the Golden Hair'. In these accounts, however, d'Aulnoy
is never mentioned by name.
43 Jeffrey Richards, *The Golden Age of Pantomime: Slapstick, Spectacle and
Subversion in Victorian England* (London, 2015), p. 65.
44 Henry Barton Baker, *History of the London Stage and its Famous Players
(1576–1903)* (London, 1904), p. 289.
45 See Emily Kilpatrick, '"Therein Lies a Tale": Musical and Literary
Structure in Ravel's *Ma Mère l'Oye*', *Context*, xxxɪv (2009), p. 81.
46 Quoted ibid., p. 94.
47 Ibid., p. 90.
48 Deborah Mawer explains: 'Exoticism is most obviously embedded in
the energetic and, at times, very forthright "Laideronnette". Mechanical
mock-Chinese (or Javanese) pentatonic figurations of semiquavers and
quavers are supported by pentatonic harmonization below, favouring
gamelan-like fourths, fifths and major seconds.' See Mawer, *The Ballets
of Maurice Ravel: Creation and Interpretation* (London, 2006), p. 41.
49 Maurice Ravel, *Ma Mère l'oye, ballet en cinq tableaux et une apothéose*:
Partition pour piano (Paris, *c.* 1912), p. 34.
50 René Chalupt, 'Laideronnette, Impératrice des Pagodes', *La Phalange*,
lɪ (September 1910), pp. 212–13.
51 Ravel, *Ma Mère l'oye*, p. 35.
52 Mawer, *The Ballets of Maurice Ravel*, p. 42.
53 For instance, when discussing Ravel's fairy suite, Deborah Mawer
remarks that 'Ravel revivifies an episode from the obscure tale of
"Laideronnette" . . . by Marie-Catherine, Comtesse d'Aulnoy.' Ibid.,
p. 42.

3 The Other Famous Cat Tale

1 Quoted in H. Philip Bolton, *Women Writers Dramatized: A Calendar
of Performances from Narrative Works Published in English to 1900* (New
York, 2000), p. 57. In his chapter on d'Aulnoy, Bolton provides the
wide repertoire of theatrical adaptations to the British stage of fairy
tales by the *conteuse*.
2 Holly Tucker has noted that 'D'Aulnoy, La Force, and Lhéritier were
united in friendship with Madame Deshoulières,' in Tucker, *Pregnant

Fictions: Childbirth and the Fairy Tale in Early Modern France (Detroit, MI, 2003), p. 158, n. 12.

3 Giambattista Basile, *The Tale of Tales; or, Entertainment for Little Ones*, trans. Nancy L. Canepa (Detroit, MI, 2007), p. 148.

4 Ibid.

5 Ibid., p. 150.

6 Lewis Seifert, 'Charlotte-Rose de Caumont de La Force: 1650?–1724', in *The Teller's Tale: Lives of the Classic Fairy Tale Writers*, ed. Sophie Raynard (Albany, NY, 2012), p. 89.

7 Ibid., p. 90.

8 Basile, *Tale of Tales*, p. 147; Charlotte-Rose Caumont de La Force, *Les Fées contes des contes* (Amsterdam, 1716), p. 42.

9 Ibid., p. 44.

10 Holly Tucker remarks: 'The tale's direct reference to age suggests that the protagonist's sequestration is connected above all to her developing body and the reproductive abilities she will soon have. While the average woman married between twenty-five and twenty-six, young girls – particularly from families for whom marriage was part of a strategy to foster an economic or political advantage – could be married off as young as twelve in the Ancien Regime.' Tucker, *Pregnant Fictions*, p. 106.

11 Gilles Corrozet, *Les Propos mémorables et illustres hommes de la Chrestienté* (Lyon, 1560; Rouen, 1599), p. 286.

12 *Le Tableau des piperies des femmes mondaines* (Paris, 1632), p. 179. *Le Tableau des piperies* was first published in 1632 and was republished in 1633, 1685 and 1686, the two periods in which the *Querelle des femmes* was most pronounced.

13 La Force, *Les Fées contes*, p. 45.

14 See *Mémoires de Mlle de Montpensier* (Paris, 1858), vol. II, p. 223; and Juliette Cherbuliez, *The Place of Exile: Leisure Literature and the Limits of Absolutism* (Lewisburg, PA, 2005), p. 44.

15 Several scholars, including Max Lüthi, Jack Zipes and Melissa Mullins, have recognized the important role La Force played in the history of 'Rapunzel', but the connection between the tale and La Force has yet to be considered common knowledge.

16 Friedrich Schulz, 'Rapunzel', in *The Great Fairy-Tale Tradition*, ed. Jack Zipes (New York, 2011), p. 484.

17 La Force, *Les Fées contes*, p. 45; Schulz, 'Rapunzel', p. 485.

18 Melissa Mullins, 'Ogress, Fairy, Sorceress, Witch: Supernatural Surrogates and the Monstrous Mother in Variants of "Rapunzel"', in *The Morals of Monster Stories: Essays on Children's Picture Book Messages*,

ed. Leslie Ormandy (Jefferson, NC, 2017), p. 145. See also Max Lüthi, in 'Die Herkunft des Grimmschen Rapunzelmäarhens (AsTh 310)', *Fabula*, III/1 (1960), pp. 95–118, who asserted in 1960 that the Grimms falsely suspected an oral folk version behind Schulz's 'Rapunzel', and who also shows the close connection between Schulz and La Force. The Grimms were aware of 'Persinette', but not as a source for Schulz's 'Rapunzel'.

19 Maria Tatar, *The Hard Facts of the Brothers Grimm* (Princeton, NJ, 1987), p. 18.

20 Elizabeth Wanning Harries, *Twice Upon a Time: Women Writers and the History of the Fairy Tale* (Princeton, NJ, 2001), p. 17.

21 On the connections between d'Aulnoy's 'The White Cat' and Diyāb and Galland's 'Prince Ahmed and Pari Banou', see Ruth B. Bottigheimer, 'Marie-Catherine d'Aulnoy's "White Cat" and Hannā Diyāb's "Prince Ahmed and Pari Banou": Influences and Legacies', New Directions in d'Aulnoy Studies, *Marvels and Tales*, XXXV/2 (2021), pp. 290–311.

22 Marie-Catherine d'Aulnoy, *Contes II* [1698], intro. Jacques Barchilon; ed. Philippe Hourcade (Paris, 1998), p. 166.

23 Ibid., p. 168.

24 Ibid.

25 Holly Tucker discusses the Russian-doll effect at length in *Pregnant Fictions*, pp. 115–16.

26 D'Aulnoy, *Contes II*, pp. 188–9.

27 Ibid., p. 189.

28 Ibid., p. 207.

29 David Blamires, 'From Madame d'Aulnoy to Mother Bunch: Popularity and the Fairy Tale', in *Popular Children's Literature in Britain* (Burlington, VT, 2008), p. 78.

30 For a succinct overview of the history of pantomime in England, see Jennifer Schacker and Daniel O'Quinn's 'Introduction' to their well-documented *The Routledge Pantomime Reader: 1800–1900* (London, 2022). See also Jeffery Richards, *The Golden Age of Pantomime: Slapstick, Spectacle and Subversion in Victorian England* (London, 2015).

31 Richards, *The Golden Age*, p. 35.

32 Adolphe Adam, *Souvenirs d'un musicien* (Paris, 1857), p. xxii.

33 Ibid. Initially, Charles X's minister did not want to grant permission for the performance since the pantomime – through its generic mix of speech, music and dance – violated the privilege given to theatre. The performance that won over the young princes allowed the play to be produced onstage in Paris.

34 See Bolton's chapter on all d'Aulnoy's tales that were staged, in
   Women Writers Dramatized, pp. 129–67.

35 On contemporary observations that harlequinades no longer
   corresponded to the spirit of the age, see Richards, *The Golden Age*,
   pp. 41–2.

36 James Robinson Planché, *The Extravaganzas of J. R. Planché, Esq.*,
   vol. II (London, 1879), p. 157.

37 Ibid., p. 176.

38 Ibid., p. 178.

39 Ibid., pp. 145–6.

40 Michèle Longino Farrell foregrounds the class-inflected meaning of
   the disembodied hands in 'Celebration and Repression of Feminine
   Desire in Mme d'Aulnoy's Fairy Tale: *La Chatte blanche*', *Esprit
   Créateur*, XXIX/3 (Autumn 1989), p. 54.

41 Planché, *The Extravagnzas*, p. 175.

42 On women playing the role of principal boy, see Rachel Cowgill,
   'Re-Gendering the Libertine; or, The Taming of the Rake: Lucy
   Vestris as Don Giovanni on the Early Nineteenth-Century London
   Stage', *Cambridge Opera Journal*, X/1 (March 1998), pp. 45–66;
   Schacker and O'Quinn, *Routledge Pantomime Reader*, pp. 6–7; Jennifer
   Schacker, 'Slaying Blunderboer: Cross-Dressed Heroes, National
   Identities, and Wartime Pantomime', *Marvels and Tales*, XXVII/1
   (2013), pp. 52–3; and Richards, *The Golden Age*, pp. 29–30.

43 Cowgill, 'Re-Gendering', pp. 57, 58.

44 Bolton, *Women Writers Dramatized*, pp. 157–8.

45 F. C. Burnand, *The White Cat! of Prince Lardi-Dardi and the Radiant
   Rosetta: A Fairy Burlesque Extravaganza* (London, 1870), pp. 8–9.

46 Ibid., p. 9.

47 Ibid., pp. 30, 32.

48 Dolores Mitchell, 'Women and Nineteenth-Century Images
   of Smoking', in *Smoke: A Global History of Smoking*, ed. Sander
   L. Gilman and Zhou Xun (London, 2004), p. 294.

49 Arnold Mortier, 'Reprise de la *Chatte Blanche*', in *Les Soirées
   parisiennes de 1875* (Paris, 1876), p. 194.

50 Théophile Gautier, 'Le Monde et le théâtre: Chronique familière du
   mois', *Revue de Paris*, X–XII (July–September 1852), p. 158.

51 Charles Monselet, 'Théâtres', *Le Monde illustré*, 21 August 1869, p. 126.

52 Émile Morlot, 'Critique dramatique: Menus-Plaisirs', *Revue d'art
   dramatique*, April–June 1887, p. 107. The Châtelet theatre is near the
   Seine, and Morlot plays on the homophones *Seine* and *scène*, referring
   to the stage.

53 Francis Chevassu, 'Les Théâtres: Châtelet', *Le Figaro*, 5 November 1908, p. 5.

54 Marie-Françoise Christout, 'Aspects de la féerie romantique de *La Sylphide* (1832) à *La Biche au bois* (1845); Chorégraphie, décors, trucs et machines', *Romantisme*, XXXVIII (1982), p. 79.

55 Ibid., pp. 79, 80.

56 Théophile Gautier, 'Théâtre de la Porte-Saint-Martin, *La Biche au Bois*', *La Presse*, 31 March 1845, n.p.

57 The word 'Petitpatapon' comes from a popular ballad, '*Il était une bergère/ Et ron et ron, petit patapon*' ('Once upon a time there was a shepherdess/ And *ron, petit patapon*'), and is onomatopoeic; '*à petit patapon*' can also signify 'slowly' ('*tout doucement*').

58 Blanchette spends only about 8 per cent of the play as the maiden in the tower, 26 per cent as the white cat, but 56 per cent as the hero, Fidèle, while Pimpondor is imprisoned for 56 per cent of the *féerie*, playing an active role for only about a quarter of the play.

59 Théodore and Hippolyte Cogniard, *La Chatte blanche* (Paris, 1852), p. 92.

60 Ibid., p. 95.

61 For more on the photographs of *The White Cat*, see G. Mareschal, 'La photographie au théâtre', *La Nature*, 5 December 1887, pp. 93–4; and Beatriz Pichel, 'Reading Photography in French Nineteenth Century Journals', *Media History*, XXV/92 (2018), pp. 9–12.

62 Richards, *The Golden Age*, p. 323.

63 Veronica Bonanni has studied Carlo Collodi's 1876 translation of several d'Aulnoy tales, including 'La gatta bianca', appearing in the collection *I racconti delle fate*, of which there were numerous editions in the twentieth century.

64 On the history of nineteenth-century French comics, see Ann Miller, *Reading Bande Dessinée: Critical Approaches to French-Language Comic Strip* (Bristol, 2007), pp. 15–18.

65 Anne Rubenstein, *Bad Language, Naked Ladies, and Other Threats to the Nation: A Political History of Comic Books in Mexico* (Durham, NC, 1998), p. 161.

66 Marie-Catherine d'Aulnoy, 'La Gatita blanca', in *Cuentos famosos ilustrados a colores*, 26 (Mexico City, 1965), p. 12.

67 D'Aulnoy, *Contes II*, p. 172.

68 D'Aulnoy, 'La Gatita blanca', p. 29.

69 D'Aulnoy, *Contes II*, p. 207.

70 D'Aulnoy, 'La Gatita blanca', p. 34.

4 The Lost Amazon Warriors

1 On maiden warrior tales, see Christine Jones, 'Maiden Warrior', in *Folktales and Fairy Tales: Traditions and Texts from Around the World*, vol. II (Santa Barbara, CA, 2016), pp. 604–7, and 'Noble Impropriety: The Maiden Warrior and the Seventeenth Century Contes de Fées', PhD diss., Princeton University, 2002; Charlotte Trinquet du Lys, 'L'homosexualité dans les contes de femmes-soldats', *Papers in French Seventeenth-Century Literature*, XLI/81 (2014), pp. 283–99, and 'Women Soldiers' Tales during Louis XIV's War Conflicts', *Marvels and Tales*, XXXIII/1 (2019), pp. 140–56; on maiden warrior tales across cultures and media, as well as the queer implications of such tales, see Chapter 4 of Anne E. Duggan, *Queer Enchantments: Gender, Sexuality, and Class in the Fairy-Tale Cinema of Jacques Demy* (Detroit, MI, 2013).

2 On this pro-woman tradition, see Armel Dubois-Nayt, Nicole Dufournaud and Anne Paupert, eds, *Revisiter la 'querelle des femmes': Discours sur l'égalité/inégalité des sexes, de 1400 à 1600* (Saint-Etienne, 2013); Anne E. Duggan, '*Les Femmes Illustres*; or, The Book as Triumphal Arch', *Papers on French Seventeenth-Century Literature*, XLIV/87 (2017), pp. 1–20; Danielle Haase-Dubosc and Marie-Elisabeth Henneau, *Revisiter la 'querelle des femmes': Discours sur l'égalité/inégalité des sexes, de 1600 à 1750* (Saint-Etienne, 2013); and Ian Maclean, *Women Triumphant: Feminism in French Literature, 1610–1652* (Oxford, 1977).

3 Jean Chapelain, *La Pucelle, ou la France délivrée: Poëme heroïque* (Paris, 1656), p. 381.

4 One example of artwork commissioned to legitimate queen regencies is the Artemisia tapestries, which blended the figure of the warrior queen Artemisia, ally of Xerxes, and Artemisia, wife of Mausolus. The version of the story upon which the series of tapestries was based was produced by Nicolas Houel around 1561–2 in honour of Catherine de' Medici; Catherine commissioned the tapestries based on the text, but their production occurred under Marie de' Medici, in about 1611–27. See Isabelle Denis, 'The Parisian Workshops, 1590–1650', in *Tapestry in the Baroque: Threads of Splendor*, ed. Thomas P. Campbell (New York and New Haven, CT, 2007), pp. 140–47.

5 For a nice overview of the diplomatic and military roles aristocratic women played during the Fronde, see Hubert Carrier, 'Women's Political and Military Action during the Fronde', in *Political and Historical Encyclopedia of Women*, ed. Christine Fauré (New York, 2003), pp. 34–55.

6 Naomi Lebens, '"We Made a Blame Game of your Game": Jean Desmarets, the *Jeu des Reynes Renommés* and the *Dame des Reynes'*, *Early Modern Women*, XII/1 (Autumn 2017), p. 131.

7 Francesco Giovan Straparola, *The Pleasant Nights*, ed. and trans. Suzanne Magnanini (Toronto, 2015), p. 174.

8 Ibid., p. 175.

9 Ibid., p. 176.

10 In early modern France the Azore Islands, which include the island of Terceira, were referred to as the Terceira islands.

11 Islands appear in d'Aulnoy's 'The Island of Felicity', 'The Prince Lutin', 'The Princess Printanière', 'The Bee and the Orange Tree' and 'The Dolphin', among others.

12 Henriette-Julie de Murat, *Histoires sublimes et allégoriques, dédiées aux fées modernes* (Paris, 1699), p. 8.

13 Sylvie Cromer discusses the notion of usurpation in her analysis of the tale in '"Le Sauvage": Histoire sublime et allégorique de Madame de Murat', *Merveilles et contes*, I/1 (May 1987), p. 11.

14 Bronwyn Reddan, *Love, Power, and Gender in Seventeenth-Century French Fairy Tales* (Lincoln, NE, 2020), p. 4.

15 Murat, *Histoires*, p. 20.

16 See Erica Harth, *Ideology and Culture in Seventeenth-Century France* (Ithaca, NY, 1983), p. 195.

17 For a summary of the debate on the attribution of the 1697 collection of Perrault's tales, see Émile Henriot, 'De qui sont les contes de Perrault?', *Revue des deux mondes*, XLII/2 (January 1928), pp. 424–41. In *Fairy Tales Framed*, Ruth Bottigheimer and Sophie Raynard suggest that the dedication 'is both enigmatic and puzzling: no daughter of Charles Perrault appears in the official church registries . . . Similarly, Perrault mentions his sons in his correspondence, but never a daughter'; see their 'Marie-Jeanne Lhéritier, *Diverse Works* 1698', in *Fairy Tales Framed: Early Forewords, Afterwords, and Critical Words*, ed. Ruth Bottigheimer (Albany, NY, 2012), p. 131. Other scholars, such as Jacques Barchilon and Peter Flinders, note that 'there may have been a fourth child', referring to the hypothetical daughter; see Barchilon and Flinders, *Charles Perrault* (Boston, MA, 1981), p. 27.

18 See Volker Schröder, 'Marie-Madeleine Perrault (1674–1701)', *Anecdota* blog, 31 December 2017, https://anecdota.princeton.edu.

19 Catherine Velay-Vallantin, 'Marmoisan ou la fille en garçon', in *La Fille en garçon* (Carcassonne, 1992), p. 63.

20 Carmeta Abbott, 'Madame de Saint-Balmon (Alberte-Barbe d'Ernecourt): *Les Jumeaux martyrs* (1650)', in *Writings by*

Pre-Revolutionary French Women, ed. Anne R. Larsen and Colette H. Winn [2000] (New York, 2017), p. 258.

21 Ibid., p. 259.

22 Marie-Jeanne L'Héritier, *Les Caprices du destin* [1717] (Paris, 1718), n.p.

23 Ibid., p. 27.

24 Ibid., p. 31.

25 Ibid., p. 35.

26 Ibid., p. 38.

27 Ibid., p. 34.

28 Ibid., p. 35.

29 See the definition in the *Dictionnaire de l'Académie française* (1694).

30 L'Héritier, *Les Caprices*, p. 48.

31 Ibid., p. 54. Trinquet du Lys remarks on the connections between the king's two wives in the tale and the two wives of Louis XIV, Marie-Thérèse of Spain and Françoise d'Aubigné, Marquis de Maintenon, in 'Women Soldiers' Tales', p. 144.

32 Martin C. Battestin, 'Fielding's Contributions to the "Universal Spectator" (1736–7)', *Studies in Philology*, LXXXIII/1 (Winter 1986), p. 89.

33 Henry Stonecastle's preface to 'Marmoisan; or, The Innocent Deceit: A Novel', *Universal Spectator and Weekly Journal*, 806 (17 March 1744), n.p.

34 Jennie Batchelor, '"Connections, which are of service . . . in a more advanced age": "The Lady's Magazine", Community, and Women's Literary Histories', *Tulsa Studies in Women's Literature*, XXX/2 (Autumn 2011), pp. 245, 263.

35 Justin McCarthy, *The Waterdale Neighbours*, 3 vols (London, 1867), vol. 1, pp. 210–12.

36 Ibid., p. 213.

37 Justin McCarthy, *A History of Our Own Times: From the Diamond Jubilee 1897 to the Accession of Edward VII*, 2 vols (London, 1905), vol. 1, p. 231.

38 On the idea of two opposing images of women in the tale, see Adrienne E. Zuerner, 'Reflections of the Monarchy in d'Aulnoy's *Belle-Belle ou le chevalier Fortuné*', in *Out of the Woods: The Origins of the Literary Fairy Tale in Italy and France*, ed. Nancy Canepa (Detroit, MI, 1997), p. 198.

39 On Perrault, Boileau and debates about women in power, see for instance Chapter 4 of my *Salonnières, Furies, and Fairies: The Politics of Gender and Cultural Change in Absolutist France*, second rev. edn (Newark, NJ, 2021), and my article 'The *Querelle des femmes* and

Nicolas Boileau's *Satire x*: Going beyond Perrault', *Early Modern French Studies*, XLI/2 (2019), pp. 144–57.

40 Zuerner discusses the notion of castrated male characters in the tale; see Zuerner, 'Reflections', p. 200.

41 Marie-Catherine d'Aulnoy, *Contes II* [1698], intro. Jacques Barchilon; ed. Philippe Hourcade (Paris, 1998), p. 218.

42 Ibid., p. 219. This scene recalls more generally the tale type of 'The Kind and the Unkind Girls'.

43 D'Aulnoy, *Contes II*, pp. 234–5.

44 Noting the role the dowager queen plays in advancing the tale's action, Trinquet du Lys remarks: 'It is only due to the actions of the queen dowager that Fortuné is sent to fight the dragon and retake the king's assets'; see 'Women Soldiers' Tales', p. 151.

45 Jean-Joseph Goux, *Oedipe philosophe* (Paris, 1990), pp. 12–13.

46 Trinquet du Lys, 'Women Soldiers' Tales', p. 151.

47 D'Aulnoy, *Contes II*, p. 244.

48 Ibid., p. 222.

49 Trinquet du Lys has a different take on the relationship with Comrade: 'Without her horse dictating her conduct and her magic helpers doing her bidding, she is completely incompetent in fulfilling her soldier's tasks'; 'Women Soldiers' Tales', p. 149. However, she emphasizes the importance of Fortuné's role as 'diplomat' in the tale.

50 D'Aulnoy, *Contes II*, pp. 262.

51 Ibid., p. 265.

52 Ibid., p. 269.

53 *Mother Bunch's Fairy Tales* (London, 1773), p. 110.

54 The tale appears to have been popular in the early nineteenth century, with reprints either alone or with 'The Wishes, an Arabian Tale' in London (1816), Edinburgh (1810), New York (1805, 1810) and Boston, MA (1812).

55 M. O. Grenby, 'Tame Fairies Make Good Teachers: The Popularity of Early British Fairy Tales', *The Lion and the Unicorn*, XXX (2006), p. 1.

56 Marie-Catherine d'Aulnoy, *The History of Fortunio and his Famous Companions* (London, 1804), p. 22.

57 'Rapt' was the legal term used to express the abduction of a woman with the intent to illegally marry her. The text is referring to this illegal practice by having the queen tie the possibility of marriage to the kidnapping.

58 Ibid., p. 35.

59 American editions include New York (1805, 1810) and Boston, MA (1812).

60 James Robinson Planché, *The Extravaganzas of J. R. Planché, Esq.*, vol. II (London, 1879), p. 189.

61 Ibid., p. 199.

62 Ibid., p. 201.

63 Ibid., p. 202.

64 For more on the attitudes towards alcohol in this period, see Henry Yeomans, *Alcohol and Moral Regulation: Public Attitudes, Spirited Measures, and Victorian Hangovers* (Bristol, 2014), pp. 46–51.

65 Ibid., p. 209.

66 On Van Amburgh performing at Drury Lane, see Brenda Assael, *The Circus and Victorian Society* (Charlottesville, VA, 2005), p. 66. On Van Amburgh as lion king, see Peta Tait, *Fighting Nature: Travelling Menageries, Animal Acts and War Shows* (Sydney, 2016), pp. 12–19. Tait discusses Carter as Van Amburgh's successor and notes that they even appeared together 'in an Orientalist theatre fantasy, *Aslar and Zolines; or, The lion hunters of the burning Zaara*, in 1843'; ibid., p. 22.

67 Tait, *Fighting Nature*, p. 20.

68 Planché, *The Extravaganzas*, p. 227.

69 H. Philip Bolton, *Women Writers Dramatized: A Calendar of Performances from Narrative Works Published in English to 1900* (New York, 2000), pp. 142–3.

70 Megan A. Norcia, *Gaming Empire in Children's British Board Games, 1836–1860* (New York, 2019), p. 52.

71 As Megan Norcia has observed, 'Many of the games produced in the later Victorian period focused on imperial policy and ably facilitated imperial consciousness in the children who would grow to be stewards of the Empire'; *Fortunio* is no exception. Ibid., p. 7.

72 Ibid., p. 248.

73 Henry J. Byron, *Lady Belle; Fortunio and his Seven Magic Men: A Christmas Fairy Tale* (London, 1864), pp. 8, 29.

74 Ibid., p. 27.

75 Ibid., p. 32.

76 Ibid., p. 26.

77 Ibid., p. 12.

78 Ibid., p. 43.

79 See Maeve E. Adams, 'The Amazon Warrior Woman and the De/construction of Gendered Imperial Authority in Nineteenth-Century Colonial Literature', *Nineteenth-Century Gender Studies*, VI/I (Spring 2010); and Adrienne Munich, *Queen Victoria's Secrets* (New York, 1996), p. 219.

Epilogue

1 Anne Claude de Caylus, *Tout vient à point, qui peut attendre; ou Cadichon, suivi de Jeannette; ou l'indiscrétion: contes . . . Pour servir de Supplément aux Contes des Fées de Madame d'Aulnoy* (Paris, 1775), pp. 3, 5.

2 In the queen's library at the Petit Trianon, Versailles, one could find a collection from 1754 of tales by d'Aulnoy, La Force and Murat, among others; and an edition from 1724 of Murat's tales. See Paul Lacroix, ed., *Bibliothèque de la reine Marie-Antoinette au Petit Trianon* (Paris, 1863), pp. 65–6.

3 Charles Baudelaire, 'To Beauty with the Golden Hair', *Revue des deux mondes*, x/5 (June 1855), pp. 1085–7.

4 See for instance Albert Feuillerat, *Baudelaire et la Belle aux cheveux d'or* (Paris, 1941), p. 3.

5 Théodore de Banville, 'A la Biche empaillée qui figurait à la Porte-Saint-Martin dans *La Biche au bois*', in *Odes funambulesques* [1868] (Paris, 1896), pp. 246–9.

6 Elizabeth Wanning Harries, *Twice Upon a Time: Women Writers and the History of the Fairy Tale* (Princeton, NJ, 2001), p. 83.

7 Caitlin Lawrence, 'Reimagining the *Conte de fées*: Female Fairy Tales in Eighteenth- and Nineteenth-Century England and their Exploration of the World In-Between', PhD diss., Baylor University, Waco, TX, 2020, in particular chapters 5 and 6.

8 Andrew Teverson, '"Mr Fox" and "The White Cat": The Forgotten Voices in Angela Carter's Fiction', *Hungarian Journal of English and American Studies*, v/2 (1999), pp. 209–22.

9 Veronica Bonanni, '"The Blue Bird" and "L'Uccello turchino". Collodi: Translator of d'Aulnoy', New Directions in d'Aulnoy Studies, *Marvels and Tales*, xxxv/2 (2021), pp. 337–52.

Sources

Source tales and critical editions

d'Aulnoy, Marie-Catherine, *Contes I* [1697], intro. by Jacques Barchilon, ed. Philippe Hourcade (Paris, 1997)
——, *Contes II* [1698], intro. by Jacques Barchilon, ed. Philippe Hourcade (Paris, 1998)
——, *Nouveaux contes de fées* (Amsterdam, 1708)
Basile, Giambattista, *The Tale of Tales; or, Entertainment for Little Ones*, trans. Nancy L. Canepa (Detroit, MI, 2007)
Le Cabinet des fées, 41 vols (Geneva, 1785–9)
Enchanted Eloquence: Fairy Tales by Seventeenth-Century French Women Writers, ed. and trans. Lewis Seifert and Domna Stanton (Toronto, 2010)
La Force, Charlotte-Rose Caumont de, *Les Fées contes des contes* (Amsterdam, 1716)
Leprince de Beaumont, Jeanne-Marie de, *Le Magasin des enfants: La Belle et la Bête et autres contes* (Paris, 1995)
L'Héritier, Marie-Jeanne, *Les Caprices du destin* [1717] (Paris, 1718)
——, 'Marmoisan ou l'innocente tromperie', in *La Fille en garçon*, ed. Catherine Velay-Vallantin (Carcassonne, 1992), pp. 17–57
——, *Oeuvres meslées* (Paris, 1696)
Murat, Henriette-Julie de, *Histoires sublimes et allégoriques, dédiées aux fées modernes* (Paris, 1699)
Perrault, Charles, *Contes* (Paris, 1981)
Peterson, Nora Martin, ed., *Miracles of Love: French Fairy Tales by Women*, trans. Jordan Stump (New York, 2022)
Straparola, Francesco Giovan, *The Pleasant Nights*, ed. and trans. Suzanne Magnanini (Toronto, 2015)
Villeneuve, Gabrielle-Suzanne de, *Beauty and the Beast: The Original Story*, ed. and trans. Aurora Wolfgang (Toronto, 2020)

——, *La Belle et la Bête* (Paris, 2012)

Zipes, Jack, ed., *Beauties, Beasts, and Enchantment: Classic French Fairy Tales*, 2nd edn (New York, 2016)

——, trans. and intro., *The Complete Fairy Tales of the Brothers Grimm* (New York, 2002)

——, ed., *The Great Fairy Tale Tradition: From Straparola and Basile to the Brothers Grimm* (New York, 2001)

Print translations and adaptations

d'Aulnoy, Marie-Catherine, *Fairy Tales: Translated from the French of the Countess d'Anois* (London, 1817)

——, 'La Gatita blanca', in *Cuentos famosos ilustrados a colores*, 26 (Mexico City, 1965)

——, *The History of Fortunio and his Famous Companions* (London, 1804)

——, *The White Cat, and Other Old French Fairy Tales, by Mme la comtesse d'Aulnoy*, ed. Rachel Field, illus. Elizabeth MacKinstry (New York, 1928)

Balzac, Honoré de, *La Dernière Fée* [1823] (Paris, 1876)

——, 'Un Prince de la Bohème', in *Oeuvres complètes* (Paris, 1879), vol. IV, pp. 21–54

Banville, Théodore de, 'A la Biche empaillée qui figurait à la Porte-Saint-Martin dans *La Biche au bois*', in *Odes funambulesques* [1868] (Paris, 1896), pp. 246–9

Baring-Gould, Sabine, *A Book of Fairy Tales* (London, 1894)

——, *Old English Fairy Tales* (London, 1895)

Baudelaire, Charles, 'To Beauty with the Golden Hair', *Revue des deux mondes*, X/5 (June 1855), pp. 1085–7

Bonnières, Robert de, *Contes des fées* (Paris, 1881)

Carrière, Joseph Médard, *Tales from the French Folk-Lore of Missouri* (Evanston, IL, 1937)

Caylus, Anne Claude de, *Tout vient à point, qui peut attendre; ou Cadichon, suivi de Jeannette; ou l'indiscrétion: contes . . . Pour servir de Supplément aux Contes des Fées de Madame d'Aulnoy* (Paris, 1775)

Chalupt, René, 'Laideronnette, Impératrice des Pagodes', *La Phalange*, LI (September 1910), pp. 212–15

The Child's Own Book of Standard Fairy Tales, illus. Gustave Doré and George Cruikshank (Philadelphia, 1868)

Daddy Gander's Entertaining Fairy Tales (London, 1815)

The Enchanter; or Wonderful Story Teller: In Which Is Contained a Series of Adventures, Curious, Surprising, and Uncommon; Calculated to Amuse, Instruct, and Improve Younger Minds (London, 1795)

The Fairiest; or Surprising and Entertaining Adventures of the Aerial
    Beings . . . The Whole Selected to Amuse and Improve Juvenile Minds
    (London, 1795)
Kletke, Hermann, *Märchensaal: Märchen aller Völker für Jung und Alt*
    (Berlin, 1845)
L'Héritier, Marie-Jeanne, 'Marmoisan, oder die unschuldige Betrügerey',
    in *Landbibliothek zu einem angenehmen und lehrreichen Zeit vertreibe*
    aus verschiedenen Sprachen zusammen getragen (Leipzig, 1772), pp. 311–56
——, 'Marmoisan; or, The Innocent Deceit: A Novel', *The Lady's Magazine;*
    or, Entertaining Companion for the Fair Sex (March 1775; April 1775;
    May 1775), pp. 148–9; 195–6; 246–8
——, 'Marmoisan; or, The Innocent Deceit: A Novel', *Scots Magazine*
    (August 1744; September 1744), pp. 372–9; 425–9
——, 'Marmoisan; or, The Innocent Deceit: A Novel', *Universal Spectator*
    and Weekly Journal, 806–11 (17 March–21 April 1744), n.p.
——, 'The Wary Princess: or, The Adventures of Finette. A Novel',
    Universal Spectator and Weekly Journal, 786–8 (29 October–12
    November 1743), n.p.
Miranda and the Royal Ram (London, 1844)
Mother Bunch's Fairy Tales: Published for the Amusement of All Those Little
    Masters and Misses, Who, by Duty to their Parents, and Obedience to their
    Superiors, Aim at Becoming Great Lords and Ladies (London, 1773; 2nd
    edn London, 1830)
Němcová, Božena, '"Cinderella" by Božena Němcová', trans. Rebecca
    Cravens, New Directions in d'Aulnoy Studies, *Marvels and Tales*,
    xxxv/2 (2021), pp. 356–69
——, and Karel Jaromír Erben, *Czech Fairytales* (Prague, 2007)
Pineau, Léon, *Les Contes populaires du Poitou* (Paris, 1891)
The Pleasing Companion: A Collection of Fairy Tales, Calculated to Improve
    the Heart: The Whole Forming a System of Moral Precepts and Examples,
    for the Conduct of Youth through Life (London, *c.* 1790)
Schulz, Friedrich, 'Rapunzel', in *The Great Fairy-Tale Tradition*, ed. Jack
    Zipes (New York, 2011), pp. 484–9

Film, stage and musical adaptations
and contemporary accounts

Adam, Adolphe, *Souvenirs d'un musicien* (Paris, 1857)
Baillot, René, *Serpentin vert, air de danse pour le piano* (Paris, 1860)
Bolton, H. Philip, *Women Writers Dramatized: A Calendar of Performances*
    from Narrative Works Published in English to 1900 (New York, 2000)

Burnand, F. C., *The White Cat! of Prince Lardi-Dardi and the Radiant Rosetta: A Fairy Burlesque Extravaganza* (London, 1870)

Byron, Henry J., *Lady Belle Belle; Fortunio and his Seven Magic Men: A Christmas Fairy Tale* (London, 1864)

Chevassu, Francis, 'Les Théâtres: Châtelet', *Le Figaro*, 5 November 1908, p. 5

Cogniard, Théodore and Hippolyte, *La Chatte blanche* (Paris, 1852)

'Fancy-Dress Ball at Marlborough House', *London Illustrated News*, 1 August 1874, p. 114

Gautier, Théophile, 'Le Monde et le théâtre: Chronique familière du mois', *Revue de Paris*, x– xii (July–September 1852), pp. 149–59

——, 'Théâtre de la Porte-Saint-Martin, *La Biche au Bois*', *La Presse*, 31 March 1945, n.p.

Kirby, James, *The Songs, Recitatives, Choruses &c. in The White Cat; or, Harlequin in Fairy Wood* (London, *c.* 1812)

Mareschal, G., 'La photographie au théâtre', *La Nature*, 5 December 1887, pp. 93–4

Monselet, Charles, 'Théâtres', *Le Monde illustré*, 21 August 1869, pp. 126–7

Morlot, **É**mile, 'Critique dramatique: Menus-Plaisirs', *Revue d'art dramatique*, April–June 1887, pp. 105–9

Mortier, Arnold, 'Reprise de la *Chatte Blanche*', in *Les Soirées parisiennes de 1875* (Paris, 1876), pp. 194–8

Planché, James Robinson, *The Extravaganzas of J. R. Planché, Esq.*, vol. ii (London, 1879)

——, trans., *Fairy Tales, by the Countess d'Aulnoy*, illus. John Gilbert (London, 1856)

——, trans., *Four and Twenty Fairy Tales, Selected from Those by Perrault, and Other Popular Writers* (London, 1858)

——, 'The Island of Jewels; A Fairy Extravaganza', in *The Extravaganzas of J. R. Planché, Esq., 1825–1871* (London, 1879), vol. iv, pp. 7–46

Ravel, Maurice, *Ma Mère l'oye, ballet en cinq tableaux et une apotheose: Partition pour piano* (Paris, *c.* 1912)

Vorlíček, Václav, dir., *Three Hazelnuts [Wishes] for Cinderella* (DEFA, 1973)

Select bibliography

Abbott, Carmeta, 'Madame de Saint-Balmon (Alberte-Barbe d'Ernecourt): *Les Jumeaux martyrs* (1650)', in *Writings by Pre-Revolutionary French Women*, ed. Anne R. Larsen and Colette H. Winn [2000] (New York, 2017), pp. 257–88

Adams, Maeve E., 'The Amazon Warrior Woman and the
De/construction of Gendered Imperial Authority in
Nineteenth-Century Colonial Literature', *Nineteenth-Century
Gender Studies*, VI/I (Spring 2010)

Assael, Brenda, *The Circus and Victorian Society* (Charlottesville, VA, 2005)

Baker, Henry Barton, *History of the London Stage and its Famous Players
(1576–1903)* (London, 1904)

Barchilon, Jacques, and Peter Flinders, *Charles Perrault* (Boston, MA, 1981)

Batchelor, Jennie, '"Connections, which are of service . . . in a more
advanced age": "The Lady's Magazine", Community, and Women's
Literary Histories', *Tulsa Studies in Women's Literature*, XXX/2
(Autumn 2011), pp. 245–67

Battestin, Martin C., 'Fielding's Contributions to the "Universal
Spectator" (1736–7)', *Studies in Philology*, LXXXIII/I (Winter 1986),
pp. 88–116

Beasley, Faith E., *Salons, History, and the Creation of 17th-Century France:
Mastering Memory* (New York, 2006)

Beauvoir, Simone de, *The Second Sex* (New York, 1989)

Blackwell, Jeannine, 'German Fairy Tales: A User's Manual. Translations
of Six Frames and Fragments by Romantic Women', in *Fairy Tales
and Feminism: New Approaches* (Detroit, MI, 2004), pp. 73–98

Blamires, David, 'From Madame d'Aulnoy to Mother Bunch: Popularity
and the Fairy Tale', in *Popular Children's Literature in Britain*
(Burlington, VT, 2008), pp. 69–86

Bloom, Rori, *Making the Marvelous: Marie-Catherine d'Aulnoy, Henriette-
Julie de Murat, and the Literary Representation of the Decorative Arts*
(Lincoln, NE, 2022)

Bonanni, Veronica, '"The Blue Bird" and "L'Uccello turchino". Collodi:
Translator of d'Aulnoy', New Directions in d'Aulnoy Studies,
Marvels and Tales, XXXV/2 (2021), pp. 337–52

Boone, Joseph Allen, *The Homoerotics of Orientalism* (New York, 2014)

Bottigheimer, Ruth, 'Cinderella: The People's Princess', in *Cinderella
across Cultures: New Directions and Interdisciplinary Perspectives*,
ed. Martine Hennard Dutheil de La Rochère et al. (Detroit, MI,
2016), pp. 27–51

——, 'Fairy Tales', in *Encyclopedia of German Literature*, ed. Matthias
Konzett (Chicago, 2000), pp. 267–70

——, 'Marie-Catherine d'Aulnoy's "White Cat" and Hannā Diyāb's
"Prince Ahmed and Pari Banou": Influences and Legacies', New
Directions in d'Aulnoy Studies, *Marvels and Tales*, XXXV/2 (2021),
pp. 290–311

——, and Sophie Raynard, trans. and notes, 'Marie-Jeanne Lhéritier, *Diverse Works 1698*', in *Fairy Tales Framed: Early Forewords, Afterwords, and Critical Words*, ed. Ruth Bottigheimer (Albany, NY, 2012), pp. 127–54

Carrier, Hubert, 'Women's Political and Military Action during the Fronde', in *Political and Historical Encyclopedia of Women*, ed. Christine Fauré (New York, 2003), pp. 34–55

Cherbuliez, Juliette, *The Place of Exile: Leisure Literature and the Limits of Absolutism* (Lewisburg, PA, 2005)

Christout, Marie-Françoise, 'Aspects de la féerie romantique de *La Sylphide* (1832) à *La Biche au bois* (1845); Chorégraphie, décors, trucs et machines', *Romantisme*, XXXVIII (1982), pp. 77–86

Cowgill, Rachel, 'Re-Gendering the Libertine: Or, the Taming of the Rake: Lucy Vestris as Don Giovanni on the Early Nineteenth-Century London Stage', *Cambridge Opera Journal*, X/1 (March 1998), pp. 45–66

Cromer, Sylvie, '"Le Sauvage": Histoire sublime et allégorique de Madame de Murat', *Merveilles et contes*, I/1 (May 1987), pp. 2–19

Defrance, Anne, *Les Contes et les nouvelles de Madame d'Aulnoy (1690–1698)* (Geneva, 1998)

Do Rozario, Rebecca-Anne C., *Fashion in the Fairy Tale Tradition: What Cinderella Wore* (New York, 2018)

Dubois-Nayt, Armel, Nicole Dufournaud and Anne Paupert, eds, *Revisiter la 'querelle des femmes': Discours sur l'égalité/inégalité des sexes, de 1400 à 1600* (Saint-Etienne, 2013)

Duggan, Anne E., '*Les Femmes Illustres*; or, The Book as Triumphal Arch', *Papers on French Seventeenth-Century Literature*, XLIV/87 (2017), pp. 1–20

——, 'Introduction: The Emergence of the Classic Fairy-Tale Tradition', in *A Cultural History of Fairy Tales in the Long Eighteenth Century* (London, 2021), pp. 1–16

——, 'Madeleine de Scudéry's Animal Sublime; or, Of Chameleons', *Ecozon*, VII/1 (2016), pp. 28–42

——, *Queer Enchantments: Gender, Sexuality, and Class in the Fairy-Tale Cinema of Jacques Demy* (Detroit, MI, 2013)

——, 'The *Querelle des femmes* and Nicolas Boileau's *Satire x*: Going beyond Perrault', *Early Modern French Studies*, XLI/2 (2019), pp. 144–57

——, *Salonnières, Furies, and Fairies: The Politics of Gender and Cultural Change in Absolutist France*, 2nd rev. edn (Newark, NJ, 2021)

Farrell, Michèle Longino, 'Celebration and Repression of Feminine Desire in Mme d'Aulnoy's Fairy Tale: *La Chatte blanche*', *Esprit Créateur*, XXIX/3 (Autumn 1989), pp. 52–64

Feuillerat, Albert, *Baudelaire et la Belle aux cheveux d'or* (Paris, 1941)

Ficová, Adéla, 'To Whom the Shoe Fits: Cinderella as a Cultural Phenomenon in the Czech and Norwegian Context', MA diss., Masaryk University, Brno, 2020

Flaubert, Gustave, *Correspondance*, vol. II: 1853–63 (Paris, 1923)

Goncourt, Edmond and Jules de, *Histoire de la société française pendant la révolution*, 3rd edn (Paris, 1864)

Goux, Jean-Joseph, *Oedipe philosophe* (Paris, 1990)

Grätz, Manfred, *Das M*ärchen in der deutschen Aufklärung*: Vom Feenmärchen zum Volksmärchen* (Stuttgart, 1988)

Gregor, Francis, 'Biographical Sketch of the Author', in *The Grandmother: A Story of Country Life in Bohemia*, by Božena Němcová (Chicago, IL, 1891), pp. 5–16

Grenby, M. O., 'Tame Fairies Make Good Teachers: The Popularity of Early British Fairy Tales', *The Lion and the Unicorn*, XXX (2006), pp. 1–24

Griffel, Margaret Ross, *Operas in German: A Dictionary* (New York, 2018)

Griswold, Jerry, *The Meanings of 'Beauty and the Beast': A Handbook* (Peterborough, CA, 2004)

Haase-Dubosc, Danielle, and Marie-Elisabeth Henneau, *Revisiter la 'querelle des femmes': Discours sur l'égalité/inégalité des sexes, de 1600 à 1750* (Saint-Etienne, 2013)

Hames, Peter, 'The Czech and Slovak Fairy-Tale Film', in *Fairy-Tale Films Beyond Disney: International Perspectives*, ed. Jack Zipes et al. (New York, 2016), pp. 139-51

Hannon, Patricia, *Fabulous Identities: Women's Fairy Tales in Seventeenth-Century France* (Amsterdam and Atlanta, 1998)

Harries, Elizabeth Wanning, *Twice Upon a Time: Women Writers and the History of the Fairy Tale* (Princeton, NJ, 2001)

Harth, Erica, *Ideology and Culture in Seventeenth-Century France* (Ithaca, NY, 1983)

Hearne, Betsy, *Beauty and the Beast: Visions and Revisions of an Old Tale* (Chicago, 1989)

Heath, Michelle Beissel, *Nineteenth-Century Fiction of Childhood and the Politics of Play* (London, 2018)

Henriot, Émile, 'De qui sont les contes de Perrault?', *Revue des deux mondes*, XLII/12 (January 1928), pp. 424–41

Hyde, William J., 'The Stature of Baring-Gould as a Novelist', *Nineteenth-Century Fiction*, XV/1 (1960), pp. 1–16

Jarvis, Shawn, 'Monkey Tails: D'Aulnoy and Unger Explore Descartes, Rousseau, and the Animal-Human Divide', New Directions in d'Aulnoy Studies, *Marvels and Tales*, XXXV/2 (2021), pp. 271–89

——, 'Trivial Pursuit? Women Deconstructing the Grimmian Model in
the *Kaffeterkreis*', in *The Reception of Grimms' Fairy Tales: Responses,
Reactions, Revisions*, ed. Donald Haase (Detroit, MI, 1993), pp. 102–26

Jones, Christine, 'Maiden Warrior', in *Folktales and Fairy Tales: Traditions
and Texts from Around the World*, vol. II (Santa Barbara, CA, 2016),
pp. 604–7

——, 'Noble Impropriety: The Maiden Warrior and the Seventeenth
Century Contes de Fées', diss., Princeton University, Princeton, NJ,
2002

Kilpatrick, Emily, '"Therein Lies a Tale": Musical and Literary Structure in
Ravel's *Ma Mère l'Oye*', *Context*, XXXIV (2009), pp. 81–98

Koehler, Julie L. J., 'Navigating the Patriarchy in Variants of "The Bee
and the Orange Tree" by German Women', New Directions in
d'Aulnoy Studies, *Marvels and Tales*, XXXV/2 (2021), pp. 252–70

——, 'Women Writers and the *Märchenoma*: Foremother, Identity, and
Legacy', in *Writing the Self, Creating Community: German Women
Authors and the Literary Sphere, 1750–1850*, ed. Elisabeth Krimmer
and Lauren Nossett (New York, 2020), pp. 182–203

——, et al., eds and trans., *Women Writing Wonder: An Anthology of
Subversive Nineteenth-Century British, French, and German Fairy
Tales* (Detroit, MI, 2021)

Korneeva, Tatiana, 'Desire and Desirability in Villeneuve and Leprince de
Beaumont's "Beauty and the Beast"', *Marvels and Tales*, XXVIII/2
(2014), pp. 233–51

——, 'Rival Sisters and Vengeance Motifs in the *Contes de fées* of d'Aulnoy,
Lhéritier and Perrault', *Modern Language Notes*, CXXVII/4 (2012),
pp. 732–53

Lawrence, Caitlin, 'Reimagining the *Conte de fées*: Female Fairy Tales in
Eighteenth- and Nineteenth-Century England and their Explora-
tion of the World In-Between', PhD diss., Baylor University, Waco,
TX, 2020

Lebens, Naomi, '"We Made a Blame Game of your Game": Jean
Desmarets, the *Jeu des Reynes Renommés* and the *Dame des Reynes*',
Early Modern Women, XII/1 (Autumn 2017), pp. 119–31

Lieberman, Marcia R., '"Some Day My Prince Will Come": Female
Acculturation through the Fairy Tale', *College English*, XXXIV/3
(1972), pp. 383–95

Lüthi, Max, 'Die Herkunft des Grimmschen Rapunzelmärhens
(AsTh 310)', *Fabula*, III/1 (1960), pp. 95–118

Máchal, Jan, 'Počátky zábavné prosy novočeské', in *Literatura česká
devatenáctého století* (Prague, 1902), pp. 309–55

Maclean, Ian, *Women Triumphant: Feminism in French Literature 1610–1652* (Oxford, 1977)

Martineau, France, 'Perspectives sur le changement linguistique: Aux sources du français canadien', *Canadian Journal of Linguistics/La revue canadienne de linguistique*, L/1–4 (2005), pp. 173–213

Mawer, Deborah, *The Ballets of Maurice Ravel: Creation and Interpretation* (London, 2006)

Miller, Ann, *Reading Bande Dessinée: Critical Approaches to French-Language Comic Strip* (Bristol, 2007)

Mitchell, Dolores, 'Women and Nineteenth-Century Images of Smoking', in *Smoke: A Global History of Smoking*, ed. Sander L. Gilman and Zhou Xun (London, 2004), pp. 294–303

Mullins, Melissa, 'Ogress, Fairy, Sorceress, Witch: Supernatural Surrogates and the Monstrous Mother in Variants of "Rapunzel"', in *The Morals of Monster Stories: Essays on Children's Picture Book Messages*, ed. Leslie Ormandy (Jefferson, NC, 2017), pp. 142–57

Munich, Adrienne, *Queen Victoria's Secrets* (New York, 1996)

Murat, Henriette-Julie de, *Journal pour Mademoiselle de Menou* (Paris, 2016)

Norcia, Megan A., *Gaming Empire in Children's British Board Games, 1836–1860* (New York, 2019)

Pasco, Allan H., *Balzacian Montage* (Toronto, 1991)

Pichel, Beatriz, 'Reading Photography in French Nineteenth Century Journals', *Media History*, XXV/92 (2018), pp. 1–19

Raková, Zuzana, *La Traduction tchèque du français* (Brno, 2014)

Raynard, Sophie, *La Seconde Préciosité: Floriason des conteuses de 1690 à 1756* (Tübingen, 2002)

Reddan, Bronwyn, *Love, Power, and Gender in Seventeenth-Century French Fairy Tales* (Lincoln, NE, 2020)

Richards, Jeffrey, *The Golden Age of Pantomime: Slapstick, Spectacle and Subversion in Victorian England* (London, 2015)

Robert, Raymonde, *Le Conte de fées littéraire en France de la fin du XVIIe à la fin du XVIIIe siècle* (Nancy, 1982)

Rubenstein, Anne, *Bad Language, Naked Ladies, and Other Threats to the Nation: A Political History of Comic Books in Mexico* (Durham, NC, 1998)

Schacker, Jennifer, 'Fluid Identities: Madame d'Aulnoy, Mother Bunch and Fairy-Tale History', in *The Individual and Tradition: Folkloristic Perspectives*, ed. Ray Cashman et al. (Bloomington, IN, 2011), pp. 249–64

——, 'Slaying Blunderboer: Cross-Dressed Heroes, National Identities, and Wartime Pantomime', *Marvels and Tales*, XXVII/1 (2013), pp. 52–64

——, *Staging Fairyland: Folklore, Children's Entertainment, and Nineteenth-Century Pantomime* (Detroit, MI, 2018)

——, and Daniel O'Quinn, eds, *The Routledge Pantomime Reader: 1800–1900* (London, 2022)

Schröder, Volker, 'The Birth and Beginnings of Madame d'Aulnoy', *Anecdota* blog, 29 March 2019, https://anecdota.princeton.edu

——, 'The First German Translation of *Les Contes des fées*', *Anecdota* blog, 20 February 2022

——, 'Madame d'Aulnoy's Productive Confinement', *Anecdota* blog, 2 May 2020

——, 'Marie-Madeleine Perrault (1674–1701)', *Anecdota* blog, 31 December 2017

Schwabe, Claudia, 'The Legacy of DEFA's *Three Hazelnuts for Cinderella* in Post-Wall Germany: Tracing the Popularity of a Binational Fairy-Tale Film on Television', *Marvels and Tales*, XXXI/1 (2017), pp. 80–100

Seifert, Lewis, 'Charlotte-Rose de Caumont de la Force: 1650?–1724', in *The Teller's Tale: Lives of the Classic Fairy Tale Writers*, ed. Sophie Raynard (Albany, NY, 2012), pp. 89–93

——, *Fairy Tales, Sexuality, and Gender in France, 1690–1715: Nostalgic Utopias* (Cambridge, 1996)

Shen, Qinna, *The Politics of Magic: DEFA Fairy-Tale Films* (Detroit, MI, 2015)

Simonsen, Michèle, *Le Conte populaire* (Paris, 1984)

Skopal, Pavel, 'The Czechoslovak–East German Co-Production *Tři oříšky pro Popelku/Drei Haselnüsse für Aschenbrödel/Three Wishes for Cinderella*: A Transnational Tale', in *Popular Cinemas in East Central Europe: Film Cultures and Histories*, ed. Dorota Ostrowska, Francesco Pitassio and Zsuzsanna Varga (London and New York, 2017), pp. 184–97

——, 'Příběh úspěšné koprodukce. Národní, mezinárodní a transnârodní prvky *Tři oříšky pro Popelku*', in *Tři oříšky pro Popelku*, ed. Pavel Skopal (Prague, 2016), pp. 36–55

Šmejkalová, Jiřina, 'Němcová, Božena (born Barbora Panklová) (1820?–1862)', in *Biographical Dictionary of Women's Movements and Feminisms: Central, Eastern, and South Eastern Europe, Nineteenth and Twentieth Centuries*, ed. Francisca de Haan, Krassimira Daskalova and Anna Loutfi (Budapest, 2006), pp. 366–9

Stedman, Allison, 'Introduction', in *A Trip to the Country: By Henriette-Julie de Castelnau, comtesse de Murat*, ed. and trans. Perry Gethner and Allison Stedman (Detroit, MI, 2011)

——, *Rococo Fiction in France, 1600–1715: Seditious Frivolity* (Lewisburg, PA, 2013)

Storer, Mary Elizabeth, *Un Épisode littéraire de la fin du XVIIe siècle: La Mode des contes de fées (1685–1700)* (Paris, 1928)

Tait, Peta, *Fighting Nature: Travelling Menageries, Animal Acts and War Shows* (Sydney, 2016)

Tartar, Maria, *The Hard Facts of the Brothers Grimm* (Princeton, NJ, 1987)

Teverson, Andrew, '"Mr Fox" and "The White Cat": The Forgotten Voices in Angela Carter's Fiction', *Hungarian Journal of English and American Studies*, V/2 (1999), pp. 209–22

Thomas, Alfred, 'Form, Gender and Ethnicity in the Work of Three Nineteenth-Century Czech Women Writers', *Bohemia*, XXXVIII (13 December 1997), pp. 280–97

Tille, Václav, 'Les Contes français dans la tradition populaire tchèque', in *Mélanges d'histoire littéraire générale et comparée offerts à Fernand Baldensperger* [1930] (Geneva 1972), pp. 284–95

Trinquet du Lys, Charlotte, *Le Conte de fées français (1690–1700): Traditions italiennes et origines aristocratiques* (Tübingen, 2012)

——, 'L'homosexualité dans les contes de femmes-soldats', *Papers in French Seventeenth-Century Literature*, XLI/81 (2014), pp. 283–99

——, 'On the Literary Origins of Folkloric Fairy Tales: A Comparison between Madame d'Aulnoy's "Finette Cendron" and Frank Bourisaw's "Belle Finette"', *Marvels and Tales*, XXI/1 (2007), pp. 34–49

——, 'Women Soldiers' Tales during Louis XIV's War Conflicts', *Marvels and Tales*, XXXIII/1 (2019), pp. 140–56

Tucker, Holly, *Pregnant Fictions: Childbirth and the Fairy Tale in Early Modern France* (Detroit, MI, 2003)

Velay-Vallantin, Catherine, 'Marmoisan ou la fille en garçon', in *La Fille en garçon* (Carcassonne, 1992), pp. 61–132

Wawn, Andrew, 'The Grimms, the Kirk-Grims, and Sabine Baring-Gould', in *Constructing Nations, Reconstructing Myth: Essays in Honour of T. A. Shippey* (Turnhout, 2007), pp. 215–42

Yeomans, Henry, *Alcohol and Moral Regulation: Public Attitudes, Spirited Measures, and Victorian Hangovers* (Bristol, 2014)

Zipes, Jack, *Fairy Tale as Myth/Myth as Fairy Tale* (Lexington, KY, 1994)

——, ed., *The Golden Age of Folk and Fairy Tales: From the Brothers Grimm to Andrew Lang* (Indianapolis, IN, 2013)

——, ed., *Spells of Enchantment: The Wondrous Fairy Tales of Western Culture* (New York, 1991)

——, *Why Fairy Tales Stick: The Evolution and Relevance of a Genre* (New York, 2006)

Zuerner, Adrienne E., 'Reflections of the Monarchy in d'Aulnoy's *Belle-Belle ou le chevalier Fortuné*', in *Out of the Woods: The Origins of the Literary Fairy Tale in Italy and France*, ed. Nancy Canepa (Detroit, MI, 1997), pp. 194–217

Acknowledgements

I would like first to express my gratitude to Vivian Constantinopoulos at Reaktion, who worked with me to make this book, which I believe needed to happen, come to fruition. The College of Liberal Arts and Sciences at Wayne State University provided generous support for this book, which I greatly appreciate. I am also indebted to Adrion Dula, Julie L. J. Koehler and Nicole Thesz for taking the time to read chapters and provide both feedback and encouragement. Working with Cristina Bacchilega on *Marvels & Tales: Journal of Fairy-Tale Studies* has helped me to grow as a scholar and editor, and I have always valued her friendship and her encouragement of my endeavours. Much of the work in *The Lost Princess* takes inspiration from Jennifer Schacker's *Staging Fairyland: Folklore, Children's Entertainment, and Nineteenth-Century Pantomime* (2018), which contributed to furthering my understanding of the incredible impact Marie-Catherine d'Aulnoy had on British popular culture and inspired me to investigate her legacy as well on the French stage. I also thank my patient and supportive husband, Víctor Figueroa, as well as Frankie and Phoebe, our two eccentric cats, who could well star in their own cat tale. Finally, I am eternally grateful to Jack Zipes, who introduced me to the marvellous world of *les conteuses*, and whose early mentorship contributed to making me the scholar that I am today.

Photo Acknowledgements

The author and publishers wish to express their thanks to the sources listed below for illustrative material and/or permission to reproduce it. Some locations of artworks are also given below, in the interest of brevity:

Alamy Stock Photo: p. 212; collection of the author: pp. 73, 129, 132 (top and bottom), 133 (top and bottom), 136, 152, 158, 215; Bibliothèque nationale de France, Paris: p. 169; from *Le Cabinet des fées*, vol. IV (Geneva, 1785): p. 190; from *The Fairiest; or, Surprising and Entertaining Adventures of the Aerial Beings* (London, 1795): p. 199; from *Fairy Tales by the Countess d'Aulnoy* (London, 1855): pp. 119, 200; from *Le Figaro* (5 November 1908): p. 141; from *The History of Fortunio* (London, 1804): p. 134; from *The Illustrated London News*, 29 December 1849: p. 95; from *La jeunesse illustrée* (26 July 1903): p. 151; courtesy of Lilly Library, Indiana University, Bloomington: p. 131 (bottom); The Metropolitan Museum of Art, New York: p. 15, 162; courtesy Musée national de l'Éducation, Rouen: p. 130; from *La Nature: revue des sciences et de leurs applications aux arts et à l'industrie*, 5 December 1887: p. 148; from *La Pucelle, ou la France délivrée* (Paris, 1656): p. 168; from the *Revue Parisienne*, 21 August 1869: p. 144; Slovak National Gallery, Bratislava: p. 164; Theatermuseum Vienna, photo KHM-Museumsverband: p. 131 (top); University of Colorado Boulder Libraries, Rare and Distinctive Collections: p. 112; courtesy Ville de Canteleu: p. 93; from *The White Cat, and Other Old French Fairy Tales, by Mme. la comtesse d'Aulnoy* (1928): p. 104; Yale Center for British Art, New Haven, CT: p. 135 (top and bottom), 206, 207.

Index

Page numbers in *italics* refer to illustrations